Studies in
Area Linguistics

Studies
in
Area
Linguistics

Hans Kurath

Indiana University Press
Bloomington and London

Published in Canada by Fitzhenry & Whiteside Limited, Don Mills,
Ontario

Library of Congress catalog card number: 72-75391
ISBN: 0-253-35530-3

Manufactured in the United States of America

Contents

Figures

Preface

The whole gamut of problems encountered in area linguistics and the techniques used in handling them are presented in the first five chapters of the book with reference to American English. Since most of those who may consult this publication will be speakers of English, the choice of this plan seems reasonable. Besides, this is the field in which I feel thoroughly at home.

American English is eminently suitable for illustrating many of the problems with which area linguistics is concerned. First of all, its dialectal structure is simpler than that of language areas with a longer history. Secondly, the sociocultural interpretation is less involved and greatly facilitated by ample information on settlement history, the growth of regional centers, the development of transportation systems, the social structure of the several regions, and the organization of schooling. Moreover, the British linguistic background and the sociocultural interrelations between North America and Great Britain from the seventeenth century to the present are rather well understood.

My choice of examples from languages other than English depends upon their relevance from the point of view of methods in area linguistics. Fortunately most of the problems confronting the area linguist can be illustrated by well documented examples available in the fields of the Germanic and the Romanic languages. I regret that I am not competent to deal critically with certain problems that have been raised in the Slavic field.

The presentation of examples from languages other than English with sufficient clarity to carry conviction is not easy. In the very nature of the case, the factual evidence consists of dialect forms elucidated with reference to standard literary forms or to other dialect forms. Glossing such forms by the foreign standard language and by English, redundant as it may seem, imposes itself. Another problem is raised by divergent practices in the rendering of phonological features. Not only do Germanists and Romanists use different notation systems, they rarely distinguish clearly between phonemic and phonic entities. Under the circumstances, the notation of the source material has to be retained. However, I have at times used the international phonetic alphabet to suggest phonic or phonemic interpretations.

The last three chapters deal with general problems of linguistic change to which area linguistics can make significant contributions: diffusion, adaptation, and parallel development.

I have taken pains to provide precise references to the works of numerous scholars I have relied on. Permission to reproduce or adapt sketch maps has been secured from the various authors and their publishers and is gratefully acknowledged.

A generous subvention for the publication of this book has been granted by the Horace H. Rackham School of Graduate Studies of the University of Michigan, for which my thanks are heartily rendered.

The maps have been drawn with skill and care by Miss Joan Enerson, cartographer of the Department of Geography of the University of Michigan. Warm thanks are rendered to Professors Charles M. Davis and Melvin G. Marcus of the geography department for sponsoring Miss Enerson's work.

I am grateful to Professor Thomas A. Sebeok of Indiana University for having invited me to contribute this volume to the distinguished series of linguistic publications of the Indiana University Press, and to the Indiana University Press for the careful reproduction of a rather intricate manuscript.

Hans Kurath

Studies in
Area Linguistics

1.

From Sampling to Publication

1.1 Selective Sampling

1.11 Introduction

Selective sampling in accordance with a stated plan is a scientific method devised for the purpose of achieving a general view of a complicated situation within a reasonable time. It is used to some extent in all scientific research, as in topographical and geological surveys, in ecological studies of animal and plant life, in delineating economic areas, in testing public opinion, and so forth.

In the study of living speech it was first employed on a large scale by G. Wenker (1876ff.), who sent his 40 test sentences to all the public schools in Germany (ca. 40,000) with the request that they be translated by a native speaker of the local dialect. Two decades later (1897) J. Gilliéron sent E. Édmont out into the field with a set questionnaire to sample the folk dialects spoken in 639 communities of France. With certain modifications and refinements, the later large-scale surveys of Italy, Spain, Romania, the United States, and England follow Gilliéron's plan of "direct" recording by properly trained observers.

The problems connected with the planning and the execution of a survey of this type are taken up below. Here we shall briefly consider its purpose, character, and potentials.

1

By choosing a limited body of linguistic items for investigation in a limited number of carefully selected communities, each of them represented by a single speaker belonging to a certain social class, or by one for each of two or more social levels, the area linguist hopes to obtain a general view of the dialectal structure of the total area within a relatively short time. He has no illusion about achieving a complete coverage of usage. He knows that linguistic features other than those that he selected may also vary, that the inclusion of additional communities may turn up unobserved variants, and that his informants are only approximately representative of their communities or of a social or age group living there. He is fully aware of the fact that the adequacy and the reliability of his sample is proportionate to the relative complexity of the linguistic and sociocultural situation in all or in parts of the area surveyed. Thus he will reserve judgment and recommend further investigation when the linguistic variants exhibit a complicated and apparently erratic dissemination as in certain transition zones or relic areas.

The area linguist will cheerfully grant that the method of systematic selective sampling has certain limitations. But he is on solid ground when he claims that no other method of gathering reliable information on usage is equally efficient and productive. Properly planned, a sampling survey will provide a general view of the dialectal structure of an area on the basis of comparable data recorded in a consistent fashion. Areas of uniform and of divided usage, clear lines of demarcation, and transition belts emerge to furnish the basis for establishing major and minor dialect boundaries, which reveal the dialectal structure of the total area surveyed.

It is of some importance to emphasize the fact that the findings of a linguistic survey carried out on this plan constitute a census of usage for a given period of time, however incomplete it may be. As such it cannot be superseded by a later survey any more than the Census of the United States for 1970 has replaced that of 1960 or 1900. Any new survey, say a generation later, will reveal changes that scholars will be able to trace in considerable detail by relying upon the data furnished by the earlier investigation.

A first sampling survey has further values and functions. It provides a framework for dealing with the usually uneven or fragmentary evidence of earlier studies and of unconventional spellings in better perspective, and it points to the need for more detailed investigations of certain areas or of specific problems. For such studies, the incomplete or insufficient data presented by the general survey inevitably contribute to the formulation of a well-oriented and economical plan.

1.12 Constructing the Questionnaire

A set questionnaire, one that prescribes the recording of specific
items and the manner of securing responses, is an indispensable
tool of systematic selective sampling. Comparable data from
community to community and from speaker to speaker, on the basis
of which the dialectal structure of the area must ultimately be
determined, cannot be secured in any other way. Constructing a
questionnaire adequate for the purpose in hand, neither too skimpy
nor too full, and so arranged and styled as to facilitate the interview,
is a complicated and time-consuming task. But care and time spent
on its preparation are richly rewarded in the end.

Questionnaires can of course be set up for limited purposes, such
as the determination of regional or social differences in the lexicon,
in verb forms, in phonemic contrasts, or in the articulation of
shared phonemes. Choosing promising items and presenting them
for the convenience of the investigator and the informant always
presents certain problems. Here our concern will be with procedures used in constructing a general questionnaire intended to cover
the regional and/or social differences in the lexicon, the morphology,
and the phonology in a given language area, the type of questionnaire
used in the surveys of France, Italy, Spain, Romania, Switzerland,
England, and the United States.

The choice of items to be included in a general questionnaire
rests upon available information, however fragmentary or ambiguous,
concerning regional or social differences within the area to be
surveyed.

As a first step, variations in vocabulary, in grammatical forms,
and in pronunciation reported in dialect dictionaries, regional word
lists, dialect grammars, phonological studies, etc., are assembled
in separate files. Then the lexical items are grouped by semantic
fields, the morphological by grammatical categories, and the
phonological on the basis of a tentative phonemic analysis of one of
the better known dialects or from the diachronic point of view. As
a third step, additional examples to illustrate known morphological
and phonological differences are chosen from the vocabulary of
everyday life, especially such as more or less naturally fall into
the semantic fields represented by the lexical items. This is of
special importance in phonological matters, since phonemes shared
by all or most of the dialects in the area are rarely reported in the
earlier literature. The survey must of course cover this aspect of
phonology as well as the reported or anticipated variants. More-

over, words whose phonemic shapes are invariable are needed to
exhibit phonic differences in shared phonemes. Taped free conversations from a number of well distributed points in the proposed
network of communities can furnish invaluable leads for the
selection of representative phonological items.

After an ample collection of "promising" items has been assembled on slips and tentatively arranged by semantic fields, the task
of producing an effective questionnaire of manageable size can be
faced. This involves (1) a rough forecast of the extent and kinds of
linguistic diversity within the area, (2) an estimate of the time
required to find and interview an informant, and (3) a rough calculation of the number of communities and informants needed for
effective regional and social representation. Last but not least, a
hard-headed estimate (4) of financial requirements and resources
for carrying out the survey, and (5) of available man power for
completing the fieldwork within a reasonable time must be brought
to bear upon this problem.

In view of all these uncertainties, a questionnaire that is both
adequate and not unduly long is hard to achieve, especially for a
first survey. Nevertheless, maximum coverage by the shortest
possible questionnaire must be the aim. If this is to some extent
conjectural—a leap into the dark, if you will—such a questionnaire
will bring to light much information that future investigators can
use in constructing more effective questionnaires, and will prepare
the way for detailed investigation of subareas revealed by the initial
survey.

Before the questionnaire is put into final shape, it should be
tested in a number of key points within the area. Even limited field
experience will disclose unproductive items and some that can be
elicited only with difficulty. These should be eliminated. It may
also suggest some important additions. Above all, it will provide a
measure of the time required for completing a single interview and
give some indication of the informants' endurance and toleration of
prolonged questioning. Allowing for a speedup of fifty percent that
may result from field experiences, the questionnaire should then be
trimmed down to manageable size.

In addition to the normal questionnaire, a reduced version containing the more important phonological or morphological items is
sometimes useful for recording the usage of auxiliary informants,
especially those that cannot spare the time for a full interview.

Supplementary lexical questionnaires dealing with regionally
restricted enterprises, such as cotton farming, viticulture, or
dairying, can be set up to supplement the lexical fields covered
by the normal questionnaire.

The arrangement of the items in the questionnaire is of crucial importance for the speedy progress of the interview and for the purpose of securing trustworthy responses. It is not the linguist's interest in the problems confronting him, but the situation in which the informant finds himself that is the controlling factor in achieving a satisfactory arrangement.

The speaker of a dialect is willing to talk about what he knows and does. He is usually not interested in what he calls a thing or an activity. Hence the questionnaire must be so arranged that the informant can talk consecutively about such topics as the dwelling, farming, the weather, the lay of the land, plants and animals, the family, social activities, and so forth. The investigator must do his best to keep the attention of the informant focused on the subject matter, even when he asks questions that must seem trivial or trying to a native speaker.

There will always be some morphological and phonological items of importance that do not fit neatly into any of the lexical fields covered by the questionnaire. If not observed incidentally in the course of the interview, responses should be elicited after the informant's interest has been aroused and his confidence gained.

In a questionnaire arranged by semantic fields, the very sequence of the items serves to narrow the choice of possible responses to the several items. Further definition of the response sought can be achieved by providing a lexical context or suggesting a specific situation verbally or by gesture. For some items illustrations or photographs can be used to cue responses. Some questionnaires prescribe a fixed phrase or sentence into which the informant is asked to insert his response; but most of them leave the precise method of eliciting trustworthy responses to the ingenuity of the trained investigator. Either method has its advantages and drawbacks.

Examples of the types of comprehensive questionnaire described above will be found in Jaberg-Jud 1928: 145–74 (Italian), Kurath-Bloch 1939: 147–58 (American English), Orton 1962: 49–101 (English Dialects), Hotzenköcherle 1962 C: 1–78 (Swiss German). These publications also contain comments on the problems involved in constructing such questionnaires. See also Pop 1950: 1136–41.

1.13 Conducting the Interview

Successful fieldwork presupposes not only adequate training in linguistics, ranging from phonology and morphology to semantics, and a general knowledge of the culture of the area in its varied manifestations, but also a sympathetic understanding of people in

all walks of life. Unless the investigator has the knack of dealing
with personalities of all kinds so as to gain their confidence, of
guiding them gently through the inevitable "dry" stretches of his
questionnaire, of humoring them when their interest lags, he will
experience serious difficulties and disappointments. Even the best-
trained linguist can be a failure in fieldwork.

The interview is channeled by the questionnaire from topic to
topic. However, the investigator is free to start the interview with
any of the semantic fields provided for: with housekeeping and
cookery, with farming, with social activities, etc., depending upon
the informant's special interests or competence. Numerals, names
of the days of the week and the months, and some other lexical
fields that are apt to strike the informant as too trivial to bother
with sometimes get the interview off to a bad start. Though they
offer an excellent opportunity for "sizing up" the phonological
characteristics of the speaker, it is often better to do them after
his interest has been aroused.

The questionnaire is normally drafted in the standard language,
or a widely used dialect, of the area to be investigated, supplemented
by regional terms as needed. In the Western world this language or
dialect usually serves also as the medium of eliciting responses
from the informants, most of whom are bidialectal or at least understand the standard language, even if they have no facility in using it
actively. There is some danger in this practice, unavoidable as it
may be, especially if the dialect is close to the standard (as in
American English), or if the informant is given to "mixing." But an
experienced fieldworker can rather easily detect such intrusions
and query the speaker. In view of the well-known fact that in Europe
and in America regional expressions of folk speech have constantly
been replaced by terms current in the standard language, particularly since the establishment of public schools, such "intrusions"
often turn out to be fully established in the speaker's dialect. Anti-
quarian interest on the part of the investigator must not be allowed
to obscure such facts. Often enough the informant will report that
his parents "used to say" so-and-so, but that he himself has given
up his childhood usage.

Peculiar circumstances may favor the use of a regional dialect
as the cue language, whether that of the informant or not. Thus
Hotzenköcherle [1962–A: 30–31] states, in substance:

> Each fieldworker conversed with his informants in his
> own dialect. Any deviation from this practice, common
> to all social classes in Switzerland, would have been
> quite unthinkable, would have led to innumerable mis-

understandings, and would inevitably have produced a fatal breakdown in the intimate relation between investigator and informant. Different dialects were used, each fieldworker speaking his own. When communication with the informant became difficult, the fieldworker adjusted himself more or less consistently to the dialect of the informant.

A similar situation may obtain in other parts of Europe, say in Scotland or Ireland. Even in parts of the eastern United States some fieldworkers found it advantageous to adapt their usage more or less to that of the informant, but without mimicking him outright.

The primary task of the fieldworker is, of course, the accurate observation and recording of the responses he elicits from the informant. Responses given freely, without hesitation or qualification, are taken down without comment, whenever the investigator feels confident that they represent normal usage. For responses offered hesitatingly, with amusement or reserve, or with any significant comment, as well as for those secured under special circumstances, the investigator must provide appropriate information. Such comments, invaluable to the editor, should be entered in a separate column set aside for this purpose.

The fieldworkers of the Linguistic Atlas of the Eastern United States were instructed to identify all such "limited" and "qualified" responses in ways that proved effective [Kurath-Bloch 1939: 143–45]. Since they may be helpful to others, the abbreviations and labels used for this purpose are listed below:

c.: an expression observed in conversation, esp. when it differs from that elicited by questioning

cr.: a spontaneous correction of the first response, whether real or an attempt at elegance

r.: a response repeated at the fieldworker's request

f.: a forced response, i.e., secured by repeated questioning

s.: a suggested response, i.e., a term or form actually pronounced by the investigator and recognized by the informant as his own

(:) preceding the recorded response marks hesitation, whatever the reason

(!) registers amusement, whatever the cause

(?) reports the observer's doubt concerning the trustworthiness of the response

(†) marks an old-fashioned or remembered expression

(→) identifies a recent expression if actually used by the informant

(⊥) marks an expression reported as heard by the informant in his community but not used by him

(*) marks an expression offered by an auxiliary informant, usually a member of the family or a local friend who happens to be present during the interview.

The identification of responses not secured by direct questioning and the indication of their status in the informant's usage furnish important information to the editor of the collections and to the scholar who undertakes to trace shifts in usage.

1.14 Recording the Speech Sounds

A decision regarding the method of recording the sounds of the dialects has to be made at the very beginning of the field survey. Both scientific and practical matters have a bearing upon this problem.

As to the scientific aspect of the problem, it is important to keep in mind that the dialects may differ (a) in the system of phonemes, (b) in the lexical incidence (etymological distribution) of shared phonemes, or (c) in the phonic manifestation of shared phonemes from place to place and from class to class (regional and social diaphones). Moreover, (d) the phonemes of any given dialect may exhibit positionally or prosodically conditioned allophones.

Though of uneven value from the structural point of view, phonemic, incidental, diaphonic, and allophonic phenomena all have their relevance in dialect research, whether synchronic or diachronic. Without adequate phonic data no single dialect or idiolect can be adequately described; nor can its historical relation to its sister dialects or its parent dialect be traced in realistic fashion [Kurath 1961].

If that be granted, as it must be, the question is simply this: How can a full record of relevant phonological information be best obtained under the conditions confronting the fieldworker charged with the task of eliciting and recording a large number of lexical, morphological, and phonological responses in a limited time? Could he reliably, or even tentatively, establish the phonemic inventory and the phonic range of the individual phonemes, say, in the first two hours and thereafter record purely phonemically? But by the time he could start phonemic recording most dialect speakers would have bid him "goodbye."

Under the circumstances, strictly phonic recording imposes itself and has been adopted in nearly all major dialect surveys since the turn of the century. Its feasibility cannot be questioned. The requirements are (1) a finely graded and flexible system of phonic notation adapted to anticipated variations within the area, such as those used in Italy [Jaberg-Jud 1928: 24–36], in the United States

[Kurath-Bloch 1939: 122–43], and in German-speaking Switzerland [Hotzenköcherle 1962–B: 79–86]; and (2) intensive training of the fieldworkers in the application of this system, preferably under field conditions, real or simulated.

The task of recording phonically, i.e., of writing down all audible shades of sounds by means of a finely graded system of notation, is not as demanding upon the investigator or as cumbersome as a casual inspection of the records might suggest to the uninitiated. Any experienced fieldworker can testify to this fact, and add that the very fullness and flexibility of the notation system often relieved him of time-consuming decisions.

The obligation to record all responses phonically does not prevent the field observer from commenting upon actual or potential structural implications of the phones he records, of pointing out the real or apparent existence of certain phonemic contrasts in connection with specific examples. He should, indeed, be encouraged to report such potentially structural phenomena in his general characterization of the speech of each informant after completing the record.

The task of establishing the phonemic structure of idiolects and dialectal types, and of describing the phonic range of the phonemes, can safely be entrusted to others. If the record is accurate and ample, there is no difficulty in making reliable decisions. If it is inadequate in one respect or another, a decision may have to be postponed. In any event, careful tabulation and leisurely analysis of the phonic field data are more apt to lead to reliable determinations than improvised decisions in the field. To the analyst, field experience is of course a helpful asset in working out the phonemic system(s).

The procedure to be followed in establishing the phonemic system(s) on the basis of phonically recorded field data is illustrated in Kurath-McDavid 1961 (see especially pp. 1–9 and 31–100). Its feasibility and effectiveness cannot be questioned, as W. G. Moulton has demonstrated in an impressive series of studies based upon the wealth of phonic data furnished by the Sprachatlas der deutschen Schweiz [Hotzenköcherle 1962]. After establishing the phonemic system of idiolects and regional dialects and describing the phonic range of the several units of the systems, he undertakes (1) to construct maps of regionally varying phonemic systems [1960, 1967 1968]; (2) to show that phonic and phonemic maps of the same underlying phonic data may exhibit divergent regional patterning [1963, 1964]; (3) to demonstrate that for dealing with diachronic problems a phonemic analysis of the phonic data is an essential prerequisite [1960, 1961]; (4) to show that the phonic range of a phoneme depends upon the neighboring units in the system [1960, 1962]; and (5) to test

A. Martinet's theory [1955] that asymmetries of vowel systems tend
to be mended by inner drives [1961].

Quasi-phonemic field recording was used by G. Bottiglioni in his
survey of Corsica [1933–42]. Rejecting "impressionistic," i.e.,
phonic, recording outright, his aim was to establish "mean" or
"average" usage in phonological as well as morphological and lexical
matters. Probing the informant's usage repeatedly and even consult-
ing other speakers in the community, he hoped to achieve an "objective" determination of "normal" local usage. Since he knew the area
well and could spend from four to eight days with each informant,
his findings would seem to have considerable validity, though
involving a subjective judgment on his part. To what extent this
method can be adapted to limited regional surveys—especially with
the necessary refinement in phonological matters—is an open
question. See S. Pop's description and criticism of Bottiglioni's
procedures [Pop 1950: 539–40, 546–47, 553–55].

It goes without saying that for specific purposes the phonemic
approach is not only possible but convenient, if not imperative, in
field recording. The existence or absence of specific phonemic
contrasts or of positional allophones in other dialects can be traced,
if the phonemic structure of one of them is known. Morphological
and lexical studies call for a speedy progression from phonic via
quasi-phonemic to phonemic recording. Conversations and texts
should of course be taken down phonemically as soon as a reliable
analysis has been worked out.

1.15 Choosing Communities

In a far-ranging general survey, observation posts must be carefully selected to achieve a general view of the dialectal structure of
the area within the limits imposed by available resources. It stands
to reason that all available information concerning the living conditions of the population, the social structure, and the sociocultural
history of the area should be brought to bear upon the problem of
establishing a network of communities. Our accumulated knowledge
about language behavior in the vicinity of dominant cultural centers
and about the effects of barriers to communication furnish additional
leads. A well informed choice of listening posts will yield a rich
harvest. The principles guiding the choice of communities should,
of course, be stated, so that the findings can be evaluated critically.

A general survey should include the larger cities, communities
of medium size, and villages; old and derivative centers and settle-

ments; points along highways and waterways as well as secluded
hamlets and homesteads. Since the selection is made in reference
to the sociocultural characteristics of the area under investigation,
the choice of types of communities will vary from area to area.

Until recently large-scale surveys have been deliberately
restricted to folk speech, especially to that of the countryside. A.
Griera [1923 ff.] was the first to include the folk speech of urban
centers in his survey of Catalonia, and this practice was followed
by Jaberg-Jud in their Italian atlas [1928: 187–88]. In the Linguistic Atlas of the United States, all population centers of any importance are regularly included [Bloch 1939: 39–40] and, in principle,
all social levels are represented [Kurath-Bloch 1939: 39–44].

Practical considerations inevitably limit the number of communities that can be investigated. Financial resources, available man-
power, and time limits of one kind or another always impose
restraint. Nevertheless, any well-designed network of communities
will bring the main features of the dialectal situation into relief and
prepare the ground for properly oriented intensive investigations in
any part of the area.

In practice, the organizer of a survey plans the network of communities, assigns priorities to desirable listening posts, and makes
his final selection after he knows how much time he must allow for
the completion of an interview. The number of communities, the
number of informants per community, and the length of the questionnaire must be brought into balance for optimum results of a sampling
survey.

Though the network of communities should be planned beforehand,
the fieldworker can be given a choice between certain communities
to facilitate his labors. Often enough he can secure helpful information locally to make a wise choice; again and again he will find easier
access to informants in one or the other of the alternate communities.

Each community represented in the survey should be briefly
characterized in the manual accompanying the published records.
Its natural setting, contacts with other communities (especially with
market towns), size and population trends, chief occupations of the
inhabitants (farming, industries, etc.) should be pointed out. Information concerning the history of each community, with bibliographical references to works consulted in making the selection, should be
provided for the convenience of those who will undertake to evaluate
and to interpret the linguistic records in their sociocultural context.
For examples of such sketches see Jaberg-Jud [1928: 37–139] and
Kurath-Bloch [1939: 159–240].

1.16 Choosing Informants

Language is the chief medium of communication between the
members of a community. To fulfill the function of communication,
the usage of the individuals constituting the community, or a social
class within the community, must be relatively uniform. This well
known fact underlies the assumption that any native speaker's usage
is in a large measure representative of the speechways of a social
or age group in his community. The area linguist shares this
assumption with all students of language who base their descriptions
upon the usage of one or several speakers. This practice can hardly
be questioned.

A further consideration has a bearing upon the essential reliability of the informant's usage as representing that of his class in a
given community. What the investigator observes and records are
ingrained habits of speech of which the speaker is largely unaware.
If he offers opinions about the way he talks, the observer will note
them as such. He will have ample opportunity to determine whether
the informant practices what he preaches. All in all, the sampling
of speech habits is simpler than the sampling of opinions in social
science and yields more reliable results.

The informant chosen to represent his community, or a social or
age group in it, should have certain personal characteristics, some
of them indispensable, others desirable. First of all he must be
intelligent (even if illiterate), communicative (but not talkative), and
tolerably well informed on the topics covered by the questionnaire.
He must have enough interest, patience, and endurance to put up with
prolonged questioning. He should, of course, be free of speech
defects and hear well enough to understand the questions readily.
Set ways and a degree of self-confidence are definite assets, as is
community pride.

Since the informant is chosen to represent his community, or one
of its social or age groups, biographical data must be secured from
him or from reliable consultants living in the community. He should
be a native of the community (preferably also his forebears) and
have lived there all or most of his life. Schooling confined to the
locality or district is a requirement for middle class and folk
speakers.

This information must be presented in the manual accompanying
the published records, along with data on the informant's age, sex,
schooling, occupation, membership in religious and other social
organizations, standing in the community, special interests, and
reading habits. Moreover, the field investigator should be encour-

aged to comment on general characteristics of the informant's speech, such as tempo, precise or slack articulation, stability or fluctuation in usage, his attitude concerning the speech of others, inclination to "improve" his usage, etc. For examples of such sketches see Jaberg-Jud [1928: 37–139], Kurath-Bloch [1939: 159–240], and Hotzenköcherle [1962–B: 97–174].

Finding suitable informants to represent the chosen communities calls for skill, tact, and sound judgment on the part of the fieldworker. He may have some information about the character of the community before he arrives, even about some of the prominent families living there. He may have a letter of introduction to a local historian or some other person who may be willing and able to help him find the kinds of informant(s) he needs. He may need a letter of identification to present to local officials. After some experience in the field, he may discover that informal contacts in the general store, barber shop, or local tavern can provide him with useful leads. The approach must, of course, be adapted to regional or local customs and sensibilities. Appeal to local pride or reference to sponsorship of a learned organization may be helpful in some communities and with some informants. Assurance that the results of the interview(s) will be held in confidence must at times be given. Procedures and experiences connected with the search for suitable informants have been discussed by two experienced field investigators, P. Scheuermeier [1932: 99–105] and B. Bloch [1935: 4–6].

The problem of selecting and securing suitable informants is essentially the same whether the sampling survey is limited to one social level or includes several of them. In Europe the practice has been to confine the survey to the speechways of the folk, and to give prominence to the oldest living generation in rural communities A predilection for historical problems, the hope of shedding light on processes of linguistic change by observing the linguistic behavior of the folk, and admiration for the soil-bound "ethos" or "world view of "natural" people have been the motives and the justification offered for this practice. Much has been accomplished within this limited perspective since the turn of the century. To advocate the application of selective sampling to the usage of the middle class and the cultured does not detract from the value of the work that has been done. It rather implies the recognition of the effectiveness of this method in dealing with living speech of any kind.

Deliberately deviating from European practice, the Linguistic Atlas of the United States included the investigation of the speechways of several social levels from the very beginning (1930). Representatives of the cultured, the middle class, and the folk are

systematically included in the survey, the last two types in nearly
every community chosen for investigation, the cultured in about one
fifth of them (chiefly in cities of some importance). This plan
rather imposed itself owing to the fact that, except for some of the
old cities on the Atlantic seaboard, American society lacks clear-
cut social classes. There is, instead, a gradation from level to
level resulting from the social mobility of the American people.
By sampling the usage of the social extremes—the cultured and the
folk—and that of the middle group(s), a broad conspectus of cultivated, middle class, and folk speech is secured region by region.
Identification of the sociocultural status of the informants is, of
course, provided. A tabulation by social levels and age groups
[Kurath-Bloch 1939: 41—44] enables the student of the field records
to choose for investigation or cartographic presentation the usage
of any type of informants or to trace social differences from
community to community.

It would be unwise to assume that a full coverage of the social
dissemination of variants is to be found in the records of the
American atlas. The author has never indulged in such an illusion. However, enough is revealed by the sampling of social
levels in American English to set the stage for properly oriented
research in social dialects, one of the major tasks of the future.
See Kurath 1964—A: 135—43.

1.17 Concluding Remarks

The method of gathering dialect data described in this chapter
would seem to be the best way to secure reliable information on
usage within a reasonable time. The effectiveness of selective
sampling as a scientific procedure cannot be questioned. Direct
observation in the field by properly trained linguists is surely
superior to information furnished by correspondents, and not only
in phonological and morphological matters: quantity is no substitute for quality, although some scholars seem to think so.

This does not mean that, with careful planning and under favorable circumstances, valuable data cannot be secured by the "indirect"
method. Thus most of the data for Netherlandish are furnished by
translation into the local dialects of 131 test sentences, five short
word lists, and five sets of morphological cue forms on the part of
carefully selected observers [Blancquaert 1948]. In 1939, W.
Mitzka sent his list of 188 Standard German cue words to about
50,000 schools with the request that the local synonyms be furnished
by a speaker of the local dialect under the supervision of a teacher.
His Deutscher Wortatlas [1951 ff.] presents the findings [rev. by

Kurath 1958]; and an imposing series of studies for which the
Wortatlas forms the point of departure has appeared under the title
Deutsche Wortforschung in europäischen Bezügen [Schmitt 1958 ff.].
In these investigations, word histories are traced in their sociocultural setting with full philological documentation [rev. by Kurath
1960]. For the lexical part of his Survey of Scottish Dialects, A.
McIntosh has adopted this practice [McIntosh 1952: 70–84; Catford
1957: 113–17], which has also been widely used in Sweden [S. Ben-
son in Germanische Dialektologie 1968: 364–67].

The manner in which lexical, morphological, and phonological
data are secured inevitably slants them in one way or another. For
this reason the student of English dialectology must be aware of
certain differences in the methods employed by the American, the
English, and the Scottish surveys, when he undertakes to compare
the data or to trace the European sources of features of American
English.

For the fieldwork in America and in England, the lexical questions
are arranged by topics (semantic fields), so as to provide a focus
for the informant and to guide his choice of terms, and the observer
is in a position to judge the ease and assurance with which he
responds. Hesitation or uncertainty on the speaker's part leads to
further probing to establish usage. When cue words are presented
by correspondence, whether topically arranged or not, the written
responses have to be accepted without the benefit of gaging the
correspondent's behavior. Lacking this information, the lexical
survey of Scotland and Northern Ireland, and that of Germany, rely
upon the mass of responses for weeding out probable errors and
identifying unsure or unsettled usage.

Although the American and the English surveys agree in providing topical settings for determining word usage, they differ sharply
in another respect. In the United States the fieldworker is free to
choose his own way of eliciting the desired response; in England the
informant is asked to "fill in" the usual term in a sentence framed
in Standard English [Orton 1962]. The English way sharply narrows
the choice, whereas the American approach may produce variants
that are not strictly synonymous. Either method has advantages
and drawbacks of which scholars must be aware.

In securing phonological data, the survey of Scotland agrees
with the atlases of England and the United States in relying upon
direct observation of the informants and in recording the syllabics
phonically ("impressionistically") within the framework of the
"cardinal vowels" of Daniel Jones. Under the circumstances,
students of English are provided with readily comparable phonic
data. Nevertheless, allowance must always be made for somewhat

different subdivisions of the phonic scale—a multidimensional spectrum—on the part of the several observers. Such differences should be pointed out by the editor [Kurath-Bloch 1939: 50–52, 126–27]. They rarely prevent the abstraction of the phonemic system, as Kurath-McDavid [1961] have amply demonstrated.

W. G. Moulton's recently expressed pessimism concerning phonic recording [1968: Lang. 44.461–65] is hardly justified. Even Ladefoged's experiment shows—contrary to Moulton's interpretation—that all fifteen phoneticians trained to D. Jones' scale of cardinal vowels identified ten phonemic entities in a language unfamiliar to them (Gaelic), although they differ considerably in recording the relevant phones. Ladefoged himself admits that in the state of our present knowledge and techniques neither an articulatory nor an acoustic identification of vowels is feasible. He concludes: "Consequently the traditional rigorous training in the performance and use of known reference points will remain for some time an essential for all who wish to make useful phonetic statements about vowel sounds" [Ladefoged 1960: 396]. To let the tape recorder do the work that fieldworkers now perform, as Moulton suggests (464), is illusory because it overlooks the fact that only trained phoneticians can report to us what the tapes contain. On the other hand, I agree wholeheartedly with Moulton that fieldworkers should be fully aware of the potential systemic relevance of phonic entities and make appropriate comments.

Although adhering to phonic recording, the Scottish survey has introduced a method of gathering the phonological data in such a way that the phonemic entities can be more easily abstracted, speaker by speaker. Instead of embedding the phonological test words in a topically arranged questionnaire, the nearly 1,000 items are presented in isolation, arranged in sequences that seemed to promise a more or less automatic discovery of phonemic entities and their sources in the parent language (Middle English or Middle Scots). The informants respond to cue words pronounced in Standard English and utter their Scottish dialect equivalents as "sentence words," i.e., stressed and with sentence final intonation [Catford 1958: 117–21]. Under these prosodic conditions, the phonic character of the syllabics may be expected to be clearer, if not exaggerated, than under weaker stress and without a pitch contour. There is no doubt that this method leads to a reliable—and quasi-automatic—phonemic analysis of the dialects, if a sufficient number of trustworthy informants can be found to submit to the ordeal of matching 1,000 semantically isolated words uttered in Standard English with their local equivalents.

In the United States such a procedure is out of the question. Here the phonological test words must be included in a topically organized

questionnaire that prevents self-conscious adaptations of the pronunciation. Since in this country the lexical and morphological items
are also recorded phonically, the evidence furnished by the phonological test words is buttressed by a wealth of supplementary data.
Moreover, prosodically conditioned allophones of the phonemes,
deliberately eliminated in the Scottish survey, are amply documented.

1.2 Editing the Field Data

Editing the materials gathered in the field interviews is a formidable task that has to be handled with care and circumspection. To
lighten the burden of the editor, the field notes should be recorded
on an open page where each item has its separate "niche" identified
by number. Responses to the question, comments of informant and
fieldworker, and incidental materials should be entered in a separate
column to forestall misunderstandings. There is much to be said in
favor of recording in duplicate in a looseleaf field book, so that one
copy—properly stamped with the community number—can be filed,
page by page, with all the other field records, and the other copy
rebound and filed by informants. The editor will want to consult the
field record of an informant whenever the response to a particular
question seems to call for comment, especially in phonological
matters.

The manuscript is best prepared on a set of sheets on which the
community numbers are printed in sequence, to match the order in
which the field notes are filed. Everything that is to be entered on
the map (or published in lists) is taken down in one column. Queries
and comments of informant, fieldworker, or editor are tentatively
jotted down in another column to form the body of notes on which
the introductory remarks of the editor will be based. When an item
is especially complicated, the original decision on what will go on
the map, and how, may have to be modified in the light of insights
gained in the process of editing the mass of material.

The first draft of the manuscript of simpler items can often be
done by an assistant in accordance with general instructions. But
even here an experienced editor will have to assume responsibility
for reviewing it and approving it for publication. Utmost accuracy
and reliability of the published record is expected of him.

Careful editing of the data furnished by the fieldworker involves
not only the preservation of the recorded responses along with
significant comments of informants and observers on the status of
the expressions offered and recorded, but also the elimination of
obvious slips and the appraisal of apparent errors of judgment on
the part of the field observer.

Whether the editor should do more than that has been a subject

of debate. Some scholars hold that "interfering" with the recorded
data—i.e., judging their reliability—must be avoided; others advocate
an expression of opinion on his part.

It is the present writer's conviction that the editor should present
all relevant information at his disposal for the convenience of those
who will inspect the record of usage more or less casually and for
the orientation of those who will undertake to interpret it in their
own linguistic or sociocultural studies. He is best qualified to perform this important task, which otherwise would have to be done
over and over again, often with more limited resources. The stand
he takes on debatable issues is, of course, subject to scholarly
criticism in the light of additional or conflicting evidence.

The special qualification of the editor to provide the essential
background information for the record of usage concerning the
items provided for in the questionnaire derives from his intimate
knowledge of the linguistic and social conditions under which the
fieldworkers do their job and from his experience in planning the
editing item by item. More often than not, he has also participated
in designing the survey and done some fieldwork himself. The
former gives him insight into the general linguistic and sociocultural situation in the area; the latter gives him a "feel" for the
conditions under which usage is elicited and recorded.

Presenting the relevant information, item by item, for proper
orientation does not impose an additional burden upon the busy
editor, since he must in any event accumulate this information for
his own purposes. Except for the simpler items for which a general
editing plan is an adequate guide, he faces the task of designing
effective and economical procedures for the presentation of the
more complicated items, each of which confronts him with special
problems. Among the factors that he may have to take into account
in planning his presentation are the following:

(1) The range of meanings of lexical items;

(2) the dissemination of synonyms, or near-synonyms, regionally,
socially, or by age groups;

(3) the situational, stylistic, and emotive connation of words
(neutral, euphemistic, jocular, derogatory, technical);

(4) the choice of terms as reflecting differences or changes in
fashion;

(5) the informant's familiarity with the "thing-meant";

(6) the status of morphological and phonological variants as
reflected in social dissemination and the informants' reaction and
comments;

(7) the fieldworker's judgment concerning the relative trustworthiness of certain responses or comments;

(8) differences between fieldworkers in eliciting responses or in phonic notation.

Since the editor must take all of these factors into consideration in designing effective editing plans for the more complicated items, there is no reason whatever for withholding this information from others. Far from it. He owes it to the reader to say how he planned his presentation of the data at his disposal. Those who consult his work must, of course, keep in mind that the evidence of usage presented in this manner is deliberately restricted to the data furnished by the sampling survey. Extraneous sources of information are not admitted.

This editorial procedure is illustrated below by several examples adapted from the Linguistic Atlas of New England [Kurath-Bloch-Lowman 1939–43].

Map 196: Horse; Gelding

The map shows the word horse, and after a semicolon gelding and stag (horse) as designations of the castrated male. When horse itself is used, either exclusively or among other meanings, in this latter sense, it is marked by a superior 2.

Horse is used in four different applications: (1) It may refer to any member of the "horse breed," including stallions, geldings and mares; (2) it may refer to male animals only, excluding mares, as in the expression a horse and a mare; (3) it may refer to geldings only. Some informants apply gelding to a horse castrated when young and either horse or stag to one castrated later.

Numerous comments of individual informants are cited in support of the definitions.

Map 284: Doughnut

The map presents the more common terms for cakes of various shapes fried in deep fat. They are of two types: (1) made of rich dough raised with baking powder or (2) of plain dough raised with yeast. Terms for (2) are identified on the map by a superior 2.

A list of terms with definitions based upon comments offered by the informants is presented: doughnut, type (1); doughnut[2], raised ~[2], riz ~[2], type (2); doughnut[3], applied to (1) and (2) indiscriminately; cruller, fried-

cake, nut cake, type (1); sinker, washer, fried hole,
jocular terms for the ring-shaped doughnut.
   More than 100 comments of individual informants
are reproduced.

Map 323: Parlor, Sitting Room

   The following information is provided.
   Older New England houses usually had a "best" room
set aside for special occasions (the reception of visitors,
weddings, funerals, etc.) and a "living" room for the use
of the family and entertaining neighbors and friends.
   The old-fashioned "best" room is (or was) rather generally called the parlor, but front room, fore room, best
room, great room, and drawing room are (or were) also
used. The accumulated "lore" about the parlor is summarized from the numerous comments and reminiscences
of the informants.
   The currency and meanings of living room and sitting
room are similarly presented.
   Complications in usage arise from differences in the
construction of the dwellings, changing fashions in
architecture, and family traditions.

   Further information about the way in which certain factors that
condition usage have been dealt with in the Linguistic Atlas of New
England can be gathered from the maps referred to below.
   (1) The effect of changing fashions: 339 bureau, 340 chest of
drawers.
   (2) The status of folk customs: 409 serenade, 410 a dance, 414
social gathering.
   (3) Neutral, polite, jocular, derogatory, and technical expressions: 190 bull, 354 privy, 450 a rustic.
   (4) The great variety of expressions for emotionally charged
activities or states: 404–7 courting, jilting, 463–64 awkward (person) 472 angry, 479–82 tired, exhausted.
   (5) The social standing of morphological variants and resulting
sensibilities: 642 climbed, 646 ate, 644 drank, 674 (he) isn't (going),
688 (he) doesn't (care), 718 double negation.

1.3 Publication of the Findings

   The edited findings of a sampling survey can be published in full
or selectively.

For full publication two different methods are used: (1) over-printing on a base map or (2) printing in the form of lists. In either case the communities represented in the survey are identified by numbers. Overprinting on a base map has been employed in the atlases of France [Gillieron-Edmont 1902–10], Italy [Jaberg-Jud 1928–40], Rumania [Puscariu-Pop-Petrovici 1938 ff.], Corsica [Bottiglioni 1933–42], and New England [Kurath-Bloch-Lowman 1939–43]. The less costly method of giving the data in lists was introduced for presenting the phonological data for French-speaking Switzerland [Gauchat-Jeanjaquet-Tappolet 1925], is being employed in the survey of the dialects of England [Orton 1962 ff.], and will be used by R. I. McDavid, Jr., in publishing the materials of the Linguistic Atlas of the Middle and South Atlantic States. Either method has its advantages and drawbacks.

Overprinting on a map is costly, especially because it requires the services of a skilled draftsman to letter the hundreds of entries in their proper locations, map by map. For quick orientation it has great advantages, particularly if the base map, printed in a light tint, contains the major political boundaries as well as the more important physiographic features of the landscape (rivers, mountain chains, etc.) that channel or hinder travel and traffic. Even a casual inspection of such a map is apt to reveal the regional dissemination of variants and thus challenge the scholar's interest. When the usage of several social levels or age groups is offered on one and the same map, as in the Linguistic Atlas of New England, the more consistent social and/or age differences in usage are also immedi-ately apparent, if the data are properly presented.

Publishing the findings in the form of lists is decidedly more economical, especially now that typewriter composition is feasible. The disadvantage is that only those that are rather intimately acquainted with the area can readily visualize the geographic dis-semination of the variants, even with the help of a foldout map showing the location of the numbered communities, an aid with which each volume must be provided. However, publishing the findings in this fashion also has its good points. The scholar who pursues specific problems in phonology or morphology, undertakes to establish dialect boundaries, or wants to determine the charac-teristic traits of a speech area, has to assemble pertinent evidence from the storehouse of data published in one form or another. He does this by charting items relevant to his purpose. There is no question but that this necessary operation can be carried out more conveniently and more speedily by drawing upon listed rather than mapped data, as the present writer can testify from ample exper-ience.

Selective publication of field data in more or less simplified form

is highly rewarding. When full publication is not feasible or must
be delayed for financial reasons, selective publication is imperative
as a means of showing the scientific implications of the project and
as a service to other scholars in the field. Even when full publication is in progress, it is often advisable to present some of the data
in simplified form in order to create a sound perspective for those
less intimately acquainted with the data and the emerging problems.

While publication in full involves the presentation of all the data
recorded in response to each of the items investigated—e.g., phonological along with lexical or morphological variants—selective
publication is focused on specific problems for which the field data
provide the material item by item. Thus one can undertake to
assemble evidence for the phonological reflexes of a group of
phonemes of the parent language, gather evidence for recurring
dissemination patterns in regional vocabulary, or compile relevant
data concerning the social behavior of certain morphological features. Such operations provide insight into the linguistic situations
within the area; they are also a necessary preliminary step toward
historical interpretation.

The variants of the selected items can be effectively displayed
on outline maps by contrasting symbols—circles, triangles, squares,
in outline or solid. Placed near the numbers showing the location
of the communities, or simply in the relative position of the communities, geographic dissemination patterns of the variants stand
out clearly. Areas of uniform usage, transition zones, enclaves,
scattered items, effectively make their appearance. This technique
of presenting variants of selected items has been widely used in the
last two decades.

The Word Geography of the Eastern United States [Kurath 1949]
contains 163 full page maps of this type (of which two are reproduced
below), 43 maps displaying heteroglossic lines based upon them, and
a map [figure 3] showing the speech areas of the Eastern States as
established by the lexical heteroglosses. In the preparation of these
maps the unpublished field records from the Middle and the South
Atlantic States as well as the fully published material for New England are drawn upon. The companion volumes on verb forms
[Atwood 1952] and pronunciation [Kurath-McDavid 1961] follow the
same general plan. So does Atwood's Regional Vocabulary of Texas
[1962]. This method has also been used in Europe: by Kloeke
[1950], Hotzenköcherle [1962], and Kolb [1966].

An important application of this procedure, involving a notable
departure from earlier practices, is to be found in the linguistic
atlases of French-speaking Belgium [Remacle-Legros 1953 ff.]
and German-speaking Switzerland [Hotzenköcherle 1962 ff.]. In

these two works, the volumes included for publication of the phonological, lexical, and morphological materials in full are preceded
by a selective presentation of typical phonic reflexes of parent
phonemes in their areal dissemination. Hotzenköcherle devotes two
large volumes—375 pages, including about 300 maps—to this task,
following a procedure briefly described in his preface to volume I.
In doing this, he orients the future users of the atlas and prepares
the way for a structural interpretation of the complicated phonic
data. See my review in Language 30. 515–20 (1963).

2.

From Heterogloss to
Dialect Boundary

2.1 Introduction

The data secured by systematic selective sampling and presented cartographically as described above furnish the basis for outlining the dialectal structure of the area surveyed.

As a first step in working out the areal structure, only items exhibiting fairly clear-cut dissemination patterns are taken into consideration. The expectation is that the items whose variants appear to be disseminated in a complicated or haphazard fashion can best be dealt with after the skeletal structure of the area has been set up tentatively.

In handling the items one by one, attention is focused on the lines that separate the variants, on the heteroglossic lines. These delimit the areas occupied by the variants, on which attention is concentrated in dealing with features peculiar to the several subareas.

When the heteroglossic lines (heteroglosses, for short) drawn for the items provided by the sample are assembled on maps, one finds that in some parts of the area they run in bundles of various sizes—close-knit or spaced. These bundles show the location of major and minor dialect boundaries and thus indicate the dialectal structure of the total area.

Every systematic sampling survey has revealed this situation, definitely disposing of the earlier notion that heteroglossic lines are more or less evenly spaced [so G. Paris 1888; perhaps also

H. Schuchardt 1928 (< 1900): 166–88]. That perhaps no two heteroglosses run precisely the same course is not in conflict with the
observation that they often do form bundles.

To evaluate the relative importance of the dialect boundaries
suggested by the bundles, it is not enough to count the heteroglosses
composing the bundles. The heteroglosses must be evaluated from
the structural point of view before a sound decision can be reached.
For this reason, heteroglosses of different kinds should be assembled
separately, so that they can be evaluated by groups. Each set will
contribute some evidence for subdividing the area; taken together
they will furnish the basis for a generalized scheme designed to
exhibit the dialectal structure of the area. This procedure is labori-
ous, and to some extent arbitrary. But there is no other method that
will do justice to the evidence yielded by the sampling survey.

From the structural point of view, heteroglosses fall into three
major classes: phonological, morphological-syntactic, and lexical.
In turn, phonological and morphological-syntactic heteroglosses are
either structural or nonstructural. Finally, the nonstructural
(subphonemic) heterophones are of two kinds: incidental and phonic.

Listed in the order in which they are discussed below, the classes
of heteroglosses and their subdivisions are as follows:

  I. Lexical
 II. Morphological-syntactic: (1) structural, (2) incidental
III. Phonological: (1) structural (phonemic); (2) nonstructural
     (subphonemic): (a) incidental, (b) phonic

2.2 Lexical Heteroglosses:
the Upper South, the Eastern States, the Midwest

The lexical heteroglosses can be more easily handled than the
morphological and the phonological. Since the lexicon of a language,
though not lacking systematization, is not as rigidly structured as
the morphology and the phonology, all heterolexes yielded by the
survey can be given the same rank and assembled on a single map.

The procedure is as follows. On an outline map on which every
community investigated is set off from its neighbors by lines so as
to provide a "honeycomb grid," the course of each heterolex is
entered segment by segment. In the end, the number of heterolexes
running between any two communities in the area is recorded on the
grid. As a result, the grouping of heteroglosses in bundles of various sizes is brought into relief.

This method is illustrated by E. J. Dearden's investigation of the
regional vocabulary in an area comprising the states of Maryland,
Virginia, and North Carolina [Dearden 1943]. In this study, all of

the varying lexical items recorded for the Linguistic Atlas of the
Eastern United States that exhibit fairly clearly defined regional
disseminations are included. The number of heteroglossic lines
running between any two communities varies from zero to twenty-
seven (see Figure 1). The most prominent bundles form a fairly
continuous, though jagged, contour running from the Blue Ridge
in Virginia southward into the piedmont of North Carolina. Less
prominent bundles separate the Eastern from the Western Shore of
Maryland, tidewater from piedmont Virginia, and eastern Virginia
from eastern North Carolina. These bundles of heteroglosses form
the primary and the secondary dialect boundaries in this extensive
area insofar as the lexicon is concerned.

In passing, it should be noted that this procedure also brings into
relief the subareas of relative uniform word usage, such as the
Piedmont of Virginia and western North Carolina.

The dialect boundaries presented by Kurath in his Word Geography
of the Eastern United States [1949] result from this procedure,
although it cannot be claimed that the method was applied with
statistical precision (see Figure 2).

A few of the heterolexes that set the Midland off from the North
and from the South are presented in Figure 3.

This method of establishing dialect boundaries has also been used
by A. L. Davis in his Word Atlas of the Great Lakes Region [1948].
Relying upon twenty-five heterolexes exhibiting a fairly clear geographic dissemination, he discovered a prominent bundle of lines
that runs in a westerly direction a short distance south of the Great
Lakes (see Figure 4). This bundle reflects the westward extension
of the dialect boundary that separates the North from the Midland in
Pennsylvania. To the north of it the New England variants of the
twenty-five lexical items are current.

The method described above is applicable to the data secured in
any sampling survey and has been used with good results in several
other investigations of the regional vocabulary of American English:
J. D. Hawkins 1935; C. T. Hankey 1960; A. H. Marckwardt 1957;
G. R. Wood 1963.

To my knowledge, the only European study of regional vocabulary
in which an actual count of heteroglosses was used to establish
speech boundaries is that of W. Wenzel [1930].

For the general purpose of determining major and minor speech
boundaries on the basis of regional vocabulary all heterolexes are
accorded the same value, so that the relative importance of such
boundaries rests solely on the number of heterolexes in any given
bundle. There can be no valid objection to this procedure.

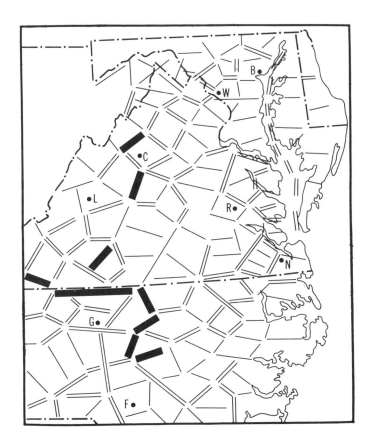

FIGURE 1: <u>Word Boundaries in the Upper South</u>
―――――――   3 to 7 heteroglosses
═══════   8 to 17 heteroglosses
▬▬▬▬▬▬▬   18 to 27 heteroglosses

<u>Cities</u>: B(altimore, C(harlottesville, F(ayetteville,
G(reensboro, L(ynchburg, N(orfolk, R(ichmond, W(ashington.

Adapted from E. J. Dearden <u>Dialect Areas of the South
Atlantic States</u>.

On the other hand, weighting the heterolexes from a certain point of view, as with reference to their expansive, stable, or recessive character, or with regard to the "ranges" of the lexicon, e.g., the vocabulary of the farm and the home, of business and politics, of literature, of science, etc., has its proper function. Such refinements in method often yield valuable insight into the sociocultural dynamics of a speech area.

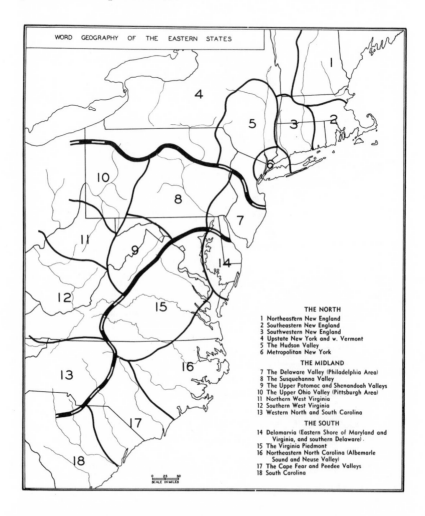

FIGURE 2: The Speech Areas of the Eastern States

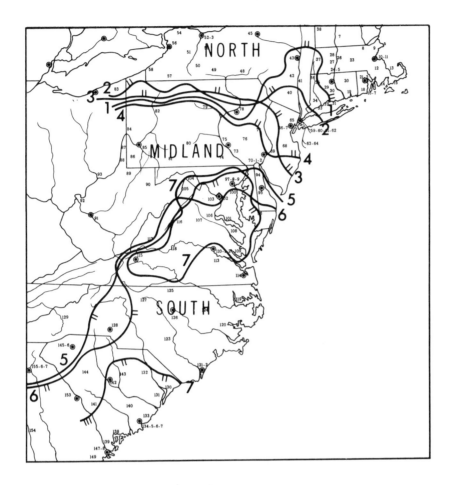

FIGURE 3: A. Northern Words

   1. buttry 'pantry' [Kurath 1949: fig. 51]
   2. spider 'frying pan' [ibid.: fig. 68]
   3. darning needle 'dragon fly' [ibid.: fig. 141]
   4. pail 'bucket' [ibid.: fig. 66]

      B. Southern Words

   5. low 'moo' [Kurath 1949: fig. 96]
   6. lightwood / laitəd / 'kindling' [ibid.: fig. 29]
   7. corn house 'corn crib' [ibid.: fig. 57]

2.3 Types of Phonological Heteroglosses

The handling of phonological and morphological heteroglosses yielded by selective sampling is much more complicated. Structural heterophones and heteromorphs must be kept apart from the non-structural.

Phonological heteroglosses fall into three distinct classes, which owing to their relative importance in the structure of the language, must be separately handled.

Phonemic heteroglosses exhibited in the data are obviously of the greatest importance, since by their very nature they occur in more or less numerous morphemes, of which only a few instances are apt

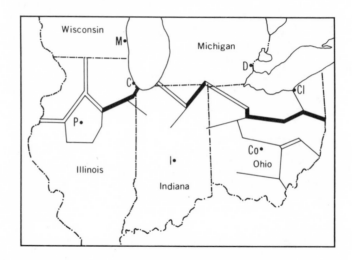

FIGURE 4:   Bundles of Heterolexes in the Great Lakes Area
━━━━━━━━━━━   more than 15 heterolexes
══════════   10 to 14 heterolexes
──────────   5 to 9 heterolexes

Cities: C(hicago, Cl(eveland, Co(lumbus, D(etroit,
I(ndianapolis, M(ilwaukee, P(eoria.

Adapted from A. L. Davis A Word Atlas of the Great Lakes Region.

to be included in the questionnaire. Separating phonemic heteroglosses from other phonological variants presupposes a phonemic
analysis of at least the major dialect types current in the area, so
that the shared phonemic units can be distinguished from the
regionally restricted ones.

When two or more plans of phonemicizing the data seem feasible,
preference is given to the one that facilitates the comparison of the
dialects. Needless to say, the plan chosen should be described and
the inventory of shared and of regionally or socially restricted
phonemes set up. This procedure has been applied, and strictly
adhered to, in dealing with the phonological data recorded in the
Eastern United States [Kurath and McDavid 1961].

Phonological variants that do not involve the phonemic structure
are of two kinds, phonic and incidental.

Shared phonemes may differ markedly in their phonic realization,
as the checked vowels / æ / of man and / ʌ / of sun, or the free vowels
/ o / of no and / e / of day in American English. Such purely phonic
heteroglosses, striking and pervasive as they may be, are of lower
rank than phonemic ones, and must be handled as a separate set.

The incidence of shared phonemes in the lexicon, i.e., in shared
words, may differ from area to area or from one social level to
another. Thus some varieties of American English have the free
vowel / u / of do, fool in room, roof, root, others the checked vowel
/ ʊ / of full; some have voiced / z / in greasy, others voiceless / s /.
Such incidental heterophones, though easily observed and by no
means negligible, should be given a rank lower than the phonic ones.
They affect neither the phonemic system nor the phonic realization
of the phonemes.

2.31 Phonemic Heteroglosses

In the Eastern United States, phonemic, phonic, and incidental
heteroglosses are only in partial agreement.

Phonemic heteroglosses set off a number of subareas on the
Atlantic Slope (see Figure 5):

(1) The semivowel / ə /, as in ear, care, door, poor, is confined
to four subareas: eastern New England, metropolitan New York,
eastern Virginia, and South Carolina-Georgia.

(2) The same subareas have contrastive vowels in such words
as heart ≠ hot, lark ≠ lock. Elsewhere postvocalic / r / survives in
heart, lark, differentiating them from hot, lock.

(3) Checked / ɵ / contrasting with free / o /, as in whole ≠ hole,
road ≠ rode, is largely confined to New England.

(4) Merging in / ɒ / of the checked vowel of cot, stock and the free
vowel of law occurs in eastern New England and in western Pennsylvania.

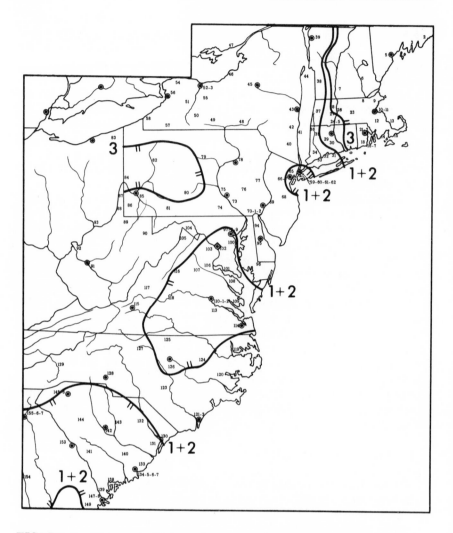

FIGURE 5: Phonemic Heteroglosses on the Atlantic Slope

1. The semivowel /ə̯ /, as in <u>ear, care, door, poor</u> [Kurath–McDavid 1961: map 156]
2. The free vowel /a ∼ ɑ̈ /, as in <u>far, heart</u> (contrasting with the checked vowel /ɑ /, as in <u>hot</u>) [ibid.: map 46]
3. <u>law, caught, stalk</u> and <u>cot, stock</u> have the same vowel, i.e. the free vowel /ɒ / [ibid.: map 15]

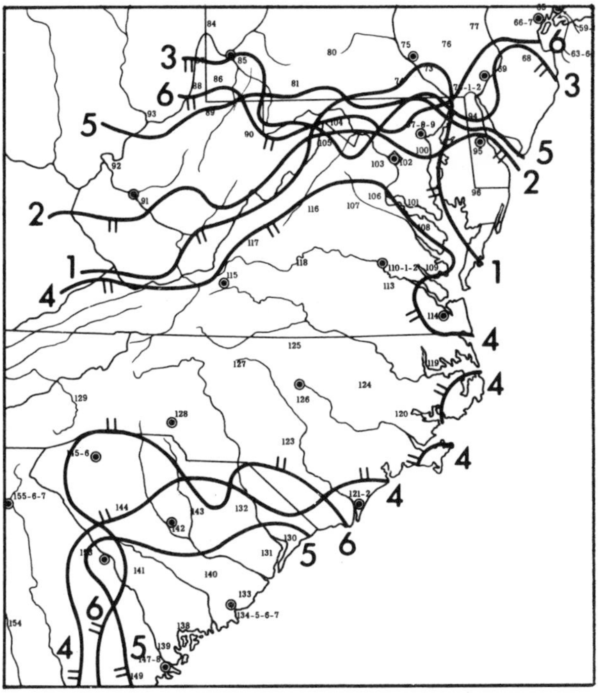

FIGURE 6: Southern Diaphones

1. The phoneme / ʌ / of sun, love articulated as a raised [ʌ] or as a diphthongal [ʌ^{ə}] (Kurath-McDavid: map 10)
2. The / æ / of ashes, half sounded as diphthongal [æ^{ɛ}] (ibid.: map 14)
3. The / u / of two, moon fronted to [ʉ] (ibid.: map 17)
4. The / ɔ / of salt, law articulated as [ɒɔ], with progressive rounding (ibid.: map 23)
5. The / ai / of high, nine sounded as [a·^{ɛ} ~ a·^{ə} ~ a·] (ibid.: map 26)
6. The / au / of down, mountain realized as [æʊ] (ibid.: map 28)

2.32 Phonic Heteroglosses

The course of some of the phonic heteroglosses agrees to some extent with that of phonemic ones.

Thus (1) unconstricted or slightly constricted / 3 /, as in thirty, is largely confined to the / ə / areas [Kurath-McDavid: Map 25].

(2) The unconstricted diphthongal articulation [31] of / 3 /, as in thirty, appears only in the / ə / areas of metropolitan New York and South Carolina-Georgia [ibid.: Map 25].

(3) Striking positional allophones of / ai / and / au /, as in nine ~ night and down ~ out, are restricted to the / ə / areas of Virginia and South Carolina [ibid.: Maps 26–29].

Other phonic heteroglosses follow an entirely different course. As a loose bundle running in a westerly direction south of the Pennsylvania line, they set the South and parts of the South Midland off from the North Midland. They agree in a general way with a prominent bundle of lexical heteroglosses. In the Lower South they agree rather markedly with phonemic heteroglosses. See Figure 6 and compare Figures 5 and 1.

FIGURE 7: Lexical Incidence of Shared Phonemes

A. Northern Features

1. root predominantly rimes with foot [Kurath-McDavid 1961: map 113]
2. broom has the vowel of full in New England, less frequently in New York State [ibid.: map 107]
3. gums often has the vowel of fool or of full in folk speech, less commonly among the middle class [ibid.: map 85]
4. goal rimes with fool, especially in New England folk speech [ibid.: map 122]
5. on (adv.) has the vowel of hot [ibid.: map 138]

B. Southern Features

6. poor rimes with pour [Kurath-McDavid: map 42]
7. bulge has the vowel of bull [ibid.: map 84]
8. creek rimes with week [ibid.: map 97]
9. coop has the vowel of foot [ibid.: map 108]
10. the vowel in Tuesday, due, new is preceded by / j / [ibid.: map 163–5]

2.33 Lexical Incidence of Shared Phonemes

Not infrequently the incidence of shared phonemes in the lexicon
varies regionally (and especially socially). Though of low rank,
these incidental heterophones must be taken into account along with
the phonemic and the phonic, when the total area is subdivided in
terms of phonological features.

Two separate bundles of incidental heterophones run westward
from the Atlantic coast: one through northern Pennsylvania, the
other south of Pennsylvania. See Figure 7. Both of these bundles
are in substantial agreement with rather prominent bundles of
heterolexes.

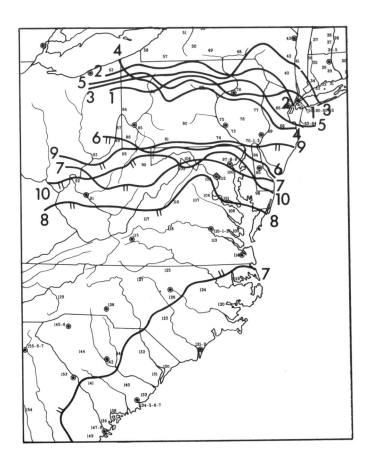

Other incidental heterophones set off subareas that are fairly congruent with lexical subareas. Thus the / a / in calf, can't [Kurath McDavid 1961: Maps 68–69], the / æ / in care, stairs [ibid.: Map 39], and the / e / in Mary [ibid.: Map 50] characterize eastern New England; the lack of contrastive vowels in such pairs as morning, mourning, horse, hoarse, and merry, Mary [ibid.: Maps 44 and 49–50] the North Midland; checked / ɑ / in long [ibid.: Map 137] is confined to the Upper South, the midfront vowel / e / in here, beard [ibid.: Maps 34–36] to the Lower South.

All in all, in the Eastern United States the phonological heteroglosses of whatever kind do not diverge markedly from the behavior of the lexical heteroglosses. They exhibit a very similar regional structure of that area, so that the grouping of the speech areas based upon the regional vocabulary is supported by the phonological data to a considerable extent.

However, phonemic heteroglosses make some of the coastal subareas—Eastern New England, Metropolitan New York, the Virginia Piedmont, and South Carolina—more conspicuous; and the loose bundles of phonic and incidental heterophones running through northern Maryland and West Virginia [Figures 6 and 7 above] set the North Midland (Pennsylvania) off from the South Midland more decidedly than does the bundle of heterolexes.

2.4 Morphological Heteroglosses

Structural differences in morphology do not exist in cultivated American English. Even incidental heteromorphs, as of the verb, are largely confined to folk speech and rather sharply recessive. Those that have been revealed by the Linguistic Atlas survey of the Eastern States are rather fully discussed by Atwood [1953].

As the accompanying illustrations show, regional verb forms exhibit the same dissemination patterns as regional words and sounds. Some past tense forms are peculiar to Northern folk speech, though / ɛt / and / dov / are also current among the middle class and not always avoided by the cultured; others are confined to Southern folk speech. See Figure 8.

There is one aspect of the morphology of the verb that seems to involve a structural difference between folk speech and cultivated speech in American English.

In folk speech (1) the past tense and the past participle are nearly always identical, as in broke, drunk, drove or driv, took or taken; and (2) the past tense and the past participle are leveled to the form of the present in come, fit, give and some other cases. This deviation from cultivated usage is clearly not structural. It only increases

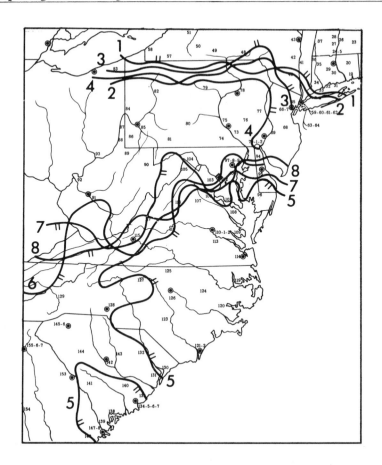

FIGURE 8: Northern Verb Forms

1. / klɪm / 'climbed,' rimes with dim [Atwood 1953: fig. 5]
2. / si / 'saw,' rimes with sea [ibid.: fig. 17]
3. / ɛt / 'ate,' rimes with let [ibid.: fig. 9]
4. / dov / 'dived,' rimes with grove [ibid.: fig. 6]

Southern Verb Forms

5. / hirn / or / hjɜn / 'heard' [Atwood 1953: fig. 12]
6. / holp / 'helped' [ibid.: fig. 13]
7. / maut / 'might' (rimes with out) [ibid.: fig. 14]
8. / rɪz / 'rose' (rimes with fizz) [ibid.: fig. 16]

the incidence of the patterns represented in cultivated speech (1) by
live-lived, find-found, hold-held, etc., and (2) by let, set, cut. Even
the not infrequent omission of the auxilliary have, as in I just heard
about it, I never seen the like of it, I been looking for you, has its
parallel in the informal speech of the upper classes. It does not
eliminate the distinction between the simple past tense and the
phrasal past perfect in folk speech.

2.5 Concluding Remarks

At this point in our discussion we may ask the crucial question:
Is the substantial agreement between lexical, phonological, and
morphological heteroglosses in American English typical?

If so, either set of heteroglosses could be taken as fairly representative of the dialect boundaries existing in any given area, and
hence of its dialectal structure. Moreover, a rather small number
of heterolexes, of heterophones, or of heteromorphs running a
similar course could serve as indicators of areal patterning. Even
a single heterogloss, unless shown to have a unique course, could be
taken to be a significant indicator, a "straw in the wind."

This would give substance to the practice of many European
scholars who intuitively select a small number of phonological
heteroglosses, or even a single one, to represent major and minor
dialect boundaries within the area investigated. Such choices are
usually made by men who have more or less extensive information
of one kind or another about the behavior of other heteroglosses.
Hence, though intuitive and not statistical, they are apt to be significant. But they are surely not definitive.

If, on the other hand, the findings of the Linguistic Atlas of the
Eastern United States should turn out to be atypical, if in other
language areas lexical, phonological, and morphological heteroglosses should be shown to diverge from each other more or less
sharply, intuitively chosen indicators would lose much of their
significance. Since no analysis comparable in scope with that of
American English has as yet been made anywhere in Europe or in
other parts of the world, the validity of selective indicators in displaying the dialectal structure of an area is still in doubt.

3.

The Sociocultural Background
of Dialect Areas
in American English

3.1 Introduction

A brief description of several attempts to achieve insight into
the dialectal structure of an area on the basis of known heteroglossic
lines, or to provide at least a tentative orientation, should throw
light on some of the problems that must be faced.

In order to characterize and to evaluate the proposed schemes,
the following factors must be taken into consideration:

(1) The character and fullness of the available data as determined by the content of the questionnaire, the choice of communities,
and the method of gathering the data.

(2) The method of establishing boundaries within the area: (a)
on the basis of congruent bundles of lexical, phonological, and
morphological heteroglosses; (b) on the basis of bundles of any of
the three types taken separately; or (c) on the basis of representative
or diagnostic heteroglosses. (d) A boundary can also be suggested
"intuitively" by a "convenient" heterogloss.

(3) Whether a diagnostic heterogloss is structural or nonstructural is another point that must be taken into account.

3.2 The Dialectal Structure of New England

Phonological and lexical heteroglosses form loose bundles running
northward from Long Island Sound to Canada. These bundles divide
New England into an Eastern and a Western dialect area (see Figure 9).

The course of these strands of heteroglosses exhibits no congruence with the boundaries of the New England states. Connecticut, Massachusetts, and Vermont are cut in half, while New Hampshire and Maine lie well within the Eastern area. Political boundaries have evidently not seriously interfered with communication between the inhabitants of the several states.

When we turn to a map showing the distribution of the population in New England (1930), we discover that of the two areas of concentration one lies to the east of the bundles of heteroglosses and the other to the west (see Figure 10). From this demographic fact we anticipate that the development of these two major dialect areas of New England is somehow connected with these two population centers and their history.

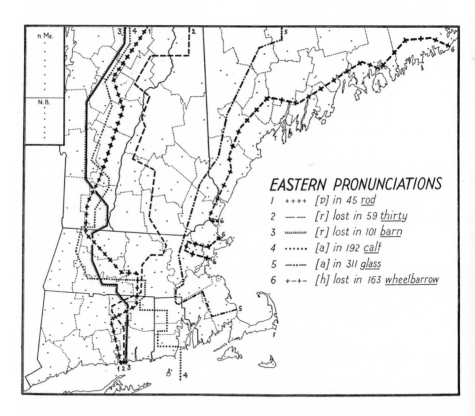

EASTERN PRONUNCIATIONS

1 ++++ [ɒ] in 45 rod
2 —— [r] lost in 59 thirty
3 ⸺ [r] lost in 101 barn
4 ...... [a] in 192 calf
5 —··— [a] in 311 glass
6 +–+– [h] lost in 163 wheelbarrow

FIGURE 9: New England: Eastern Pronunciations. From Kurath, Handbook of the Linguistic Geography of New England.

We also observe that most of the heteroglosses run through
sparsely settled areas—along the Green Mountains of Vermont and
through the hill country of central Massachusetts and eastern
Connecticut. Such areas impede communication and thus tend to
create and to stabilize existing dialect boundaries.

The Eastern concentration area extends from Narragansett Bay
(Providence, R. I.) to Casco Bay (Portland, Me.). Its dominant
center is Massachusetts Bay (Boston). The Western area of concentration extends from Long Island Sound (New Haven) to Hartford
and Springfield on the Connecticut River. Both of these centers date

FIGURE 10: New England: Population Distribution, 1930
From J. K. Wright, editor, New England's Prospect: 1933, page 23.
New York, 1933.

from early Colonial times and have continuously, and increasingly, influenced the speech of their back county.

The chronology of the settlement of New England has fortunately been worked out in considerable detail. Between 1630 and 1645 colonies were planted along the open Atlantic and on the lower Connecticut River. Expanding slowly, they did not establish contact with each other for about half a century (see Figure 11), a period during which some regional differences in usage must have become established. Half a century later (1725) these two settlement areas were in contact with each other in Connecticut and in parts of Massachusetts, but the sparsely settled hill country connecting them interfered with communication.

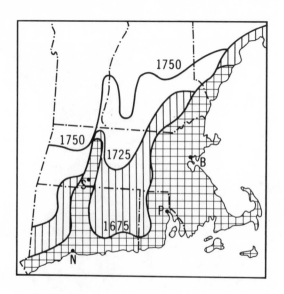

FIGURE 11: New England: Chronology of Settlement

Settled ⊞ before 1675 ⦀ by 1725 ☐ by 1750

Cities: B(oston, N(ew Haven, P(rovidence, S(pringfield

Based upon Kurath, Handbook of the Linguistic Geography of New England (foldout map).

Even more important is the fact that each of these areas developed a transportation system radiating from the old centers outward to the peripheral settlements, which served to consolidate them economically, socially, and culturally. This process of integration continued with increasing force in the nineteenth century when turnpikes and railroads were built. The network of railroads in operation in 1930 effectively portrays this situation (see Figure 12). Add

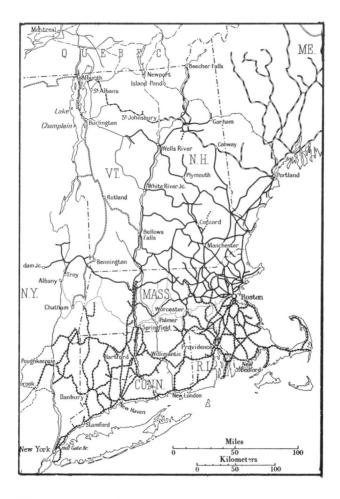

FIGURE 12: New England: Railroads
From J. K. Wright, editor, New England's Prospect: 1933, page 345. New York, 1933.

to this the prestige enjoyed by Boston-Cambridge-Concord from the
middle of the nineteenth century onward in the fields of literature
and scholarship, and you have a picture of the sociocultural forces
that have preserved Eastern New England as a highly distinctive
dialect area.

Eastern New England is of course not a wholly uniform speech
area. Settlement history is reflected, for instance, in the survival
of tempest "storm" and cade "pet lamb" from Narragansett Bay to
Cape Cod, i.e., in the colonies established in Rhode Island and in the
Plymouth area [Kurath 1949: Figure 12]. Recession of the highly
distinctive checked vowel / ɵ /, as in coat, road, home, is in progress,
as shown by its regional, social, and age distribution [Avis 1961].

This brief account of the sociocultural background of the two
major speech areas of New England must suffice. Its present purpose is to illustrate the method by which the discovery of congruences between dialect boundaries and the areas set off by them and
sociocultural boundaries and domains leads to more or less plausible
historical interpretations of areal linguistic phenomena.

3.3 The Boundary between the Northern and
the Midland Dialect Areas

A close-knit bundle of lexical, phonological, and morphological
heteroglosses runs through northern Pennsylvania, some thirty miles
south of the state line, and continues westward into Ohio. At the
eastern end (near Scranton) the heteroglosses fan out, some of them
swerving southeastward through New Jersey, others continuing eastward to pass north of New York City (see Figure 13).

The prominent dialect boundary in northern Pennsylvania clearly
reflects settlement history, channeled and reinforced by the topography. While the Pennsylvania settlements expanded up the Susquehanna Valley to the forested area in the northern part of the state,
westward across the Alleghenies to the upper Ohio and its tributaries
(Pittsburgh), and southwestward into the valleys of the Appalachians,
New Englanders migrated westward into the basin of the Great Lakes,
skirting the Dutch settlements in the Hudson Valley. New Englanders
also moved southward into eastern New Jersey. From Upstate New
York, some of them pushed southward into the wooded hill country of
northern Pennsylvania. These lines of expansion are suggested in
Figure 14. The chronology of the settlement is shown in Paullin-
Wright 1933: Plate 76A–E.

In the Hudson Valley and in New Jersey the transition area
between the North and the Midland reflects partly the complicated
history of the settlement—English over Dutch—and partly the later

effects of the chief communication route (New York-Philadelphia)
that intersects the settlement boundary between East Jersey and
West Jersey.

The speech of Upstate New York is obviously derived from that
of New England. Features peculiar to eastern New England, such
as the loss of postvocalic /r / in beard, hard, board, or the low
front vowel /a / in half, pass, aunt, survive only sporadically. The
chief reason for this is the fact that the majority of the settlers
came from rural western New England at a time when the increasing
population of eastern New England was absorbed into the developing
industries and engaged in seafaring.

In Pennsylvania the dialect boundary between the North and the
Midland, created by the population movements outlined above, was
supported in later years by the sparsely settled belt in the heavily
forested section of northern Pennsylvania.

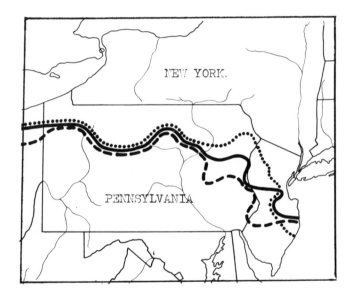

FIGURE 13: The Southern Boundary of Three Northern Words

    ━━━━━━━ Whiffletree, Whippletree 'swingletree'
    ━━ ━━ Pail
    · · · · · · · · · Darning Needle 'dragonfly'

From H. Kurath, A Word Geography of the Eastern States.

The westward extension of this boundary has been established on the basis of the sampling survey of the Great Lakes area directed by A. H. Marckwardt (see Figure 15). On lexical evidence, the dividing line between the North and the Midland runs through northern Ohio, Indiana, and Illinois to the Mississippi River (near Burlington, Iowa). To the north of it, New England regionalisms are current, of which many can be traced all the way to the North Pacific Coast, as C. E. Reed [1956, 1957] has shown.

3.4 The Structure of the Upper South

The Upper South, focused on eastern Virginia, constitutes a rather well defined subdivision of the Southern dialect area. Its northern boundary runs in an arc from the Atlantic Ocean through Delaware (north of Dover) and Maryland (north of Baltimore) to the Blue Ridge Mountains of Virginia. From there the dividing line follows the Blue Ridge southwestward to the upper reaches of the Roanoke River. To the north of this boundary lies the North Midland area, to the west of it the South Midland area. The southern limit of

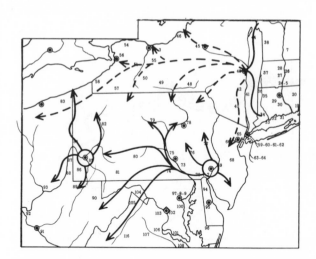

FIGURE 14: The Boundary between the Northern and the Midland Dialect Areas

The arrows suggest the westward expansion of the settlements from New England and from eastern Pennsylvania in the latter part of the eighteenth and the first two decades of the nineteenth century.

this area is less clearly defined. It has the character of a transition belt formed by spaced heteroglosses, some of which dip into north central North Carolina, while others follow the tidal inlet of the James River.

The focal area of the Upper South is suggested by three concentric lexical isoglosses shown in Figure 16 and by an important phonological feature in Figure 17.

The search for extralinguistic factors that might be responsible for the prominent dialect boundary that sets the Upper South off from the Midland reveals immediately that there is no congruence what-

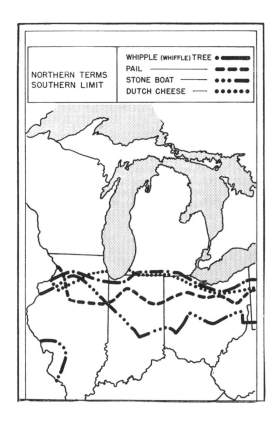

FIGURE 15: The Great Lakes Area: Northern Words
From A. H. Marckwardt, Principal and Subsidiary Dialect Areas in the North-Central States.

ever with major political boundaries, i.e., with state lines: the
linguistic boundary cuts right through Delaware, Maryland, and
Virginia. Secondly, although this boundary rests upon the Blue Ridge
Mountains in Virginia, which rise steeply out of the coastal plain to
form a rather formidable natural barrier to communication, it runs
right through the coastal plain in Maryland and Delaware. An investigation of settlement history, the character of the economy, and the
social organization of the Upper South readily leads to the discovery
of forces that have shaped this dialect area.

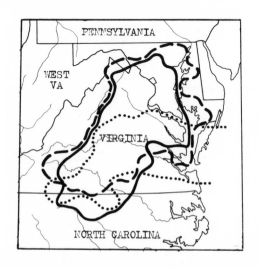

FIGURE 16: The Virginia Piedmont: Word Boundaries

━━━━━	Cuppin 'cowpen'
━━ ━━	Corn House 'corncrib'
· · · · · · ·	Cow House 'cow barn'

From H. Kurath, A Word Geography of the Eastern States.

The Upper South was settled by gradual expansion from the colonies planted on Chesapeake Bay in the seventeenth century. These movements up the river valleys were controlled to a large extent by the plantation aristocracy engaged in the cultivation of tobacco for the European market. As the fertility of the "old fields" was exhausted, new land suitable for growing tobacco was cleared. The heart of this plantation country is strikingly reflected in the concentration of Negro slaves in the Piedmont of Virginia from 1790 to 1860 [Paullin-Wright 1932: plates 67B and 68B].

From the colonial seaports of this area—Richmond on the James River, Fredericksburg on the Rappahannock, and Alexandria on the Potomac—the tobacco was shipped to England, and in return manufactured goods were imported. The common interest of the dominant plantation aristocracy consolidated the area both economically and socioculturally. The linguistic integration of this area clearly emerged from this situation.

The areas north and west of the Upper South were settled largely from, and by way of, Pennsylvania. Northern Maryland and the Valley of Virginia (west of the Blue Ridge) never were plantation

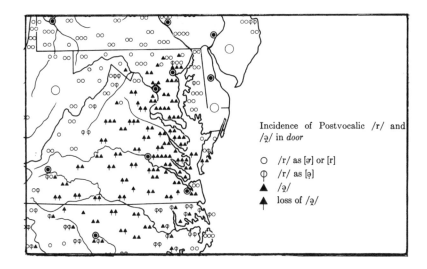

Incidence of Postvocalic /r/ and /ə/ in *door*

O /r/ as [ɚ] or [r]
Φ /r/ as [ə]
▲ /ə/
↑ loss of /ə/

FIGURE 17: The Virginia Piedmont: Postvocalic / ə /
From H. Kurath and R. I. McDavid, Jr., The Pronunciation of English in the Atlantic States.

country. The settlers, many of them Ulster Scots and Germans, engaged in general farming; wheat fields and orchards characterized the landscape. In Virginia, the conflicting economic interests between the coastal plain and the Valley of Virginia, and consequently the divergent attitudes toward slavery, created a regional antagonism that tended to keep the two dialect areas apart.

In Figure 18 the settlement paths of the South and of the South Midland, and the dialect boundary separating them, are presented schematically.

Although set off from the Midland dialect area by a well defined boundary, especially in its northern sector, the Upper South is still rather far from uniform in its linguistic usage. The Eastern Shore of Chesapeake Bay has preserved a considerable number of old local

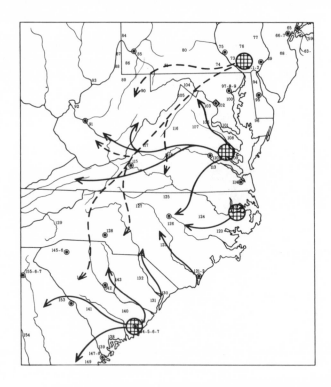

FIGURE 18: Settlement Paths of the Coastal South and of the South Midland

features. Even the points of land between the tidal inlets of the
rivers on the western shore have not yet been brought fully into line
with the dominant focal area of the Upper South—the Piedmont of
Virginia. Diffusion from this center is still in progress, as evi-
denced by the social dissemination of variants on its periphery
[Kurath 1964: 135—44].

3.5 The Lower South

The sociocultural factors underlying the dialect situation of the
Lower South, of which South Carolina is the focus, resemble those
of the Upper South in many ways. There are, however, some rather
marked differences.

The plantation economy (indigo, rice, and later cotton) controlled
the life of the people from the very beginning and created the steeply
graded social structure of the Lowcountry. Even more than in Virginia, the planter class dominated economic, political, and social
affairs and in time largely submerged the Upcountry, where Ulster
Scots and Germans from Pennsylvania had settled in considerable
numbers. This development has been admirably described by a
South Carolinian, R. I. McDavid, Jr. [1948]. The author shows how
some linguistic features once peculiar to the Lowcountry of South
Carolina have been diffused to the Upcountry from the prestige dialect of the planter class. To be sure, some other distinctive traits
of Lowcountry speech have not spread inland, as the ingliding
articulation of the vowels / e, o / of eight [e$^\partial$ t], coat [ko$^\partial$ t] in
the Charleston dialect, a feature that seems to be receding even
there.

Some phonological features peculiar to the Lower South are displayed in Kurath-McDavid 1961: maps 16, 19, 21, 25, 156.

3.6 The Pacific States

The English spoken in the Pacific States—California, Oregon,
and Washington—has been investigated by David W. Reed and by
Carroll E. Reed, partly by direct observation in the field and partly
by correspondence. Their questionnaire includes a fair number of
lexical items for which regional synonyms had been established in
the Eastern States [Kurath 1949] and in the derivative North Central
States [Davis 1948].

The evidence secured by correspondence in response to a "check
list" of words whose currency is regionally restricted in the Eastern
States is presented and analysed by D. Reed [1954] for California and
by C. Reed [1956, 1957] for Oregon, Washington, and Idaho.

The chief findings are: (1) In this vast area, extending some eleven hundred miles from Mexico to Canada, the dissemination of regional Eastern words differs little from state to state, although San Francisco Bay, the Willamette Valley of Oregon, and the Puget Sound area of Washington were separate "growing points." (2) Regional synonyms of the East are current side by side without any marked differences in their relative frequency from state to state. (3) Words used in large sections of the Atlantic Slope and/or the North Central States appear with greater frequency than synonyms restricted to subareas of the East. (4) Regional words derived from the Northern dialect area (New England and the basin of the Great Lakes) and from the North Midland (Pennsylvania and the Ohio Valley) appear with similar frequency, whereas words peculiar to the South Atlantic States are rare. (5) The distribution by age groups shows that regional words are receding sharply all the way from California to Washington.

The authors point out some of the sociocultural factors underlying the behavior of the words investigated. Other factors can easily be adduced, since the settlement history of the Pacific Coast and later developments are so well known.

The salient facts can be briefly stated. Beginning with the 1840's, California, Oregon, and Washington received their rapidly growing English-speaking population largely from the same sources: New England, the Middle Atlantic States, and the Midwest. Immigrants from abroad poured into all of the Pacific States, though California had the largest share. In time the foreigners learned the language of the dominant English stock. These sociocultural factors account for the striking similarity in word usage throughout the Pacific States.

As in other sections of the United States, the recession of the largely rural regional words reflects the mechanization of farming and the rapid urbanization since the turn of the century. Nearly three-fourths of the population of the Pacific States now live in urban areas and are quite unfamiliar with life on the farm, where regional words brought in from the East survive as valuable evidence for the provenience of the native American stock of the Far West.

Among the words that clearly establish the Northern provenience of large elements among the English-speaking settlers in the Pacific States are the following: co boss! a call to cows; angleworm "earthworm"; darning needle "dragon fly." Confined to the Northern dialect area on the Atlantic Slope [Kurath 1949: Figures 99, 140, 141] and to the basin of the Great Lakes [Davis 1948: Maps 163, 165, 239], these lexical items unmistakably reflect the westward migration of New Englanders and their descendants in the basin of the Great Lakes to the Pacific Coast.

The westward trek from Pennsylvania and the Ohio Valley—the
North Midland speech area—is shown with equal clarity by the
currency of regional Midland words in the Pacific States, among
them blinds "roller shade," greenbeans "string beans," sook! a call
to cows, for which see Kurath 1949: Figures 49, 133, 99 and Davis
1948: Maps 178, 210, 163.

The relative frequency of these Northern and Midland words
appears to be much the same in California and in Washington, which
suggests that the proportion of "Northerners" and "Midlanders" in
these two states as a whole differs little.

The behavior of regional words common to the North and the
North Midland of the Eastern States supports this inference. In
addition, it confirms the rule that the frequency with which such
words appear in the "derivative area" of the Pacific States depends
upon the extent of their currency in the "mother area." Thus whinny
[Kurath 1949: Figure 97; Davis 1948: Map 161] and skunk [Kurath
1949: Figure 137], shared by the North and the North Midland, are
much more widely disseminated in California and Washington than
the Northern and the Midland words illustrated above. In conformity
with this rule, words confined to subareas of the North or the Midland survive only in scattered instances or not at all. See the lists
in D. Reed 1954: 13–14 and C. Reed 1956: 7.

The calculation of the frequency with which regional words imported from the East occur in the Pacific States is an important
contribution of the Reeds to the method of area linguistics, which
has been applied with significant results to the regional vocabulary
of Texas by E. B. Atwood [1962]. This device has special importance
for dealing with derivative speech areas in which usage reflects
recent mixture without any clear regional dissemination of the variants.

3.7 Texas

E. B. Atwood's book on The Regional Vocabulary of Texas [1962]
is a well planned and circumspect treatment of one aspect of the
linguistic situation in the state of Texas and its neighbors—Louisiana,
Arkansas, Oklahoma, and New Mexico. Most of his data were gathered between 1950 and 1960 by his friends and students with the help
of a questionnaire. For Oklahoma, W. R. Van Riper contributed his
field materials, for Louisiana, M. Babington.

For his questionnaire Atwood selected (1) items referring to
farming and to life in the countryside for which regionally restricted
(varying) terms are current in the eastern United States [Kurath
1949]; (2) designations referring to the range cattle industry and the

topography of the western part of the state; and (3) some expressions
that seemed to be peculiar to Texas or to southern Louisiana. The
last two groups enabled him to show the Spanish and the French contributions to the vocabulary of Texas and to set off the areas in whicl
they are current. The stock of regional terms brought in from the
"mother" area of American English along the Atlantic during the
westward movement, and recent trends in their currency, naturally
are his primary concern.

The author found that most of the English regional terms used
(or formerly used) by Texans are derived from the South Atlantic
States—the Southern and the South Midland dialect areas [Kurath
1949: Figure 3], and that the extent to which they are current in
Texas stands in a fairly clear relation to the size of the areas they
occupied in the Eastern States around 1940.

Thus bucket "pail," Christmas gift "merry Christmas," (corn)
shucks "husks," dog irons ~ fire dogs "andirons," paling "picket"
(of a fence), pullybone "wishbone," which are common to the South
and the South Midland on the Atlantic slope, are widely used in
Texas; and so are nicker "whinny" and clabber cheese "cottage
cheese," although the former is not current in the Carolinas and the
latter is restricted to the South Midland and North Carolina.

Some terms that in the East are confined to the Southern speech
area (the plantation country of the coastal plain), as snap beans
"greenbeans," carry home "take (somebody) home," and low "moo"
have (or had until recently) considerable currency in Texas and
adjoining areas; so do sook! a call to cows, (quarter) till (eleven)
"to," and the phrase (I) want off "want to get off," which are peculiar
to Pennsylvania and the South Midland (West Virginia to the Upcountry of the Carolinas). See Figure 19.

Words that have limited currency in the East are infrequent in
Texas or not used at all: Virginian batter-bread "soft corn cake";
coastal Carolinian spider "frying pan," press peach "clingstone
peach," whicker "whinny"; and fire-board "mantle shelf," red-worm
"earth worm" of the southern Appalachians.

There are some exceptions to the rule that expressions current
in large sections of the Atlantic states are more widely used in
Texas than those confined to smaller areas. Thus general Southern
light-wood "kindling" is infrequent in Texas, whereas North Caro-
linians tow sack "burlap sack" has general currency. The history
of the "thing-meant" obviously has a bearing upon the frequency witl
which a term is used, and hence upon its dissemination.

The fact that words confined to different speech areas of the
Atlantic States are current side by side in Texas leads to the inference—on purely linguistic grounds—that some of the early settlers,

or their forebears, ultimately came from the Southern dialect area
(the coastal plain) and others from the South Midland speech area
(the Appalachians and the piedmont of the Carolinas). Since the
English settlements in Texas lag only one or two decades behind
those in the intervening areas—Trans-Appalachia and the Gulf
States—the connection with the Eastern "homeland" is very close:
Tennessee and Arkansas settlers who moved into Texas had only
recently crossed the Appalachians, and the cotton belt in Alabama
and Mississippi was not taken up until 1820–30 [Paullin-Wright:
plates 76E, F]. Data concerning the provenience of the early and
the later Texas settlers, though rather fragmentary, agree with
the linguistic evidence [Atwood 1962: 7–10].

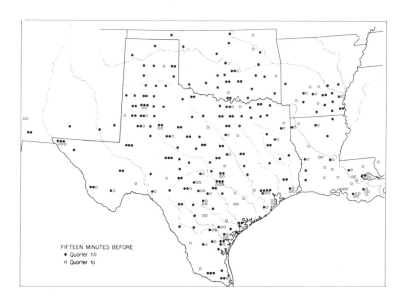

FIGURE 19: Texas: Quarter till and quarter to
From E. B. Atwood, The Regional Vocabulary of Texas.

Atwood is inclined to attribute greater influence upon the regional vocabulary of Texas to the South Midland dialect than to Coastal Southern, but the evidence is far from conclusive. Until phonological and morphological data become available, the question should in my opinion be kept open.

The author finds no lexical evidence for drawing a linguistic boundary along the Brazos River, which on sociocultural grounds— the concentration of slaves in 1860—had previously been suggested as the probable western limit of the Southern dialect area [Kurath 1949: 37]. Nor is there any clear division between the north central and the southeastern section of the state, although some South Midland words have more extensive currency in the former and some Southern words in the latter [Atwood 1962: 82].

In his analysis of the currency of regional words, Atwood introduced two procedures hitherto not employed in this country or abroad: (1) A statistical determination of the frequency of the regional terms within the total area investigated; and (2) a statistical treatment of trends in word usage as inferred from the dissemination by age groups. These calculations were carried out with the aid of an electronic computer.

As to trends in usage, it is important to remember that many of the regional words brought in from the East fall within the semantic domain of farm and home life. Their currency has declined sharply in the nineteenth century, what with urbanization, merchandising of food stuffs, mechanization of the farm, extended schooling, and changes in fashion. Atwood effectively chronicles their decline generation by generation and convincingly points out specific sociocultural factors that underly their recession. His findings are significant not only for Texas and its neighbors; they are symptomatic of trends in word usage throughout the United States.

Atwood's investigation of this aspect of regional vocabulary demonstrates the effectiveness of combining geographic dissemination with age distribution in tracing linguistic change, a method equally applicable to phonological and to morphological data. A further dimension—the social dissemination of the variants—can be added to achieve the full potential of area linguistics in its effort to deal with language in its sociocultural context.

For the Spanish contributions to the vocabulary of Texas and their regional behavior see 4.6 below.

In preparation for the sociocultural interpretation, Atwood outlines the history of the population of Texas. The salient facts are briefly mentioned below.

English settlement began in 1821 on the lower Brazos River and grew so rapidly that by 1835 the Spanish settlers were outnumbered

two to one in a total population of about 35,000. The rout of the
Mexican military forces in the battle of San Jacinto (near Houston)
led to the formation of the Republic of Texas (1836) and its admis-
sion to the United States in 1845. During the days of the Republic
the population had risen to more than 100,000; by 1861—when Texas
joined the Confederacy—it was 600,000, concentrated in the eastern
third of the state. As late as 1900 only the eastern half of the state
had more than 6 inhabitants per square mile, although the population
had increased to about 3,500,000. Between 1900 and 1930 the High
Plains of northwest Texas were occupied, largely from the older
parts of the state. Meanwhile urban centers grew apace. Whereas
in a population of 4,500,000 two-thirds were classified as rural in
1920, by 1960 three-fourths of the 9,500,000 inhabitants of Texas
lived in cities.

The expansion of the English settlements from east to west leads
to the expectation that linguistic usage became established to some
extent in the eastern section by 1861, where the planter class dominated economically and politically to such an extent that Texas joined
the Confederacy. This raises the question of the provenience of this
social class: Did the majority of the planters come via the cotton
belt from the Atlantic coast and the Gulf plain or from the southern
Upland via Tennessee?

The increase in population from 1845 to 1860 and again from
1870 onward is so phenomenal that continued influx from the outside
clearly overshadows the growth of the indigenous population. Hence
the question is to what extent the newcomers adopted the usage of
the indigenous families when it differed from theirs.

The rather late development of important cities is a significant
fact. They can hardly be expected to have had much influence upon
the speech of their rural surroundings. Their phenomenal growth
from 1920 onward implies that country folk flocked into them. What
happened, and is happening, as a consequence can only be revealed
by rather thorough future investigations of the speech of these
centers and their hinterland.

4.

The Adoption of Foreign Words in American English

4.1 Introduction

Contact with speakers of other languages residing in various parts of North America has led to the adoption of foreign words in American English. Some of these are regionally restricted, others have nationwide currency, still others are used—or at least understood—wherever English is spoken.

The circumstances under which words were adopted from the several languages—Indian, Dutch, German, French, Spanish, African—and the time of their acceptance vary greatly.

4.2 Amerindian Words

Algonkian words referring to the American fauna and flora and to the Indian way of life were adopted as soon as English colonists set foot on the Atlantic Seaboard, among them moose, raccoon, hickory, persimmon, hominy, pow wow, squaw, wigwam. For other examples see Mencken-McDavid 1963: 110–20. Stripped of their inflections and adapted to the English phonological and prosodic systems, they were carried westward to the Rocky Mountains and beyond. In the Plains and the Southwest terms were adopted from other Indian tribes, as tepee "tent" from Sioux and coyote "prarie wolf" from Nahuatl (via Mexican Spanish).

Amerindian names of rivers, mountains, cities, states, etc.,

abound all the way from the Atlantic to the Pacific. This seems to
be so natural that reference to it sounds trivial. Yet this observation has its relevance in area linguistics. As the most conservative
elements of the vocabulary, place names often provide important—if
not the only—information on the areal extent of a submerged speech
community.

4.3 Dutch Words

For the Dutch contributions to the English vocabulary, the
Linguistic Atlas survey of the Eastern States has established a set
of isoglosses that are focused on the Hudson Valley, several of
which are shown in Figure 20.

Other Dutch words have achieved more than regional—even
national—currency, among them boss, cookie, waffle, Santa Claus,
and Yankee. At the other extreme, such "homely" terms as

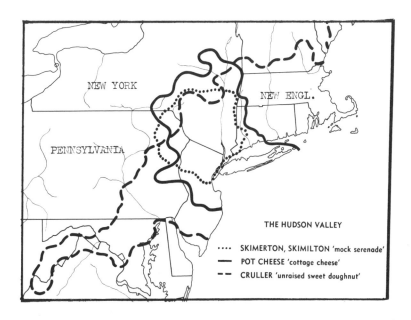

FIGURE 20: Hudson Valley Words
From H. Kurath, A Word Geography of the Eastern States.

rollechies "roulades" and winkle-hawk "right-angle tear in a gar-
ment" barely survive within the narrow confines of the Dutch settlement area on the lower Hudson River [Hawkins 1942].

The geographic extent of the Dutch settlements is clearly reflected
in place names. From south to north we encounter, among others,
Sandy Hook (N. J.), Staaten Island, Brooklyn, Yonkers, Peekskill,
Staatsburg, Rhinebeck, Catskill, Greenbush, Rensselaer (Co.), (Ball-
ston) Spa, Amsterdam. It is within this area that the largest number
of Dutch words survive in English.

The history of this section of New York State is so well known
that it can be suggested in a few words. The Dutch settlements,
established in the 1630's, were taken over by the English in 1664.
Though dominated by the English, many Dutch families continued to
speak their language well into the nineteenth century. Throughout
the Colonial period, both English and Dutch were official languages,
and continued so for some time after the Revolution. During two
centuries of decreasing bilingualism Dutch words were taken into
the English of this area. In the westward movement some of them
were carried to the Great Lakes Basin and beyond. Others were
diffused more or less widely because the things they denote were
themselves adopted by speakers of English, as the terms for foods
prepared in a special way: cruller, cookie, coleslaw, pot cheese,
waffle; stoop for a distinctive feature of the Dutch house; scow and
sleigh for vehicles used by the Dutch; boss and Santa Claus for
social customs peculiar to the Dutch. This is an excellent example
to show that the diffusion of words is entailed by the spreading of
the things they denote. Things and words go together.

4.4 Pennsylvania German Words

Pennsylvania German (PG) words have entered the English
spoken in the Great Valley of eastern Pennsylvania, the fertile farm
land of which York, Lancaster, Reading, Allentown, and Bethlehem
are the urban centers. The location of some representative isoglossic lines established by the Atlas survey is shown in Figure 21.
Their configuration effectively conveys the fact that Germanisms
are most numerous in eastern Pennsylvania—the area that has been
bilingual from Colonial times to the present—and that their number
diminished in a westerly and southwesterly direction, where German
is no longer spoken.

To the present bilingual area are confined, besides toot, the following farm words: bee! a call to chickens; laugh "whinny" (PG
laxə); shilshite "whiffletree" (PG šil-šait; cp. SG scheit "billet,
bar").

Other Germanisms are still current as far west as the Alleghenies and/or in the Shenandoah Valley and the northern Appalachians, where German farmers from eastern Pennsylvania settled in larger numbers. Thus <u>hommie</u>! a call to sheep; <u>vootsie</u>! a call to pigs; <u>sawbuck</u> ~ <u>woodbuck</u> "sawhorse"; <u>over-den</u> ~ <u>over-head</u> "hay loft" (cp. PG <u>den</u> = SG <u>tenne</u> "barn floor"); <u>thick-milk</u> "curdled milk" (transl. of PG /dikə-milix /); <u>fat-cakes</u> "doughnuts" (transl. of PG /fed-kuxə /); <u>fossnocks</u> "a kind of doughnut" (adaptation of PG /fasnaxs-kuxə / "Shrovetide cakes"). Only a few of these "homely" Germanisms show a wider diffusion, as <u>ponhaws</u> "Philadelphia scrapple" and especially <u>smear case</u> ~ <u>cheese</u> "cottage cheese."

The perseverance of Germanisms in the English of the bilingual section of eastern Pennsylvania and their gradual recession in the western part of the state and in the Appalachians can be traced in considerable detail, because we have good information both on their present dissemination and on the underlying sociocultural factors. The settlement history of this ethnic group, its way of life, and its cultural activities (among them the creation of a folk literature in their dialect from ca. 1850 onward) are well known, and their dialect

FIGURE 21: <u>Pennsylvania German Words</u>
From H. Kurath, <u>A Word Geography of the Eastern States.</u>

of German—essentially that of the Palatinate (Rheinpfalz) with some
Alemannic admixtures—has been adequately described. The whole
process of the interaction of languages in intimate contact—the
adoption of words from the receding language on the part of the
dominant language and their fading out is part of it—can be directly
observed in this case. A good beginning has been made, but much
more can be done. See, among others, the studies of C. E. Reed and
L. W. Seifert [1949, 1954] and of Kurath [1945], which rely upon data
secured by systematic sampling in the field with the aid of a set
questionnaire.

The field records of the <u>Linguistic Atlas of the Middle and the
South Atlantic States</u> provide considerable evidence for phonological
influence of Pennsylvania German upon the English current in the
bilingual area of eastern Pennsylvania, which awaits investigation
and interpretation. Some of the problems can be easily foreseen:

(1) Since PG has only voiceless fricatives, to what extent are
/ v, z / replaced by / f, s / in their English?

(2) Does the lack of the contrast / d ≠ t / in PG lead to some
confusion between / d / and / t / in their English?

(3) How do those whose first language is PG handle English / θ /
and / ð /, which have no counterparts in PG? Do they substitute their
voiceless / s / and / d /, at least occasionally?

A striking phonic effect of the PG substratum upon the English
spoken in parts of eastern Pennsylvania appears in the free mid
vowels / e / and / o / exemplified in <u>day</u>, <u>bracelet</u>, and <u>ago</u>, <u>coat</u>
[Kurath-McDavid 1961: Maps 18–21]. Differing sharply from the
upgliding / εɪ / and [ɔu ~ ou] current in Philadelphia and vicinity,
the Great Valley has the long close monophthongs [eˑ] and [oˑ] of PG.

4.5 French Words

Long before English settlers moved into the basin of the Great
Lakes and the Mississippi Valley, French explorers, fur traders,
and Jesuit fathers had established trading post, forts, and missions
at strategic points in these vast areas. Such place names as <u>Lake
Champlain</u>, <u>Detroit</u>, Sault Ste. Marie, and <u>St. Paul</u>, <u>La Crosse</u>, <u>St.
Louis</u>, <u>New Orleans</u> bear witness to this historic fact. When English
settlements were planted there in the early decades of the nineteenth
century, these French "names on the land," and many others, were
adopted by the newcomers.

Within these areas, French words for features of the landscape—
<u>butte</u>, <u>chute</u>, <u>prairie</u>, and <u>levee</u>, <u>bayou</u> (< Choctaw)—and for ways of
the voyageurs—<u>batteau</u>, <u>cache</u>, <u>chowder</u>, <u>portage</u>—were taken into
English in the eighteenth century, most of them through contacts

between the far-ranging French and English fur traders. The extensive replacement of a variety of eastern terms for the mock serenade
by shivaree (presumably via / šrivari / from French charivari) along
the Great Lakes and in the Valley of the Mississippi must clearly be
attributed to this background [Davis-McDavid 1949].

Little is known about the extent of French influence upon the
English spoken in the province of Ontario and of English influence
upon the French of Quebec in officially bilingual Canada. On the
North American continent there is no other linguistic and sociocultural situation like this. It offers an unsurpassed opportunity
for the observation of linguistic cross-influences in a rather well
known social context.

Thanks to M. Babington and E. B. Atwood [1961], we have some
information about the contributions of French to the English of
largely bilingual southern Louisiana. The authors find the usual
types of "homely" words, such as calls to domestic animals, affec-
tionate terms for members of the family, and names of favorite
dishes. Also some words referring to the environment have been
adopted, among them armoire "wardrobe," pirogue "river boat"
(< Sp. piragua < Carib), bagasse "waste from sugar cane" (< Sp.
bagazo), pooldoo "coot or mudhen" (Fr. poule d'eau).

It is of interest to note that some of these words came into
French from Spanish, the language of the rulers of Louisiana from
1762 to 1803. Among them, lagniappe "a bonus given to the customer"
(< Sp. la napa < Quechuan), is worth noting as an expression for a
practice that has spread beyond the French-speaking area into
coastal Texas [Babington-Atwood 1961: Map 11].

4.6 Spanish Words

Spanish county names along the Gulf of Mexico—Zapata, Presidio,
Refrigio, Mata Gorda, Lavaca, San Jacinto—suggest the centers of
Spanish settlements in Texas, so do the names of rivers flowing into
the Gulf—Rio Grande, Colorado, Trinity—and the names of such cities
as El Paso, Corpus Christi, San Antonio, Gonzales. Outnumbered two
to one by English settlers in the eastern half of the state when Texas
was admitted to the Union (1845), speakers of Spanish were the sole
occupants of the sparsely settled area along the Rio Grande until
after the Civil War. It is here that Mexican Spanish words, with
some of which the English settlers of central Texas had become
familiar by 1850, became established in English.

Most of the Spanish terms adopted fall into two semantic domains:
(1) words for features of the landscape not hitherto encountered by
English speaking settlers in their westward movement; (2) the termi-

nology for a way of herding cattle in open grassland, unfamiliar to speakers of English. In his Regional Vocabulary of Texas [1962] E. B. Atwood has provided extensive localized data for such terms in a series of maps. He also calculated the relative frequency of these Spanish terms in Texas as a whole.

Of the topographical terms, some are current in all of western Texas and familiar to most Americans, as canyon "deep stream bed," mesa "high flat land," arroyo "dry creek." Others are largely restricted to the southwestern part of the state, as llano "plain," acequia "irrigation ditch," chaparral "brush-covered land."

English settlers adopted the Mexican way of herding cattle in its entirety, and with it the Spanish terminology. The northward expansion of the "Cattle Kingdom" through the High Plains—with its cattle drives as far north as Wyoming—is a familiar story. The popular "Westerns" of the movie industry have made some of the Spanish terms known throughout the land, and even abroad.

Several terms within this semantic field—vaquero "cowboy" and toro "bull"—are confined to the southwestern triangle of Texas, the original center of the cattle industry, which has remained bilingual to this day. Some are more or less restricted to the grassland of the high plains, as hacienda "ranching establishment," reata "rope for lassoing cattle," remuda "group of saddle horses." Still others have spread also eastward and into Oklahoma, among them corral "horse pen," bronco ~ bronc "unbroken horse," cinch "saddle girth." See Atwood 1962: Maps 2–29. The northward spreading of some of these Spanish terms is treated by H. B. Allen [1958: 5–7].

The phonological and prosodic adaptation of the Spanish words offered little difficulty.

(1) the palatal / ñ / is replaced by the sequence / nj / in canyon; apical / r / and / rr / are rendered by constricted / r /, as in reata and corral; the velar fricative / x / is replaced by / h / in hackamore and frijoles. The initial consonants of llano and hacienda in American English are due to spelling.

(2) The Spanish stress pattern is retained, as in mésa, remúda, corrál, and háckamore (< jáquima) "rope halter of a horse." Láriat for la reáta "lasso" is an exception.

(3) Final unstressed vowels tend to be dropped when a word achieves wide currency, as in ranch, cinch, lariat, bronco ~ bronc.

5.

The Historical Relation of American English to British English

5.1 Regional Words

A considerable body of lexical regionalisms in America, brought to light by the Linguistic Atlas survey, is presented and discussed by H. Kurath in A Word Geography of the Eastern United States [1949]. Commenting on "ranges of the vocabulary," the following observations are made [pp. 9–10]:

> "Enterprises and activities that are regionally restricted have . . . a considerable body of regional vocabulary . . . . Regional and local expression are most common in the vocabulary of the intimate everyday life of the home and the farm . . . . Food, clothing, shelter, health, the day's work, play, mating, social gatherings, the land, the farm buildings, implements, the farm stocks and crops, the weather, the fauna, and the flora. These are the intimate concern of the common folk in the countryside, and for these things expressions are handed down in the family and the neighborhood that schooling and reading and a familiarity with regional or national usage do not blot out."

If this point of view is adopted, we may expect that many of the American regionalisms within this wide semantic range are derived from British regional dialects.

We are relatively well prepared for the task of tracing some American regionalisms to specific sections of the British Isles, and projects now underway will considerably better our chances. For England, J. Wright's English Dialect Dictionary [1898–1905] provides a large body of roughly localized data, and H. Orton's Survey of English Dialects [1962–71] is gradually furnishing us with a wealth of evidence recorded directly in the countryside. For North America, the collections of the Linguistic Atlas of the Eastern States present ample localized materials for a limited vocabulary; and the Dictionary of American Regional English, now in preparation under the direction of F. G. Cassidy, will vastly increase our resources.

A few examples chosen from the Word Geography of the Eastern United States will serve to illustrate some of the sources.

The evidence presented by J. Wright makes it clear that cade, cade lamb "pet lamb," current in southeastern New England [Kurath 1949: Fig. 12], was brought to this country from the Midland counties of England and became established in the Plymouth and the Rhode Island colonies. Orton's survey does not report a single instance of this expression in the north and the south of England.

The word hap "quilt," still in common use in the mountains of central Pennsylvania [ibid.: Figs. 25, 80], was brought to America by the Ulster Scots. J. Wright [1905] reports this term only for Scotland and the northern counties of England. The fact that Orton's survey of half a century later no longer found any trace of hap in northern England does not invalidate this inference, since we must reckon with the recession of regional folk words.

For the noise made by the horse, three different words are current in the Eastern States: (1) whinny ∼ whinner in the North and the North Midland, (2) nicker in the Upper South and the South Midland (Virginia and the Appalachians), and (3) whicker in the Carolinas and along Chesapeake Bay [ibid.: Fig. 97].

According to Wright and Orton, whicker is the usual term in the southwestern counties of England. It is the obvious source of the Carolina variant.

The Virginian nicker may have been imported from the southeastern counties of England, although Orton and Wright report it also from Cumberland and Durham.

For whinny, now regarded as the standard or literary term, the regional dissemination in British folk speech is as yet only partially known. According to Orton, it is in regular use in all of the northern counties. Its currency in literary English suggests that it is widely used in the Midlands, where neither whicker nor nicker are reported by Wright. Thus the extensive currency of whinny in the American North and North Midland, though supported by literary English, has its primary source in a regional dialect of England.

The "hand-picked" examples presented above are not intended
to suggest that the relationship between American and British
regionalism are often that clear and simple. In the course of 250–
300 years many recessions and expansions have taken place on both
sides of the Atlantic. As far as America is concerned, we must
keep in mind that at the time of settlement usage varied in each of
the colonies and that the relative uniformity within the several
dialect areas, as in the case of whinny ≠ nicker ≠ whicker, developed several generations after the settlement.

In passing it seems worth pointing out that such regional expressions as cade, hap, and nicker can, with proper precaution, function
as "tracers" of population movements or migration routes.

5.2 Phonological Features

5.21 The System of Syllabic Phonemes

Any meaningful discussion of the relationship of a derivative
dialect to its parent dialects in phonological matters presupposes a
phonemic analysis. Not until the phonemic systems of both dialects
are set up, is it possible to distinguish between shared and divergent
structural features, to describe differences in the phonic realization
of shared phonemes, and to point out divergences in the lexical
(etymological) incidence of shared phonemes.

In this discussion of the historical relationships of American
English to its British sources I shall rely upon the analysis of the
system of stressed vowels presented in H. Kurath and R. I. McDavid,
Jr., The Pronunciation of English in the Atlantic States [1961]. For
the justification of this analysis see especially pp. 3–9. Its usefulness as a frame of reference has been demonstrated in H. Kurath,
A Phonology and Prosody of Modern English [1964].

According to this analysis, the stressed vowels of American
English and of Standard British English fall into two classes: checked
and free. The checked vowels are restricted to preconsonantal position, whereas the free vowels are unrestricted in their distribution.

The three checked front vowels / ɪ ≠ ɛ ≠ æ /, as in bit ≠ bet ≠ bat,
bear the same relation to each other in Standard British English
(SBE) and in all varieties of American English (AE). Except for
/ æ /, they differ little in lexical incidence.

The three checked back vowels, on the other hand, differ markedly in lexical incidence: (1) SBE has / ʊ ≠ ɒ ≠ ɑ / in foot ≠ hot, fog,
loss ≠ hut; most varieties of AE have / ʊ ≠ ʌ ≠ ɑ / in foot ≠ hut ≠
hot; (3) eastern New England has / ʊ ≠ ɵ ≠ ʌ / in foot ≠ boat, stone ≠
hut in old-fashioned speech; but checked / ɵ / has been largely replaced by free / o /.

The subsystem of free vowels presented below is common to
SBE and to those dialects of AE in which postvocalic / r / is not
preserved as such. Other dialects of American English differ from
this system only in that they lack the / ɑ / of bar.

The Free Vowels

bee	i		u	do
bay	e	3	o	no
bar	ɑ		ɔ	law
buy	ai	oi	au	now
		fur		
		boy		

The lexical (etymological) incidence of the free vowels differs
little from dialect to dialect. On the other hand, their phonic character varies markedly. Thus the free vowels / i, u, e, o / of bee,
do, bay, no are upgliding diphthongs in SBE and in some regional
dialects of AE, while in other dialects of AE they are monophthongal
and even ingliding. The / ɑ / of bar is low central in SBE and in
Metropolitan New York, low front in eastern New England, low back
in eastern Virginia. The / ɔ / of law is well rounded in SBE and in
Metropolitan New York, less so in eastern New England, western
Pennsylvania, and eastern Virginia. The / au / of now ranges all
the way from [au] to [æu] and [əu] in AE. The / 3 / of fur is unconstricted in SBE and in most AE dialects spoken along the Atlantic
and the Gulf of Mexico, and constricted elsewhere in America.

The phonic variants of shared phonemes in AE are displayed in
a series of "synopses" in Kurath-McDavid 1961: 31–100.

The essential agreement of the vowel system of AE with that of
SBE may be attributed to three distinct factors.

(1) When the American colonies were planted, SBE was already
highly standardized in its phonemic system. Hence the leading
families in the several colonies must have used essentially the same
vowel system.

(2) The speech of the leading families became the model for the
unlettered majority of settlers, who, coming from different parts of
the British Isles, spoke a great variety of folk dialects, some of
which differed greatly from SBE in the system of syllabics, in the
phonic realization of shared phonemes, and in their lexical incidence.
Generally speaking, this group of settlers, or their descendants,
must have adopted the vowel system of SBE, the prestige dialect of

their community, but preserved some of their subphonemic peculiarities.

(3) The leading families in the colonial seaports—officials, merchants, financiers, religious leaders, and intellectuals—maintained close ties with the mother country throughout the colonial period and followed English fashions in speech as well as in other cultural matters. Thus eighteenth century changes of SBE found their way into the colonies on the Atlantic seaboard, notably postvocalic / ə / from earlier / r /, as in <u>fear, fair, four, poor</u>, and the free vowel / ɑ / of <u>far, hard</u>. These new prestige features spread inland from the seaports, as they still do to some extent, but did not reach the back country.

Only some of the more striking phenomena can be briefly dealt with here to throw light on the complicated task of accounting for the pervasive influence of SBE in shaping the regional varieties of AE and the survival of certain aspects of regional British folk speech.

We shall first consider some phonemic mergers and splits that had taken place in SBE by 1600—i.e., before the first settlements were established in America, but not in certain regional dialects of England. By doing this we shall see that all varieties of AE largely conform to the phonemic pattern of SBE.

5.22 Mergers and Splits

(1) In SBE and in AE, ME close / ẹ̄ / and open / ę̄ / are merged in / i /, as in <u>beet = beat</u>. Some English dialects show the same development, others not. Thus Suffolk, Lincolnshire, and Leistershire have the merger; but Yorkshire, Lancashire, and Gloucestershire preserve the contrast as [i:] ≠ [iə ~ eə].

(2) In SBE and in AE, ME open / ę̄ / and / ā / remain distinct, as in <u>wheat ≠ late</u>. This contrast is also preserved in Lincoln, Leicester, and Lancashire. But in Suffolk, Yorkshire, and Gloucester they are merged in / eə / or / iə /.

(3) In SBE and in AE, ME / ā / and / ai / are merged in / e /, as in <u>tale = tail</u>. Merging is found also in the dialects of Lincoln and Leicester. But the contrast is preserved in large parts of England: as / eə ≠ æj / in Suffolk and Gloucester, as / iə ≠ aj ~ ɛj / in Yorkshire, and as / e: ≠ ej ~ aj / in Lancashire.

(4) In SBE and in AE, ME / ọ̄ / and / ou / are merged in / o /, as in <u>stone = grown</u>. Merging occurs in Suffolk and in Leicester, but in most of the English dialects the contrast survives: in Lincoln as / uə ≠ ow /, in Yorkshire as / iə ≠ aw /, in Lancashire as / uə ≠ o: /, in Gloucester as / oə ~ uə ≠ ow /. It should be noted that in old-fashioned New England speech the contrast is partially preserved as checked / ɵ / ≠ free / o /, as in <u>stone ≠ grown</u>.

(5) In SBE, ME short / o / and the diphthong / au / have remained distinct, contrasting as / ɒ ≠ ɔ / in <u>crop, frost, dog ≠ law, taught</u>. The dialects of England exhibit sharply divergent treatments of these two ME phonemes, which is reflected in the complicated situation obtaining in the regional dialects of AE (see Wetmore 1959).

(6) In SBE, ME short / a / developed positional variants which in the latter part of the eighteenth century were phonemicized as / æ ≠ ɑ /, as in <u>hat, bag, man ≠ bath, glass, aunt</u>. In AE this split appears to some extent in eastern New England and fragmentarily in Virginia; elsewhere / æ / occurs in all positions. In most of the British dialects, ME / a / remains a low vowel, [a ~ ɑ], in all positions. Structurally, AE largely agrees in this respect with the folk dialects of England, but the phonic realization of the vowel reflects that of SBE / æ / in <u>hat, bag, man</u>.

5.23 Post-Settlement Importations

Changes that took place in the vowel system of Standard British English before the planting of the colonies on the American continent are rather fully established in all regional varieties of American English. Later changes in SBE, on the other hand, are confined to coastal areas: eastern New England, Metropolitan New York, eastern Virginia, South Carolina, and the states along the Gulf of Mexico. The most important of these changes is the development of an additional free vowel owing to the loss of postvocalic / r / as such in the latter part of the eighteenth century.

Orthoepists report "weakening" of postvocalic / r / as early as the seventeenth century and its loss as such shortly before 1800 [Jespersen 1909: 318, 360; Luick 1929: 730]. After high and mid-vowels, it is now represented by the mid central semivowel / ə̯ /, as in <u>fear, fair, four, poor</u>, and <u>beard, paired, board, moored</u>, but may be lost after the back vowel / ɔ /. In <u>far, hard</u> it merged with the low vowel to create the new phoneme / ɑ /. In AE, these developments of SBE are rather closely matched by the usage current in the coastal areas mentioned above.

In SBE the lengthened and/or lowered allophone of the descendant of ME / a /, as in <u>glass, staff, dance, aunt</u>, merged with the / ɑ / derived from earlier / ar /, as in <u>farce, starve, barn</u>. In America this merger is largely confined to eastern New England [Kurath 1964: 109–110].

5.24 Regional Variants in the Phonic Realization of Shared Phonemes

While the regional varieties of American English do not differ greatly in the structure of their vowel system and agree substantially

with Standard British English in this respect, the phonic character
of many of the shared phonemes varies considerably from region to
region, both in folk speech and in the speech of the cultured.

Some of the more striking regional <u>diaphones</u> of shared phonemes
in AE are listed below. References to maps in Kurath-McDavid 1961
are offered for the convenience of the reader, who will want to inspect the regional dissemination of the variants, which follows recurring patterns.

(1) The phoneme / e / of <u>day, bracelet</u> [Maps 18, 19] has the
diaphones [ɛɪ ~ eɪ ~ e· ~ eə];

(2) the phoneme / o / of <u>ago, coat</u> [Maps 20, 21] is realized as
[ɔu ~ ou ~ o· ~ oə];

(3) the / u / of <u>two</u> [Map 17] appears as [uu ~ u· ~ ʉ·];

(4) the / ɔ / of <u>law</u> [Map 22] has the variants [ɒ· ~ ɔ· ~ ɒɔ];

(5) the phoneme /ai / of <u>nine, twice</u> [Maps 26, 27] is realized as
[ai ~ ɑ·e ~ a·ɛ ~ əi], partly positionally;

(6) the / au / of <u>mountain, out</u> [Maps 28, 29] has the variants
[aʊ ~ æʊ ~ əu], partly in positional distribution;

(7) the phoneme / 3 / of <u>thirty</u> [Map 25] appears as a more or
less constricted [ɚ ~ ɜ] or as unconstricted [ɜ· ~ ɜɪ];

(8) the / ʌ / of <u>sun</u> [Map 10] appears as [ʌ ~ ɤ];

(9) the phoneme / æ / of <u>sack, ashes</u> [Maps 12, 13] has the diaphones [æ ~ æə ~ æɛ], partly by position.

Some connections between regional diaphones of AE with British
folk dialects seem to be rather clear, as pointed out below.

(1) The upgliding AE variants [ɛɪ ~ eɪ] of the phoneme / e /, as
in <u>day, bracelet</u> [Maps 18, 19], have their counterpart in the folk
speech of eastern England (as shown in Figure 22), which underlie
SBE. The monophthongal and ingliding AE variants [e· ~ eə] are
matched by phones current in the dialects of the west of England.

(2) In a similar way, the AE upgliding variants [ou ~ ɔu] and the
monophthongal and ingliding variants [o· ~ oə] of the phoneme / o /,
as in <u>ago, coat</u> [Maps 20, 21], are matched by regional variants in
the folk speech of England (see Figure 23).

(3) The AE variants [æu] and [ʌu ~ əu] of the phoneme / au /, as
in <u>mountain, out</u> [Maps 28, 29] also have their counterparts in English folk speech, as shown in Figure 24. The type of [æu] charac-
terizes the eastern counties, the type of [ʌu ~ əu] the west. The
variant [au ~ ɑu] of the American North and North Midland matches
SBE, its probable source.

Further light on the problems of relating American diaphones of
shared phonemes to specific British sources will come largely from
the field surveys of the folk dialects of England, Scotland, and Ire-

land. Spelling evidence can be of little help in tracing subphonemic entities.

The problem of tracing the probable British sources of phonemic, phonic, and incidental differences between the regional and social dialects of AE is especially complicated in the low vowels. In this range a tabulation of the phonic reflexes of ME / a ≠ o ≠ au / in the dialects of England is enough to suggest the complicated British background:

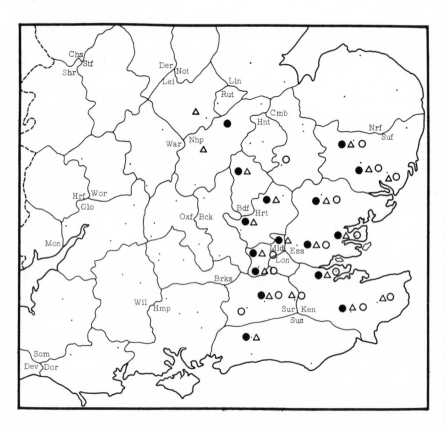

FIGURE 22: England: Diaphones of / e /
The syllabic in ● lane △ apron ○ make is articulated as an upgliding diphthong [eɪ ~ ɛɪ ~ æɪ]. Elsewhere ingliding [eə ~ ɛə ~ iə] or monophthongal [e ~ ɛ] are current.

ME / a / as in <u>apple</u>:   æ ~ a ~ ɑ
      as in <u>glass</u>:   æ ~ a ~ ɑ ~ ɒ
ME / o / as in <u>crop</u>:   ɑ ~ ɒ ~ ɒ
      as in <u>frost</u>:   ɑ ~ ɒ ~ ɒ ~ ɔ
ME / au / as in <u>law</u>:   ɑ ~ ɒ ~ ɒ ~ ɔ

When we ask why the several dialects of AE have so much in common in the organization of their vowel systems and differ so

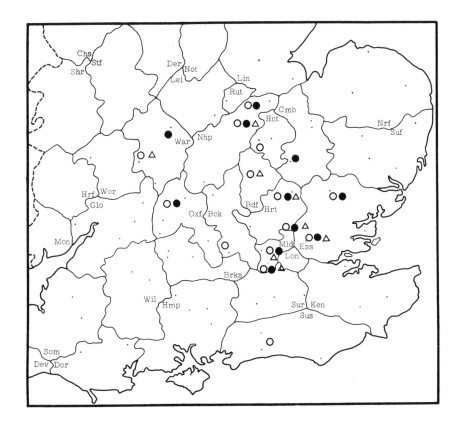

FIGURE 23: England: Diaphones of / o /
The syllabic in ○ road ● coat △ home is articulated as an upgliding diphthong [ou ~ ɔu ~ ʌu]. Elsewhere ingliding [oə ~ uə] or monophthongal [o ~ ɔ] are current.

much in the phonic realization of shared vowel phonemes, the answer
is fairly obvious. Communication is not seriously hampered by variations in the phonic character of shared phonemes as long as they
fall within a certain phonic range, as they actually do. Differences
in phonemic structure, on the other hand, would seriously interfere
with effective communication. Hence the trend toward eliminating
structural differences and tolerating substructural regional features
in the history of American English.

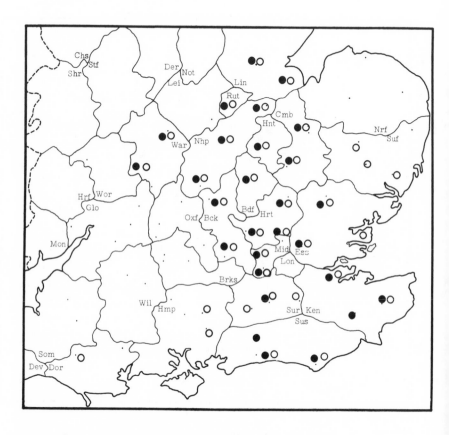

FIGURE 24: England: Diaphones of / au /
The syllabic in ● mouth ○ pound is articulated as [æu ～ ɛu].
Elsewhere [ʌu ～ əu] are current.

6.

The Patterning of
Dialect Areas

6.1 Introduction

The construction of a scheme of dialect areas on the basis of localized evidence secured by selective sampling is the immediate objective of area linguistics. The procedure leads from the determination of individual heteroglossic lines to the discovery of bundles of such dividing lines in some sectors of the area surveyed. Counting the number of heteroglosses in the several bundles and evaluating them from the structural point of view lays the foundation for dividing and subdividing the total area. The reliability of a scheme of the dialectal patterning of an area depends in part upon the adequacy of the sample and in part upon the point of view governing the structural evaluation of the heteroglosses forming the boundaries. Any such scheme has the character of an approximation to the linguistic realities and is subject to revision and open to refinements in the light of new evidence or of new insights.

Within the range of purely linguistic operations, a dialect scheme based upon localized evidence functions as a frame of reference. The dissemination of individual features can thus be described in linguistic terms without reference to physiographic, demographic, political, economic, or cultural domains. One can say, for instance, that in the Eastern United States stoop "porch" is confined to the Northern dialect area, lightwood "kindling" to the Southern area, the low vowel / a / in aunt, calf to the subarea of Eastern New England,

the checked vowel / ʊ / in coop to an area comprising the South and
the South Midland [Kurath 1949: Maps 7, 29; Kurath-McDavid 1961:
Maps 67, 68, 108]. Such descriptions are brief, clear, and to the
point, whereas premature reference to extralinguistic domains is
apt to be misleading.

The construction of a scheme of dialect areas has a further purpose: It is an indispensable preliminary to the sociocultural interpretation of the linguistic situation, both synchronically and
diachronically. However imperfect or tentative such a scheme may
be, it furnishes the basis for discovering congruences between
linguistic and sociocultural domains and their boundaries, which in
turn set the stage for more or less probable historical interpretations.

Experience has shown that dialect areas are often roughly
congruent with political or ecclesiastic domains, with trade areas
and transportation systems, with settlement areas, and even with
physiographic provinces insofar as they underly sociocultural
domains. Concentric dialect boundaries are frequently focused on
important cultural centers from which innovations spread to the
receptive hinterland. More often than not, a combination of sociocultural factors is involved in shaping a dialect area. Moreover,
with changes in social organization the linguistic patterning of the
total area also changes: the past is closely interwoven with the
present.

Every language area presents its own problems of historical
interpretation. Examples taken from the regional behavior of
American English illustrate this point (see Chapter 3). The
linguistic "profiles" of several European countries that follow should
add substantially to an understanding of current practices in area
linguistics and call attention to its unique contribution to linguistic
science. They are drawn from an extensive body of scholarly literature of the last fifty years.

6.2 Southern England

How a sampling survey carried out on a modest scale can reveal
important aspects of the dialectal structure of an area is strikingly
illustrated by Guy S. Lowman's investigation of southern England
thirty years ago (1937–38). Lowman chose sixty communities and
interviewed a single speaker of the local folk dialect in each of them.
His questionnaire consisted of nearly 400 items, chiefly phonological,
chosen from the worksheets of the American linguistic atlas. The
intention of this undertaking was to provide background material for
the historical interpretation of regional and social differences

in American English. This "American" bias in the choice of items
cannot, of course, provide a balanced view of the dialectal structure
of the area investigated. Nevertheless, the findings furnish important insights, as shown on the accompanying sketch maps, on which
the locations of the "listening posts" are indicated by dots.

The four heterophones presented in Figure 25 are highly suggestive with respect to the dialectal structure of the southern part of
England. The Home Counties (the London area) are clearly shown
to be a part of the East Midland dialect area; they are rather sharply
set off from the western area(s). South of the Thames the spacing of
the heteroglosses indicates a gradual southward expansion from the
London area.

The three heteroglosses presented in Figure 26 are highly suggestive of the relations between the London area and its surroundings.

Line 3, along with the heteroglosses shown in Figure 25, indicates
that the London area is part of an extensive eastern dialect area—a
well-known fact.

Line 2 suggests a tie-up with the industrial area of the Midlands,
which remains to be investigated. Important lines of communication,
as the railroad lines leading from London to Birmingham-Manchester
and to Nottingham-Leeds, may well be involved as favoring diffusion.

Line 1 sets off an area—the Home Counties—to which urban London usage is apt to spread by "pendular" population movements.

The field records on which the seven heteroglosses presented
above are based are part of the collections of the Linguistic Atlas of
the United States. Lowman was exceptionally well qualified to carry
out this survey for the Linguistic Atlas. He received his doctorate
under Daniel Jones in 1930 and spent seven years doing field work
for the American atlas before returning to England for a year.

Harold Orton's Basic Material of the Survey of English Dialects
will greatly increase our resources for dealing with the problem so
briefly dealt with here.

6.3 Dialect Areas of Medieval England

That a small number of securely established heteroglossic lines
can serve as a meaningful framework for suggesting the dialectal
structure of an area is also illustrated by the survey of regional
traits of Middle English as reflected in localized documents written
between ca. 1400 and ca. 1450. Carried out in preparation for editing
the Middle English Dictionary, which undertakes to document regional
usage by drawing upon appropriate texts, the results were published
by S. Moore, S. B. Meech, and H. Whitehall in Middle English Dialect
Characteristics and Dialect Boundaries [1935]. Their chief findings

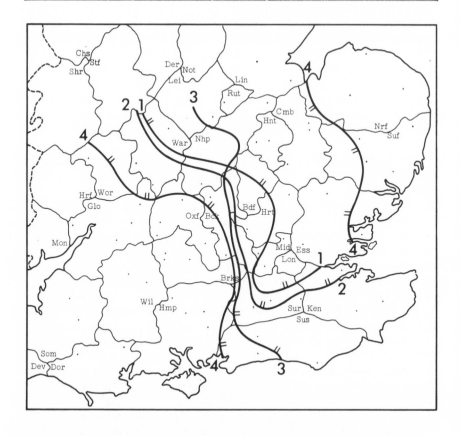

FIGURE 25: Southern England: West versus East

1. In the east, postvocalic / r /, as in ear, care, four, has developed
    into the semivowel / ə̯ /; in the west it survives as a constricted
    / r /.
2. In the east, law has a well rounded vowel, [ɔ], in the west an un-
    rounded vowel, [ɒ ~ ɑ].
3. In the east, ME / ā / and / ai, ei /, as in tale and tail, are merged
    in an upgliding diphthong [ei ~ ɛi ~ ai]; in the west, ME / ā /
    appears as an ingliding diphthong [e^ə] and ME / ai, ei / as an
    upgliding diphthong [ɛi ~ æi].
4   The syllabic of down, out is articulated as / æu ~ ɛu / in the east,
    as / əu ~ ɐu / in the west and in East Anglia.

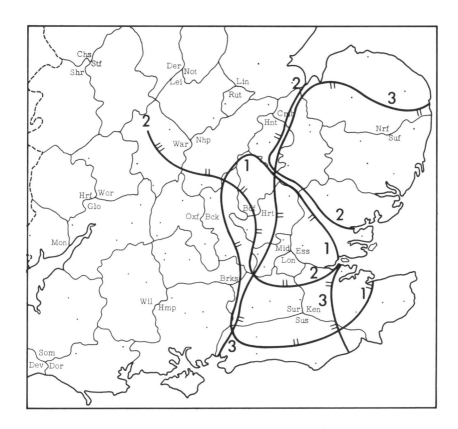

FIGURE 26: Southern England: London and Environs

1. In London and environs (the "Home Counties"), ME / ǭ / and / ou / are merged in an upgliding diphthong [ou ~ ɔu], as in stone and grown. Outside this area, they remain distinct as ingliding [oᵊ ~ uᵊ] ≠ [ou ~ ɔu], respectively.
2. In the Home Counties and in a corridor leading northward, nine and right have a "slow" rising diphthong with a low-central to low-back beginning, i.e. [ɑ·i ~ ɑ·i]. Outside of it, a "fast" rising diphthong starting in a centralized position, i.e. /ɐi ~ əi /, is current.
3. In common with the greater part of the eastern counties south of the Wash, the London area has the checked / ʊ / of foot in the word room. To the west, room has the free vowel /u / of do.

are summarized and tentatively interpreted in the Plan and Bibliography of the Middle English Dictionary [Kurath 1954].

Figure 27 presents the six most important, or striking, heteroglossic lines.

North of line 1, OE / ā / as in stān "stone" remained unrounded, to the south it became rounded to open / ǭ /. From sources other than those used by Moore [1935], we know that north of this line OE long / ā / merged with OE short / a- / in open syllables and with the diphthong / ai / from OE / æg /; south of it, OE / ā / merged with OE short / o- / in open syllables. The structural importance of this diagnostic heterogloss is thus quite clear. It sets the Northern dialect area off from the Midland area.

South of line 4 the present plural of verbs ends in -eth, north of it in -en. According to Moore this morphological heterogloss is rather closely paralleled by the line separating the southern voiced initial fricative / v- / from the voiceless / f- / to the north of it, as in foot. From other sources of information we gather or infer that in all probability initial / s / and / þ / have also become voiced within the southern / v- / area. This bundle of heteroglosses can safely be taken to reflect the dividing line between the Southern and the Midland area at ca. 1400.

Line 5 sets off a western area in which by ca. 1400 four rounded front vowels had been preserved: / y /, as in the word "hill"; / ȳ /, as in "fire"; / ö / (< OE / eo /) as in "self"; and / ȫ / (< OE / ēo /) as in "lief." To the east of this line, these vowels had merged with unrounded front vowels of the same tongue level. This bundle of structural heteroglosses should surely be recognized as the most important boundary between the West Midland and the East Midland dialects of Middle English, though it was rather sharply recessive. According to A. Brandl and H. C. Wyld, two centuries earlier this bundle of heteroglosses was located much farther east [Kurath 1954: 10].

Line 6 has no structural implications. Separating Western short / o / before nasals from Eastern / a /, as in the word "man," it is merely a convenient diagnostic feature.

Line 3 separates the variant inflection of the present singular 3: -es to the north vs. -eth to the south. In its eastern sector this line is paralleled by the heteroglosses them (< Old Norse) ≠ hem ∼ hom (< OE) and sal ≠ shal. This bundle of lines subdivided the East Midland area into a northern and a southern section, perhaps as late as ca. 1450. By ca. 1500, North Midland -es and them had been carried southward to the London area to become established in the literary language.

Other regional features of Middle English have as yet not been

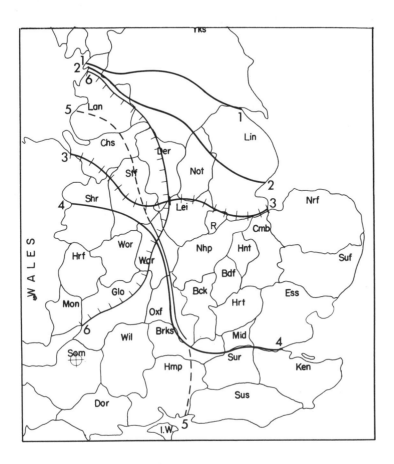

FIGURE 27: Middle English Heteroglosses.

1. The vowel in "stone": N / ā / ≠ S / ǭ / (OE ā)
2. The inflection of the pres. pl.: N -es ≠ S -en
3. The inflection of the pres. sing. 3: N -es ≠ S -eth
4. The inflection of the pres. pl.: N -en ≠ S -eth
5. The vowels in "hill, fire, self, lief": W rounded / y, ȳ, ö, ȫ / ≠
    E unrounded / i, ī, e, ē̦ / (OE y, ȳ, eo, ēo)

delimited with any precision. For the time being, their location can
be best described with reference to the skeletal structure suggested
by well known heteroglosses. This, indeed, is one of the functions
of a set of diagnostic heteroglosses.

It will be interesting to see how the extensive investigation of
Middle English localized documents and of localizable texts by Angus
McIntosh [1963] will round out and refine our conception of the
dialectal structure of Medieval England.

6.4 The Swabian Dialect Area

An important contribution to the method of delimiting speech
areas and of showing their relations to adjoining areas was made by
K. Bohnenberger. Formulated after some 30 years of field experience in connection with his fundamental article on the eastern
boundary of the Alemannic speech area [1928], he applied it in his
posthumously published book on the Alemannic dialects [1953].

The central feature of his procedure is the choice of a representative heterogloss sector by sector. This devise enables him
to describe for each sector the course of the several heteroglosses
with reference to it, pointing out whether they coincide with it or
deviate from it more or less. This, in turn, leads to the description
of dialect boundaries as sharply defined or as transition belts.
Finally, the character of any given dialect boundary, sharp or
graded, furnishes valuable leads to its interpretation in sociocultural
terms.

For the Alemannic area Bohnenberger had at his disposal about
three dozen heteroglosses whose location he had ascertained very
largely by his own fieldwork. These he assembled on a single map
(11 by 13 inches), identifying the heteroglosses and their Middle High
German sources [1953: 301–2]. Up to this point his procedure is
strictly synchronic. The map exhibits the geographic behavior of the
heteroglosses as of ca. 1900–1950. It shows that the Swabian subarea of Alemannic is set off by rather striking bundles of lines,
close-knit in some sectors and spaced in others.

At this stage, Bohnenberger selects specific heteroglosses to
represent the bundles sector by sector. Since there is no one heterogloss that runs through all the bundles that frame the Swabian dialect
area—no Swabian shibboleth comparable with Bavarian enk "you"
(plural)—this procedure imposes itself. On his map the author draws
these representative or diagnostic heteroglosses as heavy lines, a
rather effective cartographic device.

Bohnenberger's choice of diagnostic heteroglosses is diachronically oriented. His intention is to prepare the ground for a historical

interpretation of the linguistic situation obtaining at the turn of the
nineteenth century. The author is fully aware of the fact that his
choice of diagnostic heteroglosses is bound to be somewhat arbitrary
and that "mixing" the diachronic with the synchronic point of view
has its hazards. But he is convinced that there is no better way of
dealing with the situation. In any event, his procedure provides a
meaningful perspective of the Swabian dialect area in its relation to
the other Alemannic areas as well as to the adjoining Bavarian and
Frankish domains.

The accompanying sketch map (Figure 28) presents the diagnostic
heteroglosses chosen by Bohnenberger to "frame" the Swabian dialect
area and to show its relations to the adjoining speech areas. Brief
comments on their character are appended.

Line 1 separates the Swabian from the Bavarian dialect area. It
represents a bundle of heteroglosses that follow the Lech River from
the Alps to the Danube; close-knit south and north, they are spaced
along the middle course of the Lech.

Line 2 is the easternmost heterogloss in a widely spaced bundle
that forms the transition from Swabian to Frankish.

Line 3 separates Swabian from Frankish. East of the Neckar
River it is closely paralleled by other heteroglosses; farther west it
marks the southernmost extent of a transition belt.

Line 4 separates Swabian from Low Alemannic. It represents a
bundle of heteroglosses that run close together along the eastern
slope of the Black Forest and again north of Lake Constance, but
are more or less widely spaced elsewhere.

Line 5 serves to set Low Alemannic off from Frankish. It marks
the northern extent of a transition belt.

Line 6 suggests the boundary between Low Alemannic and High
Alemannic.

6.5 The German Area

The earliest dialect scheme of an extensive area based upon
heteroglosses established by a systematic selective survey is that
of F. Wrede, director of the Sprachatlas des Deutschen Reiches for
more than 20 years. It was published posthumously as Map 56 of
the Sprachatlas [1934].

As early as 1919 Wrede advocated the use of diagnostic indicators
(Merkmale) on the model of the satəm ≠ centum heterogloss in
comparative Indo-European linguistics in these words: "This kind
of device is clear, whereas, from the point of view of area linguistics,
the traditional distinction between High German and Low German is
ambiguous" [Wrede 1963 < 1919: 340].

F. Wrede's plan of subdividing the German speech area on the basis of individual diagnostic heteroglosses is presented in Figure 29 on a simulated map.

It will be observed that Wrede accepts the traditional nineteenth century grouping of the German dialects into Low and High and the subdivision of High German into Central and Upper. Equally tradi-

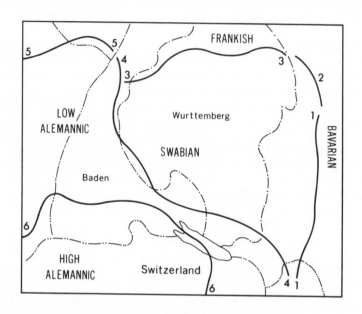

FIGURE 28: The Swabian Dialect Area
Shown in its relation to the Low Alemannic (LA), the High Alemannic (HA), the Bavarian (B), and the Frankish (F) domains.

Heteroglossic Lines
1. Swabian reflexes of MHG ir, iuch "you" (PGc pl.) ≠ Bavarian es, enk "you" (PGc dual)
2. Swabian / ā /, as in / dāg / "day" ≠ Frankish / ō / (OHG ă)
3. Swabian / ǫǝ ~ ǫi /, as in / brǫǝd / "broad" ≠ Frankish / ai ~ ā / (OHG ai ~ ei)
4. Swabian / ei /, as in / eis / "ice," and / ou /, as in / hous / "house" ≠ Low Alemannic / ī / and / ū / (OHG ī and ū)
5. Low Alemannic / pf- /, as in / pfund / "pound" ≠ Frankish / p- /
6. Low Alemannic / kh- /, as in / khopf / "head" ≠ High Allemannic / xopf /

Based on K. Bohnenberger, Die alemannischen Mundarten

tional is his subdivision of Low German into (a) Low Frankish, (b) Low Saxon, and (c) East Low German; of Central German into (a) Western and (b) Eastern; and of Upper German into (a) Alemannic and (b) Bavarian.

What, then, is Wrede's contribution to the method of subdividing the German dialects? It consists in basing each boundary, major or minor, upon a single heterogloss whose course had been established by the Sprachatlas. Thus the boundary between the Low and the High German areas rests upon the heterophone / -k ≠ -x / as reflected in ik ≠ ich; that between the Alemannic and the Bavarian areas upon the heterolex euch ≠ enk "you" (pl.); that between the Low Frankish and the Low Saxon areas upon the heteromorph -en ≠ -et (inflection of the present plural).

The scientific as well as the practical importance of this step is clear. First of all, it furnishes the investigator with guidelines for discovering and describing heteroglossic lines of similar trend on which dialect boundaries can be established. Moreover, it commits him to a consistent orientation, so essential in dealing with complicated linguistic situations.

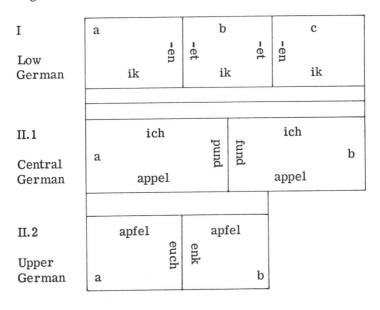

FIGURE 29: The Dialectal Structure of the German Area According to F. Wrede

Wrede's plan fulfills the limited objectives for which, indeed, he intended it. Much of what has been written by Wrede's students and by other scholars associated with the Sprachatlas group betrays his orientation, for good or ill.

Serving primarily the practical purpose of orientation, the diagnostic heteroglosses (Merkmale) chosen by Wrede involve no differences in phonological or morphological structure between the German dialects. The heteroglosses ik ≠ ich, appel ≠ apfel, and pund ≠ fund exhibit only differences in the incidence of shared phonemes. The -en ≠ -et morphemes are grammatically synonymous, denoting plurality in the present tense of the verb. The euch ≠ enk heterogloss is lexical: no grammatical difference is involved, since both variants function as plurals.

Thus Wrede's diagnostic heteroglosses are trivial in themselves. The significance they have for a scientific grouping of the German dialects depends entirely upon their presumed representative character, that is, upon the extent to which they are supported by bundles of heteroglosses running similar courses. It can be assumed that, owing to his long preoccupation with the collections of the Sprachatlas, the author had a "feel" for their relevance; and some of his "hunches" have been amply documented by later research.

No attempt has been made in later years to group the German dialects on a different basis. As a matter of fact, it will not be possible to establish a sound classification until at least the major dialect types of German shall have been analyzed from the structural point of view, so that the systemic phonological and morphological heteroglosses can be distinguished from the incidental. Moreover, the areal grouping of morphological and lexical phenomena will have to be taken into consideration.

6.6 The Netherlands

A conspectus of the linguistic situation in the Low Countries—the Netherlands and northern Belgium—is offered by A. Weijnen in De Nederlandse Dialecten [1941]. Assembling 35 phonological and 8 morphological heteroglosses for which fairly adequate data had been recorded by various scholars (including E. Blancquaert, L. Grootaers, and G. G. Kloeke), he presents them on a single map [174] without evaluating them structurally or weighing them from the diachronic point of view. Lexical heteroglosses are deliberately set aside. The result is a strictly synchronic picture, highly suggestive, though admittedly incomplete and tentative.

On this evidence, a relatively uniform central area extends all the way from the French (Walloon) language boundary northward to the Zuider Zee (from Brussels and Antwerp to Amsterdam). In the southwest, Flanders and Zeeland, especially the latter, are set off from this central area by prominent bundles of heteroglosses. The southeast (Limburg) has the character of a transition area. Less prominent bundles subdivide the northeastern Netherlands and set them off from the central area. North Holland and Friesland form another subdivision of the Netherlandish language area.

Whether the large central area is actually as uniform as it appears on Weijnen's map is subject to doubt. It seems likely that the "deviant" usage of the peripheral areas attracted the attention of scholars and that dialects of the central area, which are closer to Standard Dutch, had been less thoroughly investigated by 1941. At any rate, Kloeke [1950] published a number of phonological and lexical maps that exhibit a west-to-east gradation between the Zuider Zee and "the Rivers." Figure 30 presents some of Kloeke's data in simplified form.

If we apply Bohnenberger's method of selecting diachronically diagnostic heteroglosses to Weijnen's synchronic map, so as to prepare the way for the diachronic interpretation of the synchronic data, we might choose the heteroglosses presented in Figure 31. As a matter of fact, Dutch and Flemish scholars, preoccupied with historical problems (time depth) as they are, have used such heteroglosses, but often without critical evaluation or proper perspective.

Line 1 sets off the area in which the syllabic of muis "mouse" is an upgliding diphthong / öü /; to the east and in the southwest monophthongal / ü / (< PGc ū) is current.

Line 2 sets off the coastal area in which PGc / ō / escapes palatal mutation, as in groen / xrun / "green."

Line 3 separates the northwestern region (North Holland and Friesland) where PGc / ā / was shifted to a front vowel, mid or high, as in Anglo-Frisian: thus slēpen "sleep" ≠ slāpen.

Line 4 sets off a region adjoining the Low Saxon area of Germany (the greater part of Overijssel and Drenthe) in which the three persons of the present plural end in -t (as in Low Saxon), whereas all other dialects of northern Netherlandish have -e(n).

Line 5 delimits a region adjoining the German dialect area of Cologne (Köln): here Netherlandish ik "I" is confronted by the ich of the provinces of Limburg, which share this feature with the Cologne area.

All of these diachronically diagnostic heteroglosses are embedded to some extent in bundles of heteroglosses exhibited in present day Netherlandish. Employed with proper reserve, i.e., without plunging headlong into the remote past, they contribute a convenient and significant frame of reference for describing the course of other heteroglosses of the present and for tracing historical developments.

6.7 The Dialectal Structure Of Italy

The Linguistic Atlas of Italy [Jaberg-Jud 1928–40] has furnished the localized linguistic data for delimiting the major dialect areas of Italy and their subdivisions. As early as 1937, G. Rohlfs, who had

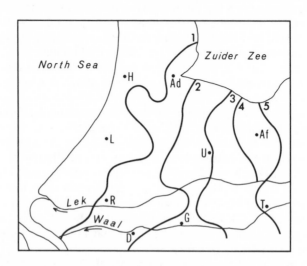

FIGURE 30: The Central Netherlands

1. West ladder ≠ East leer "ladder" [Kloeke 1950: 159]
2. West butter ∼ bōter ≠ East botter "butter" [79]
3. West hiel ≠ East hak "heel" [149]
4. West kaas ≠ East kees ∼ keis "cheese" [82]
5. West gras ≠ East gres "grass" [173]

Cities: Ad – Amsterdam, Af = Amersfoort, D = Dordrecht, G = Goringhem, H = Haarlem, L = Leiden, R = Rotterdam, T – Tiel, U – Utrecht

investigated seventy communities in southern Italy for this atlas,
drew upon these data to outline the dialectal structure of Italy and
to point out the chief sociocultural forces that brought it about
[Rohlfs 1952 < 1937: 89–107]. Some of his findings are summarized
in Figure 32.

The most prominent dialect boundary of Italy follows the crest of
the Apennines, separating Northern Italy from Tuscany. The follow-

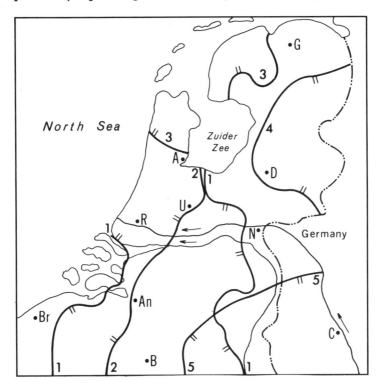

FIGURE 31: The Dialectal Structure of the Netherlands

Cities: A(msterdam, An(twerp, B(russels, Br(ugge, C(ologne,
D(eventer, G(roningen, N(ijmegen, R(otterdam, U(trecht.

Based on A. Weijnen, De Nederlandse Dialecten

ing North Italian (Gallo-Italic) phonological features have their southern limit here:

(1) The voicing of intervocalic voiceless stops, as in <u>fradel</u>, <u>formiga</u>, <u>pever</u> ≠ Tuscan <u>fratello</u> "brother," <u>formica</u> "ant," <u>pepe</u> "pepper";

(2) the simplification of geminate consonants, as in <u>spala</u>, <u>gata</u> ≠ Tuscan <u>spalla</u> "shoulder," <u>gatta</u> "cat";

(3) the loss of final vowels, as in <u>an</u>, <u>sal</u> ≠ Tuscan <u>anno</u> "year," <u>sale</u> "salt";

(4) the loss of unaccented medial vowels, as in <u>slar</u>, <u>mdor</u> ≠ Tuscan <u>sellaio</u> "saddler," <u>mietitore</u> "mower";

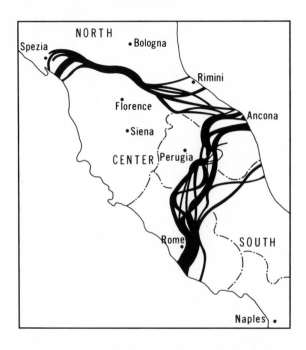

FIGURE 32: The Three Major Dialect Areas of Italy
The boundaries of 7 Northern and of 11 Southern features are shown on the map.

Adapted from G. Rohlfs, <u>La struttura linguistica dell'Italia</u>

(5) the nasalization of vowels before word final nasal clusters, as in pā ≠ Tuscan pane "bread";

(6) some lexical items, as incö ≠ Tuscan oggi "today," orp ≠ Tuscan cieco "blind."

This linguistic boundary rests on a natural barrier, the crest of the Apennines. But in ancient times this line was an ethnic boundary between the Gaulish tribes and the Etruscans. Moreover, for many centuries it was also an ecclesiastical boundary dividing the arch-diocese of Ravenna from that of Rome.

Another important linguistic boundary sets Central Italy off from the South. Here, however, the line of demarcation is not clear-cut. It is rather a transition belt formed by a large bundle of more or less congruent lines. The greater part of this belt extends from the environs of Ancona on the Adriatic across the Apennines to the Tyrrhenian Sea south of Rome. The general course of this graded boundary agrees roughly with the northern boundary of the ancient duchy of Spoleto. Even in the early Middle Ages this duchy was separated from Tuscany by a corridor, the Papal States, which pro-vided communication between the Patrimonium Petri and the exarchate of Ravenna. Thus, the natural relations between the South and Tuscany were breached in the Umbrian area. This had a deci-sive influence upon the linguistic physiognomy of this part of Italy.

The following South Italian features have their northern limits in this transition belt:

(1) The voicing of voiceless stops after nasals, as in mondone "montone, ram," tiembre "tempo, time," angora "ancora, again";

(2) the mutation of accented vowels before final -i, -u, as in acitu "aceto, vinegar," sulu "solo, only";

(3) such lexical items as frate ≠ fratello "brother," fémmina ≠ donna "woman, wife," ferraru ≠ fabbro "smith," tenere ≠ avere "have."

The three major dialect areas of Italy can easily be subdivided. In the North, for instance, the boundaries between the dialects of the Piedmont (Turin), of Liguria (Genua), of Lombardy (Milan), and of Venetia (Venice) are quite sharp.

In Italy, Tuscany has been the most important cultural center since the Middle Ages. As the prototype of the literary language, this region has had extraordinary importance in the diffusion of the cultivated vernacular (volgare illustre) to all neighboring regions.

The currency of Tuscanisms throughout Venetia is well known. Even in the Middle Ages Tuscan infusion brought about a profound transformation of the local dialects of that region. Of Tuscan origin are, for instance: (1) the generalization of the diphthong ie, cor-responding almost exactly to the Tuscan situation, as in fiele "bile," piè "foot," miele "honey"; (2) words like giorno "day," semola "bran," donnola "weasel," grembiale "apron." This has had the effect of leveling the dialects of the Venetian plain to a much larger extent than those of the other subareas of Northern Italy.

Tuscan diffusion into Lombardy has been more limited. Under the powerful leadership of Milan, this region largely maintained its linguistic independence. For instance, Lombardy is almost the only section of Northern Italy where ancient caput (Lomb. co) has not yet yielded to testa "head." However, in recent times the influence of the literary language, which is essentially Tuscan, is making itself felt in Lombardy. This infiltration is directed at the heart of Northern Italy (Alta Italia). Little by little, Milan has become an important center of diffusion for the national language. From the capital of the valley of the Po emanate the linguistic influences that have been upsetting the old idioms, gradually pushing them back to the periphery. Thus, Tuscan zio "uncle" has replaced indigenous barba, zia "aunt" has taken the place of ámeda (Tecino anda), giovedì "Thursday" has supplanted the earlier giobia. Instead of vèner one now says venerdì "Friday," instead of Lombard calegar one hears only calsular "shoemaker." In Liguria and in Piedmont, Tuscan natale "Christmas day" has replaced indigenous nadal.

On the dialect of Rome (romanesco) Tuscan influence has been profound. From Rome northward, the greater part of Latium has been exposed to Tuscan penetration for centuries. Since the fourteenth century, the old vernacular of Rome has suffered constant disintegration. The old Southern vocalism has given way to the Tuscan. One no longer says tiempo but tempo "time," not cuorpo but corpo "body," not pede but piede "foot," not ditto but detto "said," not munno but monno "mondo, world." The modern dialect of Rome is simply Tuscan superimposed on the relics of an indigenous substratum.

Various languages have left their marks in the vocabulary of different sections of Italy. North of the Apennines some Celtic words survive, and Germanic invaders—Goths and Lombards—have contributed to the regional vocabulary. In southern Italy and Sicily, French words survive from the days of Norman rule. Other French words spread into Italian by cultural diffusion during the age of chivalry. For all of these lexical admixtures the linguistic atlas of Italy provides ample localized evidence.

The only significant phonological feature of foreign origin admitted by G. Rohlfs is the voicing or "weakening" of medial Latin p, t, k in Northern Italy. This he attributes, with many other scholars, to the Celtic substratum [Rohlfs 1952 < 1930: 75–78].

For general orientation concerning the dialectal structure of

present day Italy and its sociocultural and ethnic background, the
reader should consult the amply documented and clearly written
treatment of this subject by E. Pulgram in The Tongues of Italy
(1958), esp. pp. 45–53. In this book the author also discusses the
substratum problem with special reference to Italy [esp. pp. 153–54,
203–44, 281, 337–43], in which views diverging from those advanced
or implied in the papers by Rohlfs and Hall are duly recorded. See
also Pulgram (1949), especially the extensive bibliography and the
author's critical evaluation of divergent opinions from a clearly
formulated point of view.

6.8 The Dialectal Structure of France

6.81 The Northern Area

J. Gilliéron's rejection of the regularity of phonemic change
[1919] and his denial of the existence of dialect boundaries—hence
also of scientifically definable dialects—did not go unchallenged
inside and outside of France. Moreover, essential problems in dialectology ignored or set aside by the author of the Linguistic Atlas
of France [1902–10] proved to be a challenge to scholars in the field
of Romanic linguistics and philology, among them Karl Ettmayer
[1924] of the University of Vienna.

From the first 284 maps of the LAF, Ettmayer chose ninety-
eight lexical items that exhibited rather clear regional patterning of
variants in northeastern France and adjoining parts of Belgium.
After drawing heteroglossic lines item by item, he assembled them
all on a single map [Map I]. The result was most striking. He found
that the northeastern periphery, extending from Picardy through
Belgium to Lorraine, was highly diversified in word usage, whereas
the central area, consisting of the Ile de France, Orleans and the
Champagne, was relatively uniform. This had, of course, been known
in a general way; but the cartographic presentation of the specific
data furnished by the LAF dramatized the situation (see Figure 33).

The most prominent bundles of heterolexes, as that between the
Ile de France and Picardy or that between the Champagne and Belgium to the north and Lorraine to the east, are labeled with reference to historic political domains. This device provides a terminology for describing the location and course of any single heterolexic
line with reference to these bundles. It also suggests, but does not
explicitly assert, historical connections between linguistic and
political boundaries.

To show lines of diffusion from the Ile de France, Ettmayer
selects six lexical items: (1) beau garçon "son in law," (2) journal

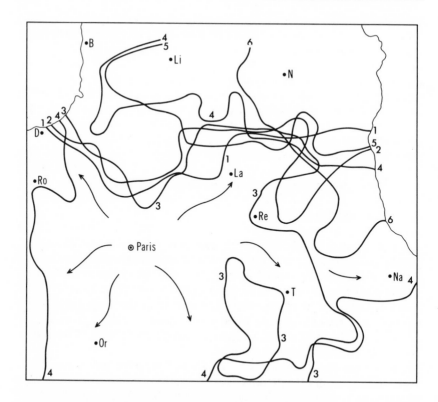

FIGURE 33: Lexical Diffusion from the Ile de France

Lexical Isoglosses
1. beau garçon "son in law"
2. journal "newspaper"
3. fouet "whip"
4. bas "drawers, breeches"
5. baril "cask, barrel"
6. soir "evening"

Cities: B(oulogne, D(ieppe, La(on, Li(lle, N(amur, Na(ncy,
Or(leans, P(aris, Re(ims, Ro(uen, T(royes.

Adapted from K. Ettmayer, Über das Wesen der Dialektbildung

"newspaper," (3) fouet "whip," (4) bas "drawers, breeches," (5) baril "cask, barrel," (6) soir "evening." Three routes of expansion are clearly brought out: (a) northwestward down the Seine (Rouen), whence in part along the coast to Boulogne; (b) northeastward through the Champagne to Laon-Reims and beyond; (c) eastward through the Champagne in the direction of Nancy. In this process a variety of regional expressions were being replaced by their Parisian counterparts at the turn of the century.

Ettmayer raises the eminently pertinent question to what extent morphological and lexical dialect boundaries agree with phonological boundaries. His findings are summarized on his ingeniously constructed Map VII, which shows that there is partial agreement between them in southern France, as south of Lyon and along the Garonne; but there are some sharp divergences elsewhere [44]. This attempt may be premature and overbold; but this problem must ultimately be faced in area linguistics. It calls attention to the partially divergent means by which phonological, morphological, and lexical features can spread.

Written almost as soon as the Linguistic Atlas of France was in print and published, Ettmayer's essay on the nature of dialect development is still worth careful reading. His perspective is sound and he boldly states his views concerning essential problems that can and must be faced in area linguistics, such as the following: the pervasive influence of dominant cultural centers and of the literary language [11]; the bundling of heteroglossic lines and their complex sociocultural background [13-14]; the expansive effects of communication routes [19]; the retarding effects of regional language loyalty on diffusion [31, 33]; the problem of distinguishing parallel regional shifts from importations [49]; the essential regularity of phonemic change despite obvious deviations from the norm [54].

6.82 The Transition Belt between Francien and Provençal

Relying upon the ample evidence furnished by Gilliéron's Linguistic Atlas of France [1902-10], R. A. Hall, Jr. [1949], undertook to determine the position of the traditionally recognized Franco-Provençal dialect area within the total linguistic structure of France. For this purpose he chose the eight striking phonological innovations of Northern French (Francien) listed below:

(1) Fronting of accented Latin ā to e after palatals, as in L cārus > cher / šɛr / "dear";

(2) fronting of accented L ā to e after nonpalatals, as in L māter > mère / mɛr / "mother";

(3) the shift of L en to an, as in L centum > cent / sã / "hundred";

(4) palatalization of L c̣ / k / before a̱, as in L campus > champ / šā / "field";

(5) palatalization of L g̱ before a̱, as in L purgāre > purger / pyrže / "cleanse";

(6) the shift of Romanic medial palatal / λ / to / j /, as in feuille / fⴰj / "leaf";

(7) the loss of preconsonantal s̱, as in L castellum > château / šato / "castle";

(8) the loss of medial ḏ (< L ṯ), as in L catēna > chaine / šɛn / "chain."

For each of these features Hall chose from seven to fourteen examples exhibiting a fairly clear regional dissemination of the variants and drew separate heteroglossic lines for them. This cartographic procedure shows at a glance whether in any given locality or district these Northern phonological innovations were adopted in all relevant words or only in some of them. The spacing of the heterophones on Hall's Maps 3, 4, and 7 demonstrates the fact that they are introduced word by word, i.e., at different times.

When all of the heterophones established on the evidence of the Linguistic Atlas for the eight features investigated are assembled on a single map, Central France appears as a transition zone between the strikingly uniform Northern (Francien) and the relatively uniform Southern (Provençal) areas. The traditionally recognized Franco-Provençal area, Hall concludes, is nothing more than the eastern section of this Central transition belt.

Hall's carefully documented study not only assigns a meaningful place to Franco-Provençal in the dialectal structure of France. It presents historically important phonological features for subdividing France into major dialect areas and of characterizing each sub-division in phonological terms. The map presented in Figure 34 below, in which the regional dissemination of five of Hall's eight features have been assembled in simplified form, shows the varying width of the central transition zone between the North and the South.

The complexities of the central transition belt that separates southern from northern France is also effectively conveyed by the compilation of numerous heterophones presented by Ettmayer [1924] on Map VI.

6.9 The Dialectal Structure of the Iberian Peninsula

The Iberian Peninsula harbors three literary languages: Spanish, Portuguese, and Catalan. Each of them is based upon a major region-al dialect.

Literary Catalan is used chiefly in Catalonia, although the Catalan

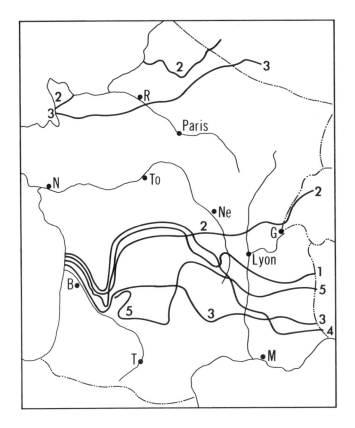

FIGURE 34: France: Outer Limits of Northern Phonological Features

1. Northern e (as in cher) ≠ Southern a (< L cārus)
2. N e (as in mère) ≠ S a (< L māter)
3. N ča- (> š, as in champ) ≠ S ka- (< L campus)
4. N loss of -d- (as in chaine) ≠ S -d- (< L catēna)
5. N loss of preconsonantal s (as in château) ≠ s preservation of s (< L castellum)

Cities: B(ordeaux, G(eneva, L(yon, M(arseille, N(antes, Ne(vers, P(aris, R(ouen, T(oulouse, To(urs

From R. A. Hall, Jr., The Linguistic Position of Franco-Provençal.

dialect is spoken also in large parts of Valencia. Spanish has been the official language since the fifteenth century.

Portuguese is the literary and the official language of Portugal. It is based upon a group of closely related dialects spoken along the entire extent of the western littoral of the Iberian Peninsula, including Galicia (part of the political domain of Spain since 1230, where Spanish is the official language).

Spanish is the literary and the official language of the entire Iberian Peninsula, except for Portugal. In Catalonia it is rivaled by literary Catalan. Spanish is Castilian in origin and was so called until the rise of Spain as the dominant political power and cultural center of the Peninsula. Castilian is the appropriate term in linguistic discussions.

The linguistic history of the Iberian Peninsula has been extensively investigated since the beginning of the present century. In his Manual de gramática histórica española [1905, 1952] and his Orígines del español [1926, 1950], R. Menéndez Pidal laid the foundation for fruitful research carried on by numerous scholars inspired by him. A great deal of systematic sampling of the modern dialects has also been done, but the Spanish Civil War (1936–39) has seriously interfered with its progress.

A Linguistic Atlas of Catalonia was organized by A. Griera i Gaja and published in part [1923–39]—858 maps. The remainder of his collection was destroyed during the Civil War. T. Navarro Tomás directed a field survey of Spain before the Civil War; unfortunately, none of his findings have been published as yet. In Portugal, M. de Paiva Boléo has energetically promoted the investigation of the dialects since the 1940's. Reports on the progress of these surveys and their character are available in Kuhn 1947, Pop 1950, Griera 1958.

Although the collections of the linguistic atlas of Spain and Portugal are presumably accessible to qualified scholars, it is regrettable that the Iberian Peninsula does not yet possess a linguistic survey, comparable with that of France and Italy, that scholars in other countries could consult. Nevertheless, the regional dissemination of some phonological features are known well enough to provide insight into some aspects of the dialectal patterning of the Peninsula. The brief sketch that follows relies largely upon the excellent and circumspect treatment presented by A. Zamora Vicente in his Dialectologia Española [1960], which also contains a comprehensive bibliography.

Three phonological heteroglosses of structural and historical importance serve to suggest the present dialectal structure of the Iberian Peninsula (see Figure 35). In the large Castilian central

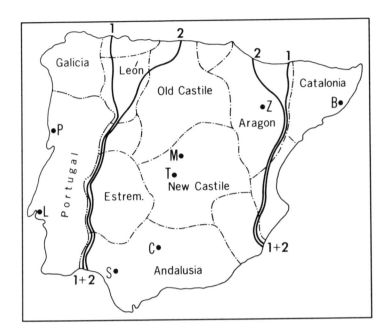

FIGURE 35: Iberian Peninsula: Major Dialect Areas

1. Latin short e and o, as in <u>mel</u> "honey" and <u>novem</u> "nine," preserved in Gallego-Portuguese along the Atlantic and in Catalan
   along the Mediterranean littoral, are shifted to ie and ue in the
   large Castilian central area.
2. Initial Latin <u>f-</u>, as in <u>fel</u> "gall," <u>folia</u> "leaves," is preserved in
   Gallego-Portuguese and in Catalan as well as in northern
   Leonese and Aragonese, but shifted to <u>h</u>- in Castilian (and thereafter lost, except in western Andalusia).

Cities: B(arcelona, C(ordova, L(isbon, M(adrid, P(orto, S(eville,
T(oledo, Z(aragossa.

Adapted from R. Menéndez Pidal, Manual de Gramática Histórica
Española and from A. Zamora Vicente, Dialectología Española.

area (1) Latin short e̲ and o̲ appear as the crescendo diphthongs ie̲
and uo̲, as in miel "honey" (< L mel), piedra "stone" (< L petra),
and in nuevo "nine" (< L novem), hueso "bone" (< L ossum). (2)
Latin initial f̲- has shifted to h̲- and is now lost in the greater part
of the area, as in hiel "gall" (< L fel), hoja "leaf" (< L folia).

In the western and the eastern littorals of the Peninsula, i.e., in
Gallego-Portuguese and in Catalan, Latin e̲, o̲, and f̲- are preserved
as such.

Other phonological features exhibit dissemination patterns that
support the present subdivision of the Peninsula into a western
(Gallego-Portuguese), a central (Castilian), and an eastern (Catalan)
dialect area. Some of these are presented in the accompanying
table, to which the numbers used below refer. Features 1 and 2 are
confined to Castilian, features 3, 4, 5 to Portuguese, and feature 6
appears primarily in Catalan. In feature 6, each of the three dialects exhibits its own reflexes. It must be pointed out, however,
that the precise regional dissemination of some of these features
has not yet been established and that diachronic considerations are
here not taken into account.

It is a striking fact that the present dialect boundary between
Portuguese and Castilian intersects the river valleys and the mountain
ranges of the peninsula at right angles. Since there is no congruence
between these two dialect areas and the natural landscape, their
origin must be sought in sociocultural factors. To some extent this
is also true of the dialect boundary between Castilian (Spanish) and
Catalan. Spanish scholars, from Menéndez Pidal [1926] to the present, have worked on this problem and achieved substantial clarifica-
tion of the dynamics that have created the three major dialect areas
of the Iberian Peninsula.

The decisive historical events are: (1) the conquest of all but
the northern section of the Iberian Peninsula by the Arabs (Moors)
in the first decades of the eighth century; (2) the gradual Reconquest
of the entire Peninsula (ca. 900–1492) by speakers of Romanic dialects that had developed in the north of the Peninsula along the Bay
of Biscay and the Pyrenees; (3) the lateral expansion of the Castilian
dialect area after the Reconquest, owing to the rise of Castile as the
dominant political and cultural power on the Peninsula.

It is important to point out that in the area dominated for centuries by the Arabs, Romanic continued to be spoken by sizable groups,
both in the cities and in the countryside. It remained the language of
the Christian congregations. In the millennium that elapsed between
the Roman colonization of the Peninsula (200 B.C.) and the Reconquest, regional differences must have developed, especially in areas
as far apart as the valley of the Ebro in the northeast, the valley of

the Guadalquivir in the south, and the Atlantic coast in the west.
Romanic words, found chiefly in Arabic texts, provide some evidence of variation in Mozarabic, as the Romanic language current
in the area dominated by the Arabs was called. Such regional differences might well have contributed to the character of the dialects
that emerged as the result of the Reconquest.

The Reconquest consisted of a series of southward thrusts from
the northern Romanic kingdoms and principalities strung out over a
thousand miles from the Atlantic to the Mediterranean, from Galicia
to Catalonia. The most vigorous and extensive of these drives was
that from Old Castil (Burgos) through the central section of the
Peninsula. In the course of about three centuries this southward
expansion reached the Atlantic at the mouth of the Guadalquivir in

Some Regional Heterophones

	Latin	Portuguese	Castilian	Catalan
1. -lj-:	mulier "woman"	molher / λ /	mujer / x /	mullier / λ /
	fília "daughter"	filha	hija	fillia
2. -ct-:	octō "eight"	oito	ocho / č /	vuit
	pactum "pact"	peito	pecho	peyta
3. au:	paucus "little"	pouco	poco	poc
	laudāre "praise"	louvar	loar	lloar
4. -l-:	volāre "fly"	voar	volar	volar
	color "color"	côr	color	color
5. -n-:	plēnum "full"	cheio	lleno	ple(n
	panis "bread"	pāo	pan	pa(n
6. l-:	lupus "wolf"	lobo	lobo	llop / λ /
	lactem "milk"	leite	leche	llet
7. pl-:	plānus "level"	chão / č /	llano / λ /	pla(n
cl-:	clavis "key"	chave	llave	clau
fl-:	flamma "flame"	chamma	llama	flama

Andalusia. Crossing the Sierra de Guadarrama into the valley of the
Tagus, Castile conquered Toledo in 1085, which became the capital
of Castil (later of Spain); Seville was taken from the Arabs in 1248,
Granada not until 1492.

To the west, the Castilian thrust was flanked by a southward
drive of the kingdom of León into the valleys of the Tagus and the
Guadiana (Estremadura); to the east of it, the kingdom of Aragon
expanded southward. On the Atlantic littoral, the Arabs were pushed
back from Galicia and northern Portugal, along the eastern shore of
the Peninsula from Catalonia (part of the Frankish March maintained
by the Carolingian emperors to contain the Arabs of the Ebro valley).
These five parallel thrusts created five major dialect areas: the
Gallego-Portuguese, the Leonese, the Castilian, the Aragonese, and
the Catalan. Each of these dialects is essentially a descendant of a
Romanic dialect that survived in the north of the Peninsula, as modified by the regional Mozarabic underlay in the several reconquered
areas.

With the rise of Castil as the dominant political power, especially
after its union with Aragon (1479), and owing to its cultural predominance from the sixteenth century onward, the Castilian dialect spread
eastward into Aragonese and westward into Leonese territory.
Moreover, with the acquisition of all parts of the Peninsula, with the
exception of Portugal, the Castilian literary language—now called
Spanish—became the official language of all of Spain.

The northern section of the Iberian Peninsula has been remarkably conservative in speech. Here Leonese and Aragonese have
escaped Castilianization to a considerable extent, as in the triangles
between heteroglosses 1 and 2 shown in Figure 35.

All varieties of Spanish spoken on the American Continent, from
the West Indies to Central and to South America, are derived from
the Castilian dialects of the Iberian Peninsula. Castilian was far
from uniform at the time the several American colonies were established. In fact, several important phonological changes were still in
progress even in literary Castilian during the sixteenth century, as
the merging (ca. 1550) of the earlier voiced fricatives / ð, z, g / with
voiceless / θ, s, x /, respectively, with the result that / θ / became
current not only in plaza (< Lat. platea) but also in haçer "make"
(< Lat. facere); / s / not only in pasar "pass" (cp. Lat. pass-us) but
also in casa "house" (< Lat. casa); and / x / not only in nexo (< Lat.
nexus) but also in hijo "son" (< Lat. filium).

While the merging of these three voiced fricatives with their
voiceless counterparts and the further merging of / θ / with / s / in
southern Castilian (i.e., in Andalusia)—as in haçer "make" and casa
"house"—became fully established in all parts of Spanish America,

presumably through continued contacts with the mother country, some other phonological features of Castilian that varied regionally or by social levels still vary in American Spanish. Thus the shift of palatal / λ / to the palatal semivowel / j /, as in llano "level," lluvio "rain," became established in the greater part of Spanish America, but not in the Andean highlands from southern Columbia to northern Chile [Zamora 1960: Map XXI].

Zamora, relying upon investigations of many scholars (see his bibliography, 381–86) summarizes the prevailing view with regard to the historical background of American Spanish in these words:

> "The Spanish transplanted to America in the "dawn"
> of the conquest was preclassical . . . [It] continued to
> receive new "layers" of spoken Spanish and, preserving
> close cultural and spiritual ties, experienced the same
> changes as the mother country. Hence there are few
> changes that separate American Spanish from Castilian"
> [Zamora 1960: 333].

Zamora adds the observation that in colonial times this sustained influence was exerted, or mediated, by the viceroyal courts. Literary Spanish, highly standardized by 1600, continued to have its effects upon the language of the several countries after they achieved independence.

In a general way, American Spanish and American English stand in the same relation to their European sources. Some dialectal differences imported at the time of the settlement survive regionally, fashionable innovations in the language of the mother country continued to be imported in certain centers during the Colonial period, and the literary language of the European homeland is an ever present dominant influence.

7.

Transplanted Languages

7.1 Introduction

For tracing the complicated history of transplanted languages, a combination of linguistic and sociocultural evidence is required. The techniques of structural linguistics must be applied to the synchronic and the diachronic phenomena; areal evidence, both in its geographic and its social dimension, must be brought to bear upon this problem.

Field surveys of the current dialects of the parent language and of the transplanted language, the structural interpretation of the findings, and the regional and social patterning of the variants constitute the most promising point of departure. The structure of the parent language at the time of the transplantation and its subsequent changes should be considered next. Finally, changes in the transplanted (colonial) language after the settlement, whether indigenous or imported from the parent stock as the result of continuing contacts, should be determined.

After the purely linguistic relationships between the parent language and its offshoot have been established as far as the available data permit, the sociocultural factors that may account for them are investigated.

The most important points to consider are: (1) the regional and the social provenience of the settlers; (2) the location of early settlements and the chronology of lines of expansion; (3) the social organization of the colony and its subdivisions; (4) commercial and cultural

contacts with the "homeland" during and after the settlement period;
(5) the status of the literary language shared with the homeland
during the colonial period and after the achievement of political and
cultural independence; (6) the influence of the natural environment,
of other ethnic groups, and of sociocultural innovations upon the
lexicon.

The multiplicity and the variety of factors that shape the history
of transplanted languages are such that sharply divergent developments may be expected. To illustrate this point, I have chosen to
discuss four typical cases in fields familiar to me for which rather
good evidence is available: American English, Pennsylvania German,
Afrikaans, and Gullah.

The development of American English in its relation to British
English is treated above (Chapter 5). The salient facts are as follows.
(1) The phonology and morphology of Standard British English were
already highly standardized when colonies were planted in North
America. However, regional variations in the Standard were more
prevalent than at present and folk dialects still predominated among
the middle and the lower classes of society. (2) The folk dialects
spoken by the majority of the settlers gave way to varieties of
Standard British English current among the elite of the several
colonial centers. (3) These regional variants of SBE were carried
inland during the seventeenth and the eighteenth centuries as the
colonies expanded. After Independence was achieved, the dramatic
"Westward Movement" of the population spread them to the Rocky
Mountains and the Pacific coast in little more than half a century,
blending them progressively. As a result, the major dialect areas
of American English are strikingly congruent with settlement areas.
(4) The use of the same literary language has served to keep American English close to British English. Nevertheless, many new words
and new applications of old words were introduced to cope with
features of a different natural environment and with the many sociocultural changes. (5) Contact with speakers of other languages has
led to the adoption of a considerable number of foreign words.

In principle, the history of American Spanish and American
Portuguese is not unlike that of American English.

A radically different development is illustrated by Pennsylvania
German. As pointed out in some detail below, it differs markedly
from Standard German in its phonology. In the lexicon and in
morphology the differences are less striking, but still rather considerable. This divergence between Pennsylvania German (essentially
a Rhine Frankish folk dialect of west central Germany) and Standard
German (based on East Central German) would tend to keep the two
apart. However, it was primarily the sociocultural setting that dis-
couraged the importation of Standard German features. From the

beginning until the present, Pennsylvania German has been the
spoken vernacular of a highly integrated farming area. Literary
German, heard in church, read in Luther's Bible and in the daily
press, and taught in grammar school for many generations, was a
thing apart. It never became the medium of communication in the
family or between neighbors. Embedded in an English-speaking
country, Pennsylvania German adopted a fair number of English
words and modeled some of its expressions on English idioms. But
its integrity as a Rhine Frankish dialect (Pfälzerisch) has survived
through two and a half centuries.

Afrikaans, now one of the two official languages of the South
African Republic, has had a unique development. Its vowel system
is essentially that of Standard Dutch, tinged with some dialectal
features peculiar to the provinces of South and North Holland
(Rotterdam, Amsterdam). The consonant system exhibits rather
marked changes: contrastive voiced fricatives are lost and final
consonant clusters have been simplified. The most drastic deviation from Standard Dutch is found in the morphology of the verb,
which is stripped of most of its inflections. None of these simplifi-
cations are attested in the folk dialects of the Netherlands. They
came into being in the Cape Colony (Capetown).

The sociocultural background of this pidginized Dutch of South
Africa is rather clear. The population of Capetown, established as
a port of call by the Dutch East India Company in 1652, had a highly
mixed population in which the Dutch-speaking minority constituted
an elite. Africans (chiefly Hottentots) were numerous and inter-
marriage between Europeans and Africans was not uncommon.
Under these circumstances a simplified Dutch became the medium
of communication between the diverse elements. This spoken
vernacular was fully established in the Cape Colony when the Boers
made their trek into the Orange Free State and the Transvaal in the
nineteenth century. The striking regional uniformity of Afrikaans
from Capetown to Johannesburg, a distance of 800 miles, testifies
to this fact.

The original domain of Gullah, an English-based pidgin language,
was the slave trade carried on by the Royal African Company in the
seventeenth and the eighteenth centuries. In North America it
became established on the plantations worked by African slaves and
has survived to this day along the coast of South Carolina and
Georgia.

The lexicon of Gullah is almost entirely English. On the other
hand, the phonemic system is simplified, and the noun and the verb
have lost their grammatical categories and the inflections expressing
them. Dealing with Africans speaking a variety of mutually unintelli-

gible languages, the slave trader used a simplified English, which was ultimately acquired by the slaves and their masters on the American plantations as their medium of communication. The policy of the plantation owners to purchase slaves speaking different African languages—for fear of organized revolt—supported this practice.

An authoritative account of the character and the genesis of pidgin and creole languages is available in R. A. Hall's recently published book on this subject [1966].

7.2 Pennsylvania German

7.21 Phonological Features

The German spoken in southeastern Pennsylvania since colonial times is essentially a descendant of Rhine Frankish, a major regional dialect of German spoken along the middle course of the Rhine in an area comprising the political domains of the Palatinate (Rheinpfalz) and Hesse-Darmstadt, with such cities as Zweibrücken, Kaiserslautern, Mannheim, and Darmstadt.

The most striking Rhine Frankish features in the phonology of Pennsylvania German (PG) are pointed out below and illustrated by a few examples. Standard German (SG) equivalents, given in conventional orthography, will serve to set the characteristic features of PG off from SG.

(1) The rounded front vowels and diphthongs of Middle High German are merged with the unrounded vowels and diphthongs of corresponding tongue positions and movements:

PG kind, šdig; fil, fīs; bed, keb šnē, šē;
SG Kind, Stück; viel, Füsse; Bett, Köpfe; Schnee, schön;

PG wēdsə, bēm, frēd
SG Weizen, Bäume, Freude.

(2) The diphthongs / ei, ŏu, ou / of MHG are merged with old monophthongs:

PG glēdər, frēd; gēd, ēl; kāfə, nāsə, jār
SG Kleider, Freude; geht, Öl; kaufen, Nase, Jahr.

(3) Contrastive MHG / ī ≠ ei / and / ū ≠ ou / are preserved as / ai ≠ ē / and / au ≠ ā / in PG, while they are merged in SG:

PG paif ≠ flēš; gaul ≠ bām
SG Pfeife, Fleisch; Gaul, Baum.

These developments have produced a simple and symmetrical system of syllabic sounds, which PG shares with Rhine Frankish:

$$
\begin{array}{llll}
\text{i} & \text{u} & \bar{\text{i}} & \bar{\text{u}} \\
\text{e} & \text{o} & \bar{\text{e}} & \bar{\text{o}} \quad\quad \text{ai, oi, au} \\
& \text{a} & & \bar{\text{a}}
\end{array}
$$

Characteristic features of the Rhine Frankish and the Pennsylvania German consonant system are:

(1) the lack of /t / and /pf /:

PG dĭr, budər; parə,   ebəl
SG Tür, Butter; Pfarrer, Apfel.

(2) The weakening of the old strong stops /p, k / to voiceless /b, g / in all positions except initially before a stressed vowel:

PG pund, blūg, šdrumb,   karix, glē,   šang,   drugə
HG Pfund, Pflug, Strumpf, Kirche, klein, Schrank, troken.

(3) The weakening of intervocalic /b, g / to the voiced fricatives /w, j /:

PG glāwə   lējə
SG glauben, legen.

(4) The loss of word final /n / after /ə / and after a long vowel or diphthong:

PG esə, gnoxə,   štē,   wai
HG essen, Knochen, Stein, Wein.

7.22 Regional Differences

Although the same phonemic system obtains throughout the German-speaking section of eastern Pennsylvania, there are some regional differences in the incidence of shared phonemes. Lehigh County (Allentown) and Lancaster County (Lancaster)—northerly and southerly parts of the original German settlement area—exhibit such differences as the following:

Leh   kĭx,   fōgəl, wolə, sodšd,   laid, dūnə
Lanc. kĭx,   fogəl, welə, sedšd,   ligd, dinə
SG   Küche, Vogel, wollen, solltest, liegt, tun

The Lehigh variants are clearly Rhine Frankish, the Lancaster variants just as clearly Alemannic.

The relatively few morphological differences between Lehigh and Lancaster usage have corresponding Frankish and Alemannic European source:

Leh.	ix sēn,	er sēt,	i͞r hen,	i͞r wolə,	gə-larnd
Lanc.	ix gsē,	er gsēt,	dir hend,	dir weləd,	g-larnd
SG	ich sehe,	er sieht,	ihr habt,	ihr wollt,	ge-lernt.

Similarly, the diminutive suffix / -xə, -xər / (cp. SG -<u>chen</u>) of Lehigh comes from Rhine Frankish, the / -li, -lin / (cp. SG -<u>lein</u>) of Lancaster from Alemannic.

Figure 36 exhibits the areal dissemination of some phonological and morphological variants for which the <u>Sprachatlas</u> provides the European background, as shown in Figure 37.

Lexical variants in PG have a similar regional pattern, as shown in Figure 38. However, the dividing lines follow the valley of the Schuykill River in Berks County rather than the northern boundary of

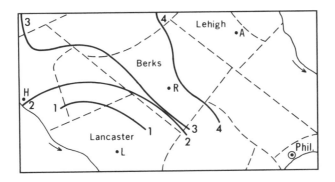

FIGURE 36: <u>Pennsylvania German: Some Morphological and Phonological Variants</u>

1. "(we) do": Lehigh / dūnə / ≠ Lancaster / dinə / [Reed-Seifert: Map 54]
2. The prefix of the past participle before the resonants / m, n, l, r, w /: Le. / gə- / ≠ La. / g- / [ibid.: Map 61]
3. The diminutive suffix (plural): Le. / -xər / ≠ La. / -lin / [ibid.: Map 90]
4. The pronoun of the second person plural: Le. / i͞r / ≠ La. / di͞r / [ibid.: Map 62]

Cities: A(llentown, H(arrisburg, L(ancaster, P(hiladelphia.

From C. E. Reed and L. W. Seifert, <u>A Linguistic Atlas of Pennsylvania German</u>.

Lancaster County. Whether the Lancaster regionalisms are predominantly of Alemannic origin is an open question, since neither
the S̲p̲r̲a̲c̲h̲a̲t̲l̲a̲s̲ [Wrede–Mitzka 1926–   ] nor the W̲o̲r̲t̲a̲t̲l̲a̲s̲ [Mitzka–
Schmitt 1951ff.] furnish relevant evidence. The following words,
which are largely confined to Lancaster County, are presumably
Alemannic: /ēxərli / "squirrel," /fed / "lard," /harəbš̌d /
"autumn," /kiwəl / "pail" [Reed–Seifert: Maps 84, 70, 71, 72].

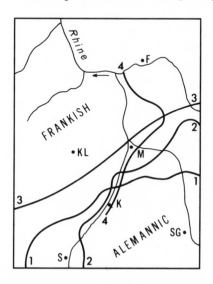

FIGURE 37: Pennsylvania German: Frankish and Alemannic Variants Underlying the Variants

1. Fr. dūn ≠ Al. d̲i̲n̲ ∼ d̲i̲a̲n̲ ∼ d̲e̲n̲ ∼ d̲e̲a̲n̲ [Reed Seifert: Map 54a]
2. Prefix of the past participle before the resonants: Fr. g̲ə̲-̲ ≠ Al. g̲-̲
    [ibid.: Map 61a]
3. Diminutive suffix: Fr. -̲c̲h̲e̲r̲ ≠ Al. -̲l̲i̲n̲ [ibid.: Map 90a]
4. Pronoun of the second person plural: Fr. i̲r̲ ∼ ē̲r̲ ≠ Al. d̲i̲r̲ ∼ d̲e̲r̲
    [ibid.: Map 62a]

Cities: F(rankfurt, K(arlsruhe, KL = Kaiserslautern,
         M(annheim, S(trassburg, SG = Stuttgart.

From C. E. Reed and L. W. Seifert.

7.23 Sociocultural Background

In two centuries of increasingly intimate contacts with speakers of English and a century of fairly general bilingualism, English words and idioms modeled on English have become established in Pennsylvania German. Their currency varies from place to place and from person to person, but some are in fairly general use. Writers of PG verse, anecdotes, and comedies (since ca. 1860) may tend to avoid Anglicisms (except for humorous effects), but twentieth-century writers like C. F. Iobst and L. A. Moll freely use such everyday English words as breakfast, supper, parlor, fence, shop, store, election, jury, and exclamatory expressions like anyhow, good-bye, never mind, sure, well. They also employ "handy" English idioms recast entirely in German vocabulary, as the following: dead to the world, feel proud, goodlooking, get away with it, and: How are you? He'll get over it. I stood my ground. Blends are not infrequent as

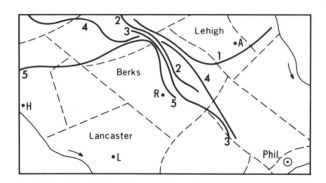

FIGURE 38: Pennsylvania German: Some Lexical Variants

1. North / šogl / (SG Schaukel) ≠ South / wīg / (SG Wiege) "cradle" [Reed-Seifert 1954: Map 82]
2. N / ludsr / ≠ S / ladárn / "lantern" [ibid.: Map 77]
3. N / blafd / ≠ S / gaudsd / "barks, of a dog" [ibid.: Map 79]
4. N / šwom / ≠ S / wis / (SG Wiese) "meadow" [ibid.: Map 80]
5. N / šēb / ≠ S / garəb / (SG Garbe) "sheaf" [ibid.: Map 76]

Cities: A(llentown, H(arrisburg, L(ancaster, P(hiladelphia.

From C. E. Reed and L. W. Seifert.

/ špriŋ-ēg / "spring harrow," / bār-štub / "bar room," / uf gədresd /
"dressed up," and / du bišd nox sori / "you'll be sorry," / ix hab mai
maind uf gəmaxd / "I've made up my mind."

It is of some importance to note that English elements taken into
Pennsylvania German are adapted to the native phonological, morphological, and syntactic systems, which have remained remarkably
stable since colonial times. Bilingual speakers (as most Pennsylvania Germans are at the present time) may of course pronounce a
word like taxes in the English manner or switch from German to
English in the middle of a sentence. But this practice does not "mix"
the structural features of the two languages.

The English of bilinguals in eastern Pennsylvania may show some
German influence in pronunciation, as a monophthongal articulation
of the syllabics of rain and bone, or the unvoicing of stops and fricatives in rob, leg, save, rise. Some German expressions also survive
in their English and a few of them have even been adopted by English
monolinguals of Pennsylvania, among them saddle horse "near-
horse," thick-milk "curdled milk," ponhaws "scrapple," and smear-
case "cottage cheese" [Kurath 1949: Figures 23, 24]. These Germanisms are rapidly fading out in areas in which German is no
longer spoken to any extent [Kurath 1945].

In dealing with Pennsylvania German we are in the enviable
position of having reliable linguistic evidence and ample information
on the sociocultural setting in which this spoken language became
established and survived through several centuries as an enclave in
English-speaking America.

Linguistic evidence is provided by voluminous writings in the
dialect since the middle of the nineteenth century [H. H. Reichard
1918; E. F. Robacker 1943]. We have a dictionary of PG with more
than 16,000 entries [Lambert 1924]. We know a great deal about the
phonological and morphological structure of the language, owing to a
field survey of the PG heartland of eastern Pennsylvania [C. E. Reed
1949; Reed-Seifert 1954]. Regional differences in vocabulary have
also been investigated [Seifert 1946; Reed-Seifert 1954; Buffington
1948]. For the European background the Sprachatlas provides information and more is forthcoming through the publication of Rheinpfäl-
zisches Wörterbuch, edited by E. Christmann.

The history of the people that speak this language has been traced
in great detail, chiefly in the voluminous publications of the Pennsylvania German Society (1891 ff.) and the Pennsylvania German Folk-
lore Society (1936 ff.). Only the most essential facts will be mentioned here.

Shortly after the founding of William Penn's Quaker colony on the
Delaware (1680), German Protestants (Lutherans, Reformed) and

Sectarians (Dunkers, Mennonites, Moravians) settled in the rich
farmland of the Piedmont as far west as the Blue Mountains, an area
extending for 100 miles from the valley of the Delaware (Easton,
Bethlehem, Allentown) to the valley of the Susquehanna (Lancaster,
York). On Penn's invitation, they left their homes along the middle
course of the Rhine (the Palatinate and Hesse-Darmstadt) to escape
religious persecution and oppressive manorial services. Along with
them came Sectarians from Elsace, Baden, and Switzerland. By
1750 they were fully established as a well-integrated cultural community, differing in many ways from their English speaking neighbors
to the east and to the west.

Although preserving a sentimental attachment to the remote
European homelands from which they had fled, they soon had little in
common with them because of the revolutionary changes in their
lives. As Americans they participated fully in the War for Independence and wholeheartedly supported the Union in the Civil War.

In their daily life the Pennsylvania Germans preserved much of
the folk culture they had brought with them, from farming methods
and home industries to social gatherings and religious practices.
Benjamin Rush (1745–1813), the famous Philadelphia physician and
statesman, described their lives admirably in his Account of the
Manners of the German Inhabitants of Pennsylvania [1910]. Last
but not least, they clung to their spoken language, essentially a
Rhine Frankish dialect with some admixtures of Alemannic in parts
of the area. This German dialect, popularly known as Pennsylvania
Dutch, is still widely current today.

Those who spoke the Pennsylvania German dialect at home, in
dealing with their neighbors, and in doing business in the regional
market towns were not unfamiliar with Standard German, which was
regularly used in church services and read to them from Luther's
Bible well into the nineteenth century. Many of them learned High
German in grammar schools and academies and read it in the
regional German newspapers. But Standard German was a language
apart from their normal medium of communication and had little
influence upon it. When words were taken into their spoken language,
they were adapted to it in sounds and in grammatical forms.

Until the middle of the nineteenth century the Pennsylvania German dialect was not reduced to writing. By ca. 1860 it came to be
used in nostalgic verse, later in humorous sketches, still later in
translations of English and German poetry. Those who employed it
as a literary language were, of course, not the common people, but
college-trained churchmen, teachers, doctors, lawyers, and newspaper editors of Pennsylvania German descent, all of them native
speakers of the dialect.

7.3 Afrikaans

7.31 The Vowel System

Relying upon evidence furnished by the Linguistic Atlas of North and South Netherland [1939ff.], G. G. Kloeke undertook to pinpoint the sources of certain features of the Afrikaans vowel system in his book entitled Herkomst en Groei van het Afrikaans [1950]. As editor of the Atlas he had access to a large body of localized dialect data gathered by him and other scholars in the Netherlands and in the Netherlandish (Flemish) section of Belgium from the 1920's onward [see E. Blancquaert 1948: esp. 37–55, the questionnaire].

Kloeke points out the following characteristic features of Afrikaans that are confined to the western section of the Netherlands:

(1) The lack of palatal mutation before PGc / i, j /, as exemplified in groen (cp. E green, G grün) and soeken (cp. E seek); in hoor (cp. E hear, G hören) and skoon (cp. G schön); in naast (cp. E next, G nächst) and swaar (cp. G schwer).

(2) The unconditioned ("spontaneous") fronting of / o /, from PGc / u- /, to / ö / (written eu), as in neut "nut" (cp. OE hnutu, G nuss), seun "son" (cp. OE sunu, G sohn). The corresponding Standard Netherlandish forms noot, zoon are at variance with the older folk usage of the western Netherlands from which the variants of Afrikaans are derived. It is of interest to note that, in agreement with Standard Dutch, Afrikaans has "unfronted" / ō / in koning "king," vogel "bird," and woon "reside." The complicated background of this situation is dealt with in some detail by Kloeke [85–100, esp. 98–99] and by Vereecken [1938, esp. 60–64 and Maps 2, 3, 5]. This problem makes it clear that in the attempt to relate traits of a colonial dialect to the dialect of its homeland, changes that occur in the source dialect after the settlement must not be overlooked.

In Figure 39 the areal dissemination of a third feature shared by Afrikaans with the western Netherlands is also delimited, the diphthongal syllabic / öü / as in huis "house," which Kloeke discussed in masterly fashion in an earlier publication [1927]. Kloeke's findings regarding this feature are dealt with by L. Bloomfield in his Language [1933: 329–31].

Kloeke undertakes to narrow down the homeland of Afrikaans to the province of South Holland and the adjoining district of North Holland—the area in which Rotterdam, the Hague, Leiden, Haarlem, and Amsterdam are situated. This is done by means of specific areal and diachronic linguistic evidence. Among the features that Afrikaans shares primarily or only with the province of South Holland are the following: (1) the merging of WGc / ā / and lengthened WGc / a- / in long / ā /, as in schaap "sheep" and water "water" [Kloeke 56–59], whereas North Holland has / ē ≠ ā / as in skeep ≠ waater; (2) the diminutive suffix with the characteristic vowel / i /, spelled ie [135–38].

The close connections of Afrikaans with the dialects of the western Netherlands would seem to imply that the majority of the early settlers of Capetown and its environs came from that area. But that expectation turns out to be unfounded. Hollanders and Zeelanders never made up more than one fourth of the total population. Kloeke assumes, for apparently good reasons, that a close-knit minority from the province of South Holland (Rotterdam) soon con-

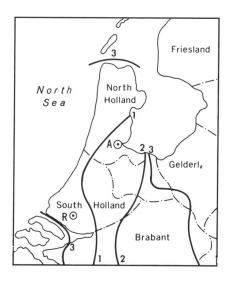

FIGURE 39: Western Features of Netherlandish

1. Eastern limit of / ō̄ / < / ō- / (PGc / u- /) in zeug "sow" (cp. OE sugu) [Kloeke 1950: 95].
2. Eastern limit of / u / from unpalatalized / ō / (PGc / ō / in zoeken "seek" (cp. OE sēcean) [ibid.: 55].
3. Eastern and southwestern limits of the diphthong / öü / from / ū / in huis "house" (cp. OE hūs) [ibid.: 48].

Cities: A(msterdam, R(otterdam.

stituted an elite whose usage was adopted by Netherlanders speaking other dialects and by the motley crew of North Germans, French Huguenots, and others. The slow growth of Capetown, established in 1652 by the Dutch East India Company as a port of call and a supply station along the route to the East Indies, facilitated this development. After half a century the white population of Capetown was still under 1,500!

Another important factor in establishing the western phonological type of Netherlandish in South Africa was its closeness to literary Netherlandish, which after the Spanish conquest of Brabant (1585) had come more and more under the influence of Holland (Amsterdam). Used in religious services and read in the Statenbijbel (translated 1625–35) by devout Protestants, literary usage both supported and supplemented the western features of Afrikaans.

The English conquest of South Africa during the Napoleonic wars encouraged the use of Afrikaans in daily life; and the "Boers" who emigrated (1830–   ) from the Cape of Good Hope to settle the Orange Free State and the Transvaal have clung to it steadfastly.

Evidence for the characteristic features of Afrikaans is decidedly limited until the latter part of the nineteenth century and consists mainly of deviations from Standard Dutch in locally written documents. When it came to be one of the official languages of the South African Union (1910) it was already highly, though not wholly, standardized. Descriptions of this spoken colloquial language began to appear in the twentieth century, soon followed by prescriptions aimed at making written usage more uniform.

Kloeke's primary concern is with the problem of establishing the sources of distinctive phonological features of Afrikaans by tracing them to folk dialects of the western Netherlands. In support of the phonological evidence for western or "coastal" origin, he adduces the phonological shape of the diminutive suffix and such western dialect words as aker "acorn" [171], hiel "heel" [149], and wiel "wheel" [150], of which the last two are also current in Standard Netherlandish. Morphological features of Afrikaans are referred to only in passing.

7.32 Simplification of the Consonant

When we look at Afrikaans as a colonial language we find that it differs rather strikingly from such other transplanted languages as American English and American Spanish. The latter preserve not only the vocabulary and the essential features of the phonemic system of their European source language, but also the morphological system, whereas the phonological and the morphological systems of Afrikaans suffer rather radical changes, as briefly outlined below.

The basic vocabulary of Afrikaans is predominantly Dutch. There are, of course, new coinages and semantic extensions of old words to unfamiliar things, and some words are imported from contact languages (Hottentot, Portuguese, etc.).

The vowel system is little changed, but the lexical incidence of phonemes shared with Standard Dutch often deviates owing to existing differences in the imported Dutch dialects or to unsettled usage in earlier Standard Dutch. These are the phonological features used by Kloeke [1950] in tracing features of Afrikaans to the provinces of South and North Holland.

There are two notable changes in the system of consonants and in phonotactics.

(1) The voiced fricatives / v, z, ɣ /, contrasting in Standard Dutch with voiceless / f, s, x /, as initially in vin "fin" ≠ fijn "fine," zuiver "neat" ≠ suizen "whistle" and medially in razen "rave" ≠ wassen "grow," hagel "hail ≠ lachen "laugh," are merged with / f, s, x /. This simplification apparently came about in contact with languages that lack this contrast, probably facilitated by the fact that Dutch lacks this contrast in final position (where only / f, s, x / occur) and in most of the consonant clusters.

(2) In all final consonant clusters consisting of an obstruent and / t /, the / t / is lost, as in hoof (SDu. hoofd) "head," wes (SDu. west) "west," lig (SDu. licht) "light," naak (SDu. naakt) "naked."

7.33 Simplification of the Verb

As a result of the phonological simplification of such final clusters ending in / t /, the inflectional / -t / of the third person singular present and of the preterit and past participle of weak verbs was lost in many cases. With the loss of final unstressed / ə / and / ən / in other verb forms, the verb became largely uninflected. A few examples culled from texts in T. H. le Roux, Afrikaanse Taalstudies [1945: 150–54], will serve to illustrate this revolutionary simplification of the verb forms in Afrikaans.

The uninflected ("unmarked") verb form is used after any subject, nominal or pronominal, singular or plural. It is not a tense form. With few exceptions, its source is the base morpheme of the Dutch present tense and/or infinitive, as shown in the following examples: bied (< SDu. bieden) "offer," haal (< halen) "fetch," hef (< heffen) "heave, raise," loop (< lopen) "run," styg (< stijgen) "climb," sweef (< zweven) "hover," vaar (< varen) "fare, ride," gaan (< gaan) "go," sien (< zien) "see."

The phrase consisting of uninflected het "have" and the past participle of the verb (with prefix ge-, unless the verb has an unstressed prefix, such as ver-) refers to the past. Examples: het

gedra "wore, has worn," het geval "fell," het gewoon "dwelled,
resided," het geglo "believed," het gebring "brought," het gedink
"thought," het verbind "bound (them) together," het vertel "told." It
should be emphasized that the base morpheme of the past participle
is identical with the unmarked verb.

Verb phrases containing the infinitive are kan wees "can be,"
sal maak "shall make," wil skryf "will write," te loop "to run."

The passive phrase consists of is or word and the past participle:
is los gesny "is ~ was cut away," word los gelaat "is ~ was let go."

The loss of contrastive voiced fricatives and of final /t / after
obstruents must surely be attributed to contacts with speakers of
other languages, since there is no parallel in the dialects of the
Netherlands. That the elimination of ablaut variation in the strong
verb, presumably following the loss of inflectional / -t /, resulted
from the same sociocultural situation in the Cape Colony can hardly
be doubted.

It is reasonable to assume that this phonologically and morphologically simplified colloquial Dutch came into being in Capetown at an
early date as a medium of communication between speakers of a
variety of Dutch dialects and speakers of other languages including
Low German, Scandinavian, Portuguese, and—last but not least—
Hottentot, the language of the indigenous population with whom some
of the early settlers intermarried and who furnished most of the
domestic servants. The need for such a medium, the basis of
modern Afrikaans, persisted, since Dutch settlers continued to be
in the minority, what with the later influx of Bantus, Hindus, and
East Indians.

With the trek of the Boers (1830–   ) into the high plains of the
Orange Free State and the Transvaal to escape British domination,
this creolized colloquial Dutch spread throughout the present domain
of the South African Republic and became one of the official languages
of the Union of South Africa in 1910.

7.4 Gullah

7.41 Introduction

Gullah, also called Geechee, is a Creole language spoken by
Negroes along the coast of South Carolina and Georgia. It is based
on English but exhibits marked morphological and phonological
features derived from languages spoken along the Gulf of Guinea in
West Africa. This language has been investigated by Lorenzo D.
Turner, a Negro scholar, who succeeded in gaining the confidence
of a people highly distrustful of all outsiders. In many months of

fieldwork he recorded their usage by means of a modified version of the worksheets of the Linguistic Atlas of the Eastern United States and recorded their spontaneous emotional speech on phonograph records. Some of his findings are presented in his book on Africanisms in the Gullah Dialect [1949], on which the following discussion is based.

The vocabulary of Gullah is predominantly English. The spontaneous monologs of eight speakers in six different places, transcribed by Turner [260–89] from his phonograph records, contain hardly half a dozen items of African origin in a corpus of about 1,300 words.

The fact that Turner [190–204] discovered some 200 words of African origin, freely used by speakers of Gullah among themselves, is not in conflict with this observation. These Africanisms include terms for the fauna of their American environment, for foodstuffs, for utensils, for religious practices and beliefs, for members of the family, and for parts of the body of man and animal. In addition there are emotionally tinged adjectives and verbs, and the numerals from 1 to 19. It is highly significant that about a dozen of these African words acquired currency outside the present Gullah area, chiefly in the Lower South: buckra "white man," cooter "box turtle," goober "peanut," gumbo "okra," hoodoo ~ voodoo, chigger, juke (-joint, -box), okra, pinder "peanut," shout "religious ring dance," yam "sweet potato."

The structure of the subject phrase, the predicate phrase, and the sentence is essentially English:

/ dat ol man gwain kʌs əm, yu no /

"That old man is going to curse them, you know."

/ dɛm pipl wat go dɛ hafə tə bai ɒl dɛm tıŋ /

"The people that go there have to buy all these things."

The only recurring syntactic feature that deviates from English is the equational sentence without the copula:

/ ai satisfai / "I'm satisfied"

/ de se wi tu ol / "They say we are too old."

7.42 Morphological Simplification

On the other hand, the head of the subject phrase (the noun) and the head of the predicate phrase (the verb) are predominantly uninflected. This usage is clearly carried over from West African languages, which lack the categories of number and case in the noun and of number, person, and tense in the verb.

A few examples will illustrate this striking "African" feature of Gullah. (1) Nouns: / tu kret / "two crates," / ɒl dɛm tıŋ / "all these things," / ɪn gɒd han / "in God's hand," / dɪ mɒsə həus / "the master's house." (2) Verbs: / i gi mi grɪts / "She gave me grits." / gɒd sew mi / "God saved me." / di rustə də kro / "The rooster was crowing." / ai ha fə wɒk ɒn mai han / "I had to walk on my hands."

Inflected noun and verb forms appear only sporadically. They are outnumbered by uninflected forms about six to one in Turner's texts.

7.43 Simplification of the Phonemic System

The phonemic system of Gullah shows some clear influence of the African substratum, especially in the vowels.

Most English consonants have fairly close counterparts in West African languages, but the fricatives / θ, ð / and contrastive / v ≠ w / are lacking. Hence / θ, ð / are replaced by / t, d /, so that thin, then are homophonous with tin, den, respectively. The fricatives / v / and / w / are merged either in a bilabial fricative or in / w /, so that vest and west sound alike. These adaptations result in the loss of three consonants. There are also some purely phonic changes, as the replacement of the assibilated plosives of chin and gin by plain palatals.

For the English high and mid vowels, both front and back, some of the African languages spoken along the Gulf of Guinea have fairly close counterparts, but none of them seems to have more than one low vowel. In this phonic range, the four vowels of English are reduced to two in Gullah: (1) front / æ / and central / ɑ / are merged in a low front / a /, so that hat and heart are homophonous, i.e. / hat /; (2) low back / ɒ / and raised low back / ɔ / are merged, so that cot and caught sound alike, i.e. / kɒt /.

None of the African languages spoken along the Gulf of Guinea seems to have any mid central vowels, whereas English has two, as in hut / hʌt / and hurt / hɜt /. These are merged in Gullah, so that hut and hurt are homophonous, i.e. / hʌt /.

These adaptations result in the loss of three English vowel phonemes in Gullah and the addition of one vowel to the African system.

The Gullah Vowel System

beat	i			u	boot
bit	ɪ			ʊ	foot
bait	e			o	boat
bet	ɛ	ʌ		ɒ	caught = cot
		a			

hut = hurt
hat = heart

The background of this simplification of low and central vowels appears with clarity from the vowel system of African languages

spoken along the Gulf of Guinea [Westermann and Ward 1933: Ewe
158, Yoruba 166, Fante 172, Bambara and Malinke 181], the home of
many, perhaps the majority of the slaves.

West African Vowel Systems

i	u	
ɪ*	ʊ*	*lacking in Ewe and Yoruba
e	o	
ɛ	ɔ	
	a	

7.44 Sociocultural Background

Gullah came into use on the plantations of coastal South Carolina
and Georgia, an area extending some 250 miles from the tidal inlet
of the Peedee River (Georgetown) in South Carolina to the inlet of
the Altamaha in Georgia. This lowland area, including the so-called
Sea Islands (St. James, South Carolina, to St. Simon, Georgia), was
admirably suited for the cultivation of rice, since the many rivers
flowing into the Atlantic provided the fresh water for periodically
flooding the rice fields. On the other hand, the cultivation of rice
as a colonial cash crop demanded a large investment of capital in
readying the land and a considerable labor force for tending the
crop. The answer was the plantation system, which dominated the
economy of coastal South Carolina from the very beginning.

The labor force was imported from Africa through the agency
of the Royal African Company, "which had the charter for all the
trade in slaves on the African Coast" [Petty 1943: 19]. By 1720,
Negro slaves outnumbered the white population in the Charleston
area as a whole, though not in the city itself [Petty: 25]. When the
first federal census was taken (1790), Negro slaves greatly outnumbered the whites on the rice plantations of South Carolina
[Petty: 69].

The social organization of the rice plantation, as also that of the
indigo plantation, was such that a special medium of communication
was imperative for the conduct of the day-by-day operations. The
white master and his family, the overseer, and perhaps some white
craftsmen, lived apart from the Negro field hands, who had their
own "quarters." And yet, the master or overseer had to direct the
work of the Negroes. On the other hand, the slaves spoke mutually
unintelligible African languages and were in need of a language to
communicate among themselves, both at work and in their quarters.
Under these circumstances the simplified pidgin English developed
in the slave trade was adopted on the plantations.

Among Negroes it has been handed down by word of mouth to this
day, especially on the Sea Islands along the coast of South Carolina
and Georgia.

8.

Diffusion

8.1 Introduction

The diffusion of linguistic features from one area or social class to another and their adaptation to the system of the receiving language or dialect are complementary aspects of one and the same event. Both aspects must be considered in dealing with this phenomenon. Diffusion is socioculturally motivated. The manner in which spreading elements are adapted depends upon the structure of the recipient language or dialect.

The spreading of linguistic features from class to class and from community to community presupposes communication by means of the spoken or the written word, i.e., by hearing or by sight. Although all kinds of linguistic features can spread in either way, phonological traits are diffused largely by hearing.

Frequent and intimate communication facilitates diffusion. However, communication is only the necessary condition for the spreading of linguistic features. It does not determine the direction of the "flow," which results from sociocultural factors and the socioculturally conditioned attitudes of the communicating speakers.

Within a socially divided or graded community, whatever its extent, diffusion from the higher to the lower social levels is the rule. The prestige and the usefulness of the "upper" dialect are the determining factors. A social revolution within the community may of course alter the direction of the spreading.

The sociocultural prominence of a speech area often induces a receptive attitude in neighboring communities, an inclination or desire to imitate the usage of a neighbor of superior standing. The motive may be admiration or the hope of improving one's lot. From this results the interregional spreading of prestige dialects. Since the upper classes of society normally have the wider range of contacts, interregional diffusion is mediated largely by this element in the population.

When the balance of sociocultural prominence shifts from one center or area to another, the direction of diffusion may also change. Thus the northwestward spreading of Austro-Bavarian features during the Middle Ages and Early Modern times is followed after the Reformation by transregional diffusion from East Central Germany throughout the German-speaking area.

Viewed from the angle of the receiving dialect, diffusion is a process of adapting foreign linguistic elements to the native system. Meaningful word stems are freely introduced, but their phonemic shape is usually brought into line with the native system, and they are made to conform to the indigenous morphology.

In this process the phonemes of the donor dialect (or language) are replaced by their nearest counterparts of the receiving dialect. The extent of such replacements depends upon the degree of divergence between the phonemic inventories of the two dialects (languages) and upon the divergent use of distinctive features in the two phonemic systems.

Thus two phonemes of the donor dialect may be merged in one, and allophones of one of its phonemes may be rendered by two different phonemes in the receiving dialect. Whether the donor dialect has contrastive vowel length or not, a recipient dialect having contrastive quantity will inevitably impose it upon the imported elements. Conversely, functional vowel quantity of the donor dialect is discarded, if the receiving dialect lacks this feature.

The "tyranny" of the native system is equally evident in the prosodic features. Stress accent replaces pitch accent, and vice versa; tonal patterns of words are imposed or dropped, fore stress takes the place of end stress, and vice versa. In this manner the foreign elements are adapted to the native prosodic system.

Native word classes and their grammatical categories are regularly imposed upon the adopted word stems and expressed by native inflections. Bilinguals may of course retain some foreign inflections, and a few of them may ultimately enter the usage of monolinguals, as the Latin plurals alumn-i, -ae in English.

This manner of adapting foreign elements to the native system is characteristic of monolingual speech communities, whatever their size. Since monolingualism prevails in large parts of the world, this phenomenon has often been observed. Nevertheless, the structural point of view has rarely been applied to it with any consistency.

The dialect or language of another region or another class can, of course, be acquired fully or at least to such an extent that it can serve as a satisfactory medium of communication. If so, it may replace the indigenous dialect or language or gain currency alongside of it. In the latter case the roles of the two speechways are socially determined, the acquired dialect or language being used in transacting public affairs, the other in the home and in communication with one's neighbors. Bidialectalism and bilingualism are not uncommon in Europe and in other parts of the world.

When after a period of bilingualism one of the languages is given up, the surviving one may exhibit some traits of the one that was submerged. Thus English has retained some phonological features derived from Medieval French in addition to a considerable body of French words; and the West Romanic languages (North Italian, French, Spanish) are said to show certain reflexes of the replaced Continental Celtic (Gaulish). Whether the replaced language was an overlay (superstratum), as French in England or Frankish in northern France, or an underlay (substratum), as Celtic in southwestern Europe, is immaterial. What counts is a more or less prolonged period of ethnically and/or socially conditioned bilingualism.

The area linguist is in a highly favorable position to trace the regional diffusion of linguistic features and the sociocultural dynamics underlying it. Dealing with living speech, he has potentially unlimited access to basic factual evidence. Also, he can observe in great detail the manner in which alien features are adapted to the native system, and can face the intricate problem of distinguishing imported innovations from parallel developments in dialects and in genetically related languages with some promise of success.

For these reasons the study of living speech has the potential of providing insights into the dynamics of linguistic change, insights that are relevant to problems confronting the scholar who concerns himself with earlier periods of linguistic history for which evidence is more limited or circumstantial.

One of the problems of area linguistics that has rarely been broached as yet is the interrelation between social dialects. Broad general statements are not wanting; but well-documented studies of larger areas will not be possible until we possess the results of sampling surveys of cultivated and of middle class speech comparable in scope with the existing atlases of folk speech.

The rate and the extent of the diffusion of linguistic features from community to community and from area to area is conditioned by the

"density" of intercommunication. Ease of travel and lack of sociocultural barriers favor transregional diffusion; political, economic,
and ecclesiastic boundaries tend to impede or to prevent it. Hence
the frequent congruence of dialect and language boundaries with
sociocultural barriers.

Since the upper classes of society enjoy the widest range of contacts with their neighbors, interregional diffusion is largely mediated
by them. Their speechways "vault" from the dominant center to the
elite of the subsidiary centers, whereupon they may infiltrate the
lower social levels and spread out into the hinterland.

Free and frequent communication between the social groups of a
speech community facilitate the spreading of innovations, social
barriers retard or prevent their diffusion throughout the speech
community. Usage within the community tends toward uniformity
when communication is free; otherwise social dialects come into
being and tend to be preserved.

The critical sketches of well-documented cases that follow are
intended to illustrate the processes of diffusion and adaptation of
linguistic features under a variety of sociocultural circumstances.
The following factors are taken into consideration: (1) the geographic
dissemination (spread) of the feature in question at a given time, i.e.,
the synchronic evidence; (2) the chronology of its appearance from
place to place, i.e., the diachronic evidence; (3) the location of socioculturally dominant centers or areas from which the diffusion is
presumed to radiate; (4) communication routes: highways, waterways,
etc.; (5) barriers to communication: features of the landscape,
political, and economic boundaries; (6) the adaptation of the spreading
feature to the recipient dialect.

8.2 Diffusion of Reflexes of Postvocalic / r / in the Upper South

The method of dealing with diachronic phonological change in area
linguistics can be effectively demonstrated by tracing the behavior of
the reflexes of postvocalic / r / in the Upper South. This fascinating
and intricate problem has been analyzed and discussed in great detail
by William R. Van Riper [1957] as part of his treatment of the history
of postvocalic / r / in four dialect areas along the Atlantic coast:
Eastern New England, Metropolitan New York, the Upper South, and
the Lower South. In the discussion that follows I shall rely largely
on his findings.

The circumstances for handling this problem are unusually favorable. The basic areal data of the present (ca. 1940), both spatial and
social, are ample, and the sociocultural setting of the present and the

past is known in considerable detail. Although diachronic evidence
for the change of / -r / to / ə̰ / in the Upper South is still lacking,
the British background is fairly clear. Besides, the westward
spreading of / ə̰ / through the cotton belt along the Gulf States and
the valley of the lower Mississippi from 1810 onward presupposes
that / ə̰ / was fully established in the Lower as well as the Upper
South before 1800.

The areal data for the Upper South are furnished by the field
survey for the Linguistic Atlas of the Eastern States carried out by
G. S. Lowman, Jr. Some 200 communities were investigated in this
area, and each community was usually represented by two speakers
belonging to different social levels or age groups. Folk speech and
common (middle class) speech were recorded in most of the communities, cultivated speech in about one fifth of them (mostly in
cities). On the map reproduced in Figure 40 the responses are
presented in the sequence folk–common–cultivated for each community, the numbers standing for cultivated speakers being under-
lined.

The evidence for the heterophones / -r / ≠ / -ə̰ / is summarized
by Van Riper on the basis of their incidence in 33 words. Some
speakers consistently use the postvocalic / r /, others the derivative
/ ə̰ /. Others again fluctuate between them, favoring one or the other
of the variants.

The areal patterning of the variants is very striking. The western
sections of Maryland, Virginia, and North Carolina consistently have
/ r /; eastern Virginia and adjoining parts of Maryland and north
central North Carolina have / ə̰ /, with few exceptions; fluctuation and
divided usage characterize the greater part of eastern and central
North Carolina.

The focus of the derivative / ə̰ / in such words as ear, beard,
chair, care, door, poor is clearly in eastern Virginia. In the same
area we find also [ɔ<ɔə̰] in corn, forty and [ɑ̨<ɑə̰] in car, barn, which
we need not consider here any further.

Turning to the area of fluctuating and divided usage in North
Carolina, we find that all the cultured informants interviewed—as
far west as Charlotte and as far south as Wilmington—consistently
use / ə̰ /, whereas other speakers either fluctuate between / r / and
/ ə̰ / or use only / r /, the latter especially on the points of land
jutting out into the Atlantic and south of the Cape Fear River. Here
the social dissemination of / ə̰ / clearly shows that this variant has
prestige and is being diffused southward and eastward from the focal
area. Inconsistent and divided usage along the lower Potomac River
and in Baltimore also suggest diffusion of / ə̰ /. North and west of
Baltimore, however, along the important dialect boundary between

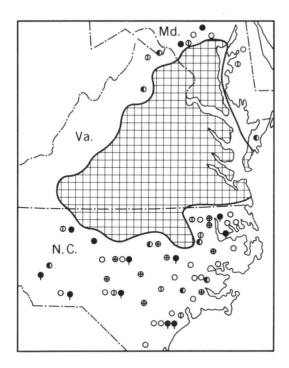

FIGURE 40: The Upper South: Loss of Postvocalic /r /

In the shaded area /r / is lost in this position. On the periphery of this prestigious focal area speakers vary and fluctuate. Here some cultured speakers consistently LACK /r / in this position, others not. Middle class speakers fluctuate uneasily.

The percentage of the LOSS of /r / in 33 test words is shown, speaker by speaker, as follows:

- ● 91 to 100%
- ◗ 76 to 90%
- ⊕ 51 to 75%
- ◑ 26 to 50%
- ○ 13 to 25%

Adapted from M. R. Van Riper, The Loss of Postvocalic /r / in the Eastern United States.

the South and the Midland, the trend seems to be toward / r /. It is worth noting, in conclusion, that in Virginia the variant / ə̣ / has not crossed the Blue Ridge Mountains.

The search for sociocultural drives that may underly the dissemination patterns of / ə̣ / from postvocalic / r / in Virginia leads to two discoveries. (1) All of the colonial seaports in Virginia lie within the focus of the / ə̣ / area: Alexandria on the Potomac River, Fredericksburg on the Rappahannock, Richmond on the James, Petersburg on the Appomattox, and Norfolk on Chesapeake Bay. It is here that commercial relations and close cultural contacts were maintained with England throughout the Colonial period. (2) The plantation country served by these seaports in the export of staples and the import of manufactured goods coincides to a remarkable extent with the focal area of / ə̣ / from earlier / r /. We obtain a reliable picture of the area dominated by the plantation economy from the percentage of slaves in the total population. From 1790 to 1860 Negro slaves outnumbered the whites in the piedmont of Virginia, the center of the present / ə̣ / area. (See Paullin-Wright 1932: plates 67 and 68; 68–B is reproduced here in Figure 41.)

The close social and cultural ties of the planter class of Colonial Virginia with England is well known. If English fashions in architecture, furnishings, and dress were admired and imitated, why not also the speechways of cultured Englishmen? That the loss of postvocalic / r / as such was fairly widespread in eastern Virginia before 1800—as also in South Carolina—can be safely inferred from the fact that / ə̣ / is characteristic of all of the plantation country along the Gulf of Mexico and in the lower Mississippi valley, settled by westward expansion between 1810 and 1840.

Any notion that the "weakening" of postvocalic / r / to / ə̂ / could be attributed to the Negro majority in the plantation country is untenable on two grounds: (1) / ə̣ / is clearly a prestige pronunciation in the South; (2) it appears in New England and Metropolitan New York, areas that had few Negroes.

The date of the loss of postvocalic / r / as such in words like ear, fair, far, four, poor has not yet been established for the American South. N. E. Eliason [1956: 209–10] cites such telltale unconventional spellings as farther for father, storke for stock, polk for pork, caulk for cork, fouth for fourth and forth, vey for very for North Carolina, but unfortunately without date. For New England the early loss of / r / before consonants is clearly documented in such seventeenth and early eighteenth-century spellings as horsers for hawsers, northen for nothing, pasneg for parsonage, and Bostorn for Boston [Krapp 1925: 228–30]. Such scattered instances can, of course, not tell us how widespread this feature was in New England.

Before turning to the British background we must consider the areal patterning of the postvocalic variants / ə / and / r / in North America as a whole. The variant / ə / appears in four geographically separated areas along the Atlantic seaboard, each of them centered on one or more Colonial seaports. Except for the cotton belt along the Gulf of Mexico, occupied by the westward expansion of the plantation economy after 1800, this / ə / is confined to the Atlantic Slope. From this situation we may infer, tentatively, that in the North and the Midland this phonological trait did not yet have general currency in its present domains when the settlements expanded westward; and furthermore, that / ə / for earlier / r / spread rather late, and

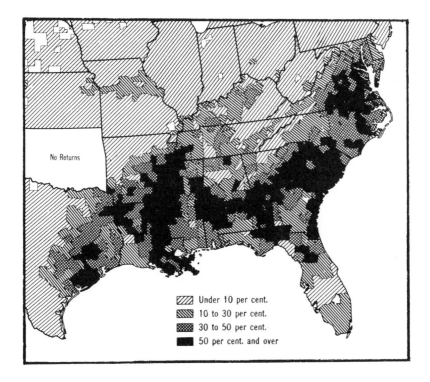

FIGURE 41: The South: Concentration of Slaves in 1860

From C. O. Paullin and J. K. Wright, Atlas of the Historical Geography of the United States.

independently in each of the four areas. Whether this development
was indigenous in the several areas or was prompted from overseas
cannot be decided on American linguistic and sociocultural evidence
alone. A decision can only be reached by a consideration of the
British background, which is fortunately rather clear.

In the British Isles the / r / after vowels is now regularly preserved in Scotland and Ireland, whatever its phonic realization.
England is rather sharply divided: / r / survives in the west from
the English Channel to Lancashire and also south of the lower Thames;
the derivative / ə / dominates all of eastern England from the Thames
to Durham (see Figure 25). It is important to note that the London
area is peripheral to the geographic domain of / ə /. Little is known
about the chronology of this areal patterning, except that / ə / is
spreading into Surrey and Kent.

We have some chronological evidence for the development of
postvocalic / r / in Standard British English. The dramatist Ben
Jonson (1573–1637), a native of Westminster, observed that / r /
was "firm" at the beginning of words and "more liquid" in other
positions, which clearly recognizes the existence of positional allophones. "Mute r" is mentioned by grammarians in mart, parlor,
partridge before 1750. John Walker states (1775) that aunt, haunch
sound as if written arnt, harnch, and (1791) that lard, card are nearly
like laad, caad, especially in London, where / r / "is sometimes
entirely sunk" [Jespersen 1922: 318, 360]. On the basis of this evidence, the "weakening" of / r / after vowels was taking place, or had
taken place, in the London area before the American Revolution and
was being accepted in cultivated speech.

In Colonial America, this innovation of SBE would be adopted in
the seaports by leading families who had close contacts with England,
infiltrate the lower social levels, and then spread to the hinterland,
a process that continued after independence and is still in progress
in some of the coastal areas.

But this is not the whole story. The spelling evidence referred
to above shows that in eastern New England postvocalic / r / had
been lost as such in the speech of some New Englanders by the
middle of the seventeenth century—long before this feature was
recognized in Standard British English. One can hardly escape the
conclusion that it was brought to America by early colonists from
the east of England, the area that lacks postvocalic / r / at present.
If usage was divided, some New Englanders pronouncing an / r / and
others not, the diffusion of / ə / as a prestige feature supported by
SBE usage from the latter part of the eighteenth century onward
becomes understandable.

Although spelling evidence for early loss of / r / after vowels in the Upper and the Lower South is still lacking, developments in these areas may well parallel that in New England.

We shall briefly consider the effect of this change of / r / after vowels upon the phonemic system in American English.

In dialects that preserve / r / after vowels, it is articulated in that position by constricting the body of the tongue laterally, retracting it, and raising it close to the roof of the mouth, the tip of the tongue remaining inactive. The degree of constriction varies greatly from region to region. Full relaxation of the constriction results in an unsyllabic / ə /-like sound in the coastal areas dealt with above. Simple as this change in articulation actually is, it has marked phonemic implications. Some have considered it a positional allophone of prevocalic / r /, so that rear and roar, articulated as [riə and roə], would not only begin with / r / but also end in it. Others [Trager-Bloch] have taken it as a positional allophone of / h /, so that here and hair, articulated as [hiə] and [heə ~ hæə], would have / h / both at the beginning and at the end. Neither of these interpretations is acceptable, because [ə] has no distinctive feature in common with prevocalic / r / or with / h /. Daniel Jones [1956] appears to treat these ingliding diphthongal sounds as phonemic units. In my own discussion of this problem I have found it convenient to treat unsyllabic [ə] as a positionally restricted semivowel / ə / [Kurath 1964; Kurath-McDavid 1961].

It should be noted that in dialects that do not preserve postvocalic / r / as such the sequence / ar > aə / has produced the new phoneme / ɑ /, as in far, hard.

8.3 The Spreading of Diphthongal Reflexes
of Middle High German / ī, ū, ǖ /

This phonological phenomenon is discussed by K. Wagner in Deutsche Sprachlandschaften [1927]. His diffusional interpretation has been widely accepted by German dialectologists.

At the time of the Sprachatlas survey (1876–85), diphthongal reflexes of the Middle High German long high vowels / ī, ū, ǖ /, as in Eis, Maus, Mäuse "ice, mouse, mice," respectively, were current in German as far north as a line running somewhat to the north of Koblenz (on the Rhine), Kassel (on the Weser), Magdeburg (on the Elbe), and Berlin (on the Havel), but not in the greater part of the Alemannic southwest (Switzerland and adjoining sections of Elsace, Baden, and Wurtenberg). See Figure 42.

The evidence of spellings in localized and datable documents and regional literary texts is said to show that these three phonological features have been current in this entire area since the sixteenth

century. However, the diphthongal reflexes of / ī, ū, ǖ /, whatever
their precise phonic character, make their appearance within this
extensive domain at very different times: first (1200–1300) in the
Bavarian dialect area along the Danube (Vienna to Regensburg and
Munich); next (a 1400) in the East Frankish area along the Main
(Bamberg, Würzburg) and in Bohemia (the Emperial Chancelry at
Prag); a century later (a 1500) in the East Central German area of
Saxony (Meissen, Dresden, Leipzig), in the Rhine Frankish area
(Frankfurt, Mainz), and in Swabian (Augsburg, Stuttgart); finally

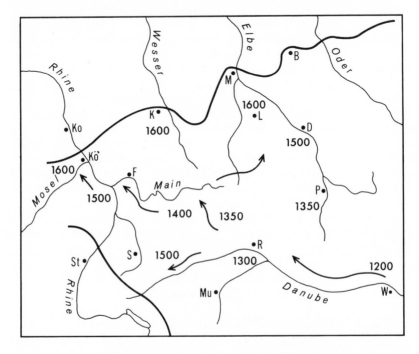

FIGURE 42: Diffusion in Germany: The Spreading of Diphthongal
Reflexes of MHG Long Vowels i, ū (a 1200–1600)

Cities: B(erlin, D(resden, F(rankfurt, K(assel, Ko(blenz, Kö(ln,
L(eipzig, M(agdeburg, Mü(nchen, P(rague, R(egensburg, St(rassburg,
S(tuttgart, W(ien.

Adapted from K. Wagner, Deutsche Sprachlandschaften

(a 1600 or later) along the present margin of the diphthongal area from the valley of the Mosel (Koblenz, Trier) to northern Hesse (Kassel) and Brandenburg (Berlin).

If the rough chronology of the regional appearance of diphthongal reflexes of the long high vowels / $\bar{\text{i}}$, $\bar{\text{u}}$, $\ddot{\bar{\text{u}}}$ / in such words as Eis, Haus, Mäuse is accepted, as it generally is, we seem to have here an instance of the gradual diffusion of a striking phonological feature from the Bavarian dialect area northward to the Frankish area along the Main and the Rhine and westward to the adjoining part of the Alemannic area, a process extending through several centuries. Add to that the secondary spreading of this feature from Frankish to East Central German in the fifteenth century—long after the German colonization of Saxony—and you have an impressive instance of trans-regional diffusion.

To account for this striking phenomenon in sociocultural terms, German dialectologists adduce the following factors.

(1) The extensive Austro-Bavarian area (some 300 miles from east to west) was unified early, both politically, culturally, and linguistically. Under the Hapsburgs and the Wittelsbachs this area had great prestige and influence. In fact, before the Reformation the Bavarian dialect bid fair to become the literary language of the German nation. Hence the adoption of the diphthongs in the neighboring Frankish and Alemannic areas.

(2) The important trade routes leading from the valley of the Danube to those of the Main and the Rhine facilitated the northward spreading of Bavarian dialect features. It is clear that from the Middle Ages onward, trade with the Near East and Italy (Venice) followed this route.

This interpretation of the spreading of the diphthongal reflexes of MHG / $\bar{\text{i}}$, $\bar{\text{u}}$, $\ddot{\bar{\text{u}}}$ / is rather convincing. And yet, the possibility of independent parallel development in the several dialect areas cannot be discarded outright.

For one thing, the long high vowels / $\bar{\text{i}}$, $\bar{\text{u}}$, $\ddot{\bar{\text{u}}}$ / changed to upgliding diphthongs in other West Germanic languages in which outside influence is out of the question. For Netherlandish, Kloeke [1927] shows that this process started ca. 1200 in the south (Antwerp) and that by ca. 1500 the diphthongal reflexes had gained currency in the north (Amsterdam). In English the diphthongization of ME / $\bar{\text{i}}$ / and / $\bar{\text{u}}$ /, as in ice, mice, and house, took place from ca. 1400 onward [Luick 1914–27: 563].

Secondly, in the Middle Ages all of the German dialects in which diphthongization has made its appearance had essentially the same system of syllabics, including the long vowels / $\bar{\text{i}}$, $\ddot{\bar{\text{u}}}$, $\bar{\text{u}}$; $\bar{\text{e}}$, $\ddot{\bar{\text{o}}}$, $\bar{\text{o}}$; $\bar{\text{a}}$ / and the upgliding diphthongs / ei $\sim$ ai, öü, ou $\sim$ au /. This might well support the possibility of similar changes in the pronunciation of the long high vowels in the several dialects without outside influence.

Finally, for the Swabian dialect of Alemannic in which the reflexes of / i, ū / are / ei, ou / over against Bavarian / ai, au /, K. Bohnenberger [1928: 279] maintains that the diphthongization is indigenous rather than imported. In support of his view he cites the important fact that in morpheme final position, as in speien "spew," bauen "build," / ei, ou / appear not only in Swabian but in all the Alemannic dialects as far south as the Bernese Alps in Switzerland [see now Hotzenköcherle 1962: vol. I, Maps 148, 152]. Remote from the Bavarian dialect area, this positional diphthongization is surely indigenous.

It is of considerable interest to observe that the diphthongs derived from the old long high vowels / ī, ǖ, ū / do not seem to merge with the reflexes of the MHG diphthongs / ei ~ ai, eu ~ öü, ou ~ au / in any of the German folk dialects [Kluge 1918: 29]. In Standard German, based largely upon the East Central German dialect, they are nevertheless merged: / ī / with / ei / as in Wein - Bein, / ū / with / ou / as in Haufen - laufen, and / ǖ / with / eu ~ öu / as in Häute - Leute. This matter deserves to be investigated from the structural point of view.

8.4 Northward Diffusion in the Rhineland

The sociocultural interpretation of the complicated linguistic situation in the Rhineland by Theodor Frings [1956 < 1922: part I, 1–54] is one of the landmarks in German area linguistics. His findings are summarily presented in Figure 43. Between the diagnostic heterophonic lines 4 and 3 lies the territory of the archbishopric of Cologne (Kurköln), between lines 3 and 2 that of the archbishopric of Treves (Kurtrier), south of line 2 that of the archbishopric of Mainz and of the Palatinate (Rheinpfalz).

Frings chooses the historically interrelated consonant shift lines as convenient indicators of the location of heteroglossic bundles, i.e., of dialect boundaries. Except for machen ≠ maken (line 4), they are of little importance in themselves from the synchronic point of view. Their significance lies in their diagnostic function.

The das ≠ dat line (2) is paralleled by the heterophones korb ≠ korf "basket," uns ≠ ūs "us"; the dorf ≠ dorp line (3) coincides roughly with haus ≠ hūs "house," wein ≠ wing "wine"; the machen ≠ maken line (4) agrees rather closely with offen ≠ open "open," Wasser ≠ water "water," han ≠ hebb "have," fönf ~ fünf ≠ fif "five"; and the heteroglosses öch ~ üch ≠ ow "you," wir ≠ wej "we," mir ≠ mej "me," exhibit the same general trend as the ich ≠ ik line (5). See Maps 3, 4, 5, 6, 7 in Frings.

The regional dissemination of the High German reflexes / f, s, x / of the postvocalic Proto-Germanic plosives / p, t, k / furnish the clue to the interpretation of their history in the Rhineland. As far north as the S machen ≠ N maken line (4), which crosses the Rhine south of Düsseldorf (at Benrath), most of the words had the "shifted" HG consonants at the time of G. Wenker's survey for the Sprachatlas (1876).

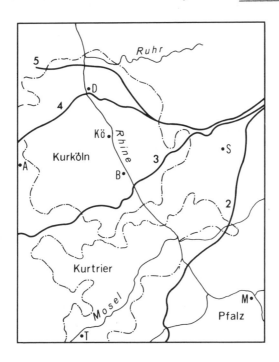

FIGURE 43: Diffusion in the Rhineland

2. Southern das ≠ Northern dat "that"
3. S dorf ≠ N dorp "village"
4. S machen ≠ N maken "make"
5. S ich ≠ N ik "I"
[1. S apfel ≠ N appel "apple" crosses the Rhine south of Worms]

Cities: A(achen, B(onn, D(üsseldorf, K(oblenz, Kö(ln, M(ainz, S(iegen, T(rier.

Adapted from Theodor Frings, Sprache und Geschichte I: Maps 2 and 14.

But "unshifted" / -t / survived in dat "that," wat "what," allet "all,"
as far south as the valley of the Mosel River (the domain of Trier).
On the other hand, "shifted" /x / appeared north of the machen ≠
maken line in the pronoun ich "I" and some other pronomenal forms.
The relics of "unshifted" /t / in the valley of the Mosel and the
outposts of "shifted" /x / north of Düsseldorf clearly point to northward diffusion of the "shifted" High German (i.e., South German)
consonants.

Frings asserts that in the Rhineland the dissemination of High
German /f, s, x / from West Germanic /p, t, k / revealed by the
Sprachatlas for the latter part of the nineteenth century had been
reached in the early Middle Ages (ca. 1000), at least essentially.
However, although northward diffusion is beyond question, its
chronology can hardly be reliably established, because local documents in the vernacular do not make their appearance until ca. 1250.

Linguistic evidence presented by Frings shows that the dialect
area set off by the diagnostic heterophones 3 and 4 falls within the
boundaries of the ecclesiastic domain of Köln, and that between lines
2 and 3 lies the domain of Trier. These ecclesiastic-political
domains (set off in Figure 43 by broken lines) were relatively stable
from the Middle Ages until ca. 1800. As such they played an important role in shaping the dialectal structure of the Rhineland. Each
of them has some unique linguistic traits [Maps 13 and 6] and a distinctive configuration of regional features.

Frings envisions the transregional northward diffusion of
southern features in the following terms. (1) The sociocultural
predominance of the politically and linguistically unified southeastern
(Austro-Bavarian) area along the Danube created a receptive attitude
in the areas along the Main and the middle course of the Rhine. (2)
The highways of commerce along the Rhine, leading from the Mediterranean to the North Sea, mediated communication with the southeast. (3) Southern traits were adopted in the centers along these
highways and then diffused to the limits of the several political
domains, thus creating the regional dialectal patterning of the Rhineland. Presented with considerable ingenuity and eloquence, his
interpretation carries conviction, although the evidence of the
Sprachatlas has serious limitations and chronological linguistic
evidence for the crucial period is all but lacking.

In passing, it should be pointed out that Frings is not interested
in evaluating heteroglosses or in pointing out that the adoption of the
High German fricatives /f, s, x / does not introduce any phonemes
foreign to the Rhineland. In native words this area actually had /f /
in af "off," /s / in glas "glass," /x / in dach "day," lachen "laugh,"
etc.

8.5 Northward Diffusion in Eastern Germany

In eastern Germany, High German features have been spreading northward into the Low German area—from Saxony into Brandenburg —since early modern times. At the time of the <u>Sprachatlas</u> survey (ca. 1880) this process was in full swing. Using <u>Atlas</u> data, K. Wagner [1927: 66–69] describes this northward diffusion between the Saale-Elbe and the Oder in considerable detail and in sound perspective. From the divergent behavior of the heteroglossic lines, their spacing from south to north, he infers that High German features are adopted piecemeal and spread into Low German territory at different rates.

A striking example of the word by word adoption of High German consonants is shown in Figure 44. The areal divergence in the lexical incidence of the High German fricative / x / in <u>kochen</u> "cook," <u>machen</u> "make," and <u>ich</u> "I," respectively, is ample evidence of the fact that the shift from / k / to / x / is not indigenous to Brandenburg. The spacing of these / x ≠ k / heterophones from south to north makes it equally clear that Brandenburg is adopting this feature from Saxony, though aided by the German <u>Schriftsprache</u> taught in the schools.

Other examples of the northward diffusion from Saxony along the Elbe and the Oder are presented by A. Bach [1950: 211–13].

8.6 The Southward Diffusion of Central Bavarian
Phonological Features

A clear case of socioculturally motivated diffusion leading to revolutionary changes in the system of syllabic phonemes of the recipient dialect is found in the Bavarian section of German-speaking Europe.

For the Bavarian dialects we possess a considerable body of reliable evidence secured by direct field observation and several structurally oriented monographs. Additional data reported to the <u>Sprachatlas</u> and the <u>Wortatlas</u> at Marburg by correspondence are also available. The discussion that follows relies primarily on the evidence presented by E. Kranzmayer in his <u>Historische Lautgeo-graphie des gesamtbairischen Dialektraumes</u> [1956] with its thirty-one sketch maps.

The Bavarian dialect area comprises the greater part of Bavaria and nearly all of Austria. It has four major subdivisions [Kranzmayer 1956: Hilfskarte 1]:

(1) A large Central area extending from the environs of Vienna to Munich, including the valley of the Danube and the lower course of its southern tributaries issuing from the Alps.

(2) A Northern area in Bavaria extending northward to the water-shed between the Danube and the River Main (including Regensburg and Nuremberg).

(3) A Southern area in Austria, extending from Tyrol (north and south of the Brenner Pass) through Carinthia into the southwestern part of Styria.

(4) A transition zone between the Central and the Southern areas along the northern slope of the Alps and in the province of Styria.

Kranzmayer's outline of the dialectal structure of the Bavarian area is based on phonological data presented in twenty-six separate

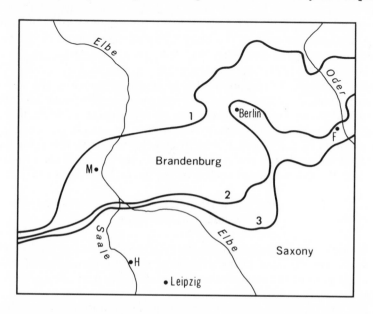

FIGURE 44: Eastern Germany: Northward Diffusion of the High German Fricative /x /

1. in kochen ≠ koken "cook"
2. in machen ≠ maken "make"
3. in ich ≠ ik "I"

Cities: Berlin, F(rankfurt, H(alle, L(eipzig, M(agdeburg.

Adapted from K. Wagner, Deutsche Sprachlandschaften

maps with reference to their Middle High German sources. These data are largely phonic, although phonemic implications can fairly easily be inferred in some instances. In his text of 143 pages the author frequently distinguishes between phonic and phonemic entities, especially in dealing with diachronic problems. All in all, some of the more striking systemic differences between Central and South Bavarian can be gathered with some assurance from his presentation and discussion.

Fortunately, we have a number of investigations devoted to the phonemic structure of several Central Bavarian dialects and of one South Bavarian dialect to guide us in comparing the phonemic system of Central Bavarian (CB) with that of South Bavarian (SB). More than half a century ago, A. Pfalz [1913] described a CB dialect spoken northeast of Vienna in phonemic terms—a truely remarkable performance that has had a strong influence upon the Vienna group of dialectologists, as did his later publications [1925, 1936]. A phonemic analysis of the dialect of Vienna, written as a doctoral dissertation under the direction of E. Kranzmayer, has been published by the American B. J. Koekoek [1955]. Another American-trained scholar, H. L. Kufner, has dealt in structural terms with the dialect of Munich [1961, 1962] and of a village about fifty miles to the east of it [1957]. For South Bavarian we have only one structurally oriented phonology, that of a family dialect spoken in a village near the city of Villach in the Austrian province of Carinthia [Kurath 1965]. Situated south of the formidable crest of the Alps, Carinthia has faithfully preserved many old SB characteristics. In my brief comparison of this SB dialect with CB, I shall rely primarily upon the work of Pfalz and Koekoek for the CB dialectal type.

Central and South Bavarian have nearly the same system of consonants: resonants: / m, n, ŋ, l, r, w, j /; fricatives: / f, s, š, x /; lenis plosives: / b, d, g /; fortis plosives: / p, t, k /. But there are rather marked differences in the distribution of some of these shared phonemes: (1) in CB the resonants / n, l, r / are restricted to prevocalic position, but not in SB. (2) In SB / b / is restricted to postvocalic position, but not in CB. (3) In CB the fortis plosives / p, t, k / are restricted to postvocalic position, but not in SB.

The only structural difference in the consonants is found in the fricatives, where CB has fortis / ff, ss, šš, xx /, as in the words corresponding to Standard German offen, Wasser, waschen, machen. In SB these merged with lenis / f, s, š, x /.

In the system of syllabic phonemes, CB and SB differ markedly.

They share the following syllabics: (1) the monophthongs / i, e, ε, a, ɔ, o, u /, as in Fisch, Bett, lecken, zäh, Graf, oft, Luft; (2) the upgliding diphthongs / ai, oi, au /, as in weiss, bleuen, Maus; (3) the ingliding diphthongs / iə /, as in SB <u>lieb</u>, CB <u>Wirt</u>; / ɛə /, as in SB <u>Zehe</u>, CB <u>wert</u>; / ɔə /, as in SB <u>rot</u>, CB <u>Garten</u>; / uə /, as in SB <u>gut</u>, CB <u>Wurst</u>.

As indicated by the examples, CB and SB often differ in the lexical incidence of these diphthongs.

Whereas South Bavarian has no qualitative syllabic phonemes peculiar to it, Central Bavarian has a considerable number of them:

(1) The rounded front vowels / ü, ö, ǫ /, as in <u>Bild</u>, <u>Hölle</u>, <u>hell</u>, which result from the "vocalization" of / l /. SB preserves the old sequences / il, el, ɛl /.

(2) The nasal syllabics / ĩ, ẽ, ã, õ, ũ, ɛ̃ə /, as in <u>Sinn</u>, <u>schön</u>, <u>Bein</u>, <u>schon</u>, <u>Sohn</u>, <u>Wien</u>, which result from the "vocalization" of / n /. Here SB preserves the old sequences / in, en, an, on, un, ɛən /.

(3) The upgliding diphthongs / ui, oe, ɔɛ /, as in <u>Pult</u>, <u>Wolf</u>, <u>Walzer</u>, derived from the sequences / ul, ol, ɔl /, which SB retains.

The system of monophthongal oral syllabics in CB and in SB are shown below: CB has rounded front vowels, SB does not. SB has phonemically short and long vowels, CB only positional variation in duration.

Central Bavarian			South Bavarian			
i	ü	u	i	u	ī	ū
e	ö	o	e	o	ē	ō
ɛ	ǫ	ɔ	ɛ	ɔ	ɛ̄	ɔ̄
	a			a		ā

The duration of the syllabic phonemes is regulated in different ways in CB and in SB.

In CB all stressed syllabics are prolonged unless they are followed by a fortis plosive or fricative. Examples containing short syllabics before fortis / p, t, k / and / ff, ss, šš, xx / are:: <u>Köpfe</u> / ghepf /, <u>Witze</u> / wits /, <u>Ecke</u> / ekx / and <u>offen</u> / offə /, <u>Fässer</u> / fessə /, <u>fischen</u> / fiššə /, <u>machen</u> / mɔxxə /. Since in CB the duration of syllabics is regulated by position, it is not phonemic.

In SB the duration of stressed syllabic phonemes depends largely, but not wholly, upon context. Here vowels are long unless they are followed by a consonant cluster. They are also short before the fortis plosives / p / and / k /, as in <u>täppisch</u> / tɛpət /, <u>eckig</u> / ekət /, before the velar nasal / ŋ /, as in <u>lang</u> / loŋ /, and irregularly before / m /, as in <u>dumm</u> / tum /, <u>zusammen</u> / tsom /. On the other hand, long vowels occasionally appear before morphologically complex consonant clusters owing to leveling in the paradigm of verbs. Hence vowel duration is phonemic in SB, although largely controlled by the context.

The loss of the postvocalic resonants / n, r, 1 / and the conse-
quent rise of numerous new syllabics constitute one of the most
important phonological innovations in the Central Bavarian dialect
area since the Middle Ages. At present (ca. 1925–50) these features
are current in the valley of the Danube from Vienna to Regensburg
and in the valleys of its tributaries, except for the upper reaches of
the rivers issuing from the Alps (Salzach, Inn, Isar). In the province
of Styria, south of the Semmering pass, postvocalic / n / is lost
throughout and postvocalic / r / in the northeastern section; but
postvocalic / 1 / is preserved (see Figure 45).

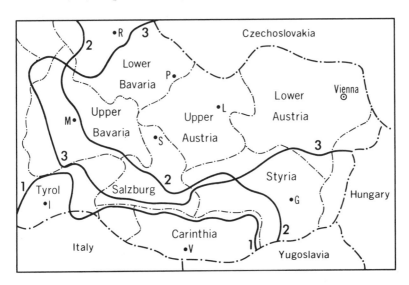

FIGURE 45: Central Bavarian: The Loss of Postvocalic / n, r, 1 /
and its Southward Diffusion

1. Loss of / n / [Kranzmayer: Map 23]
2. Loss of / r / [ibid.: Map 6]
3. Loss of / 1 / [ibid.: Map 7]

Cities: G(raz, I(nnsbruck, L(inz, M(unich, P(assau, R(egensburg,
S(alzburg, V(illach.

Adapted from E. Kranzmayer, Historische Lautgeographie des
gesamtbairischen Dialektraumes.

The heterophonic lines resulting from the loss vs. the preservation of / n, l, r / in postvocalic position run close together along the crest of the Alps that separate the province of Salzburg from Carinthia; but in Styria (south of the crest of the Alps) and in Upper Bavaria and Tyrol they are more or less widely spaced. In these graded areas, one may safely infer, change is still in progress. An investigation of the usage of age groups and of social classes in these transition zones would presumably show that / n, r, l / are receding. Since such evidence is as yet not available, we must be content with an inference from the location of the socioculturally dominant centers of the Danube valley and conclude that Central Bavarian usage is spreading into the South Bavarian dialect area and that this process has been in progress for some time. The Danube valley with its ancient population centers has dominated the Alpine valleys in economic, political, and cultural matters from the early Middle Ages onward. Ancient trade routes lead from the Vienna area across the Semmering pass into Styria and from Bavaria via the valley of the Inn across the Brenner Pass. Along these routes Central Bavarian features have been diffused.

In the valley of the Danube the phonological development discussed here is very old. According to Kranzmayer [1956: pp. 120, 123] loss of postvocalic / l / and / r / is attested in the Danube valley, especially in Lower Austria, shortly before 1300. Evidence for the loss of / n / seems to be even earlier.

The Central Bavarian loss of the resonants / n, r, l / as such in postvocalic position changed only the distribution and the lexical incidence of these consonants. On the other hand, their "vocalization" revolutionized the system of syllabic phonemes in CB. The magnitude of these changes can be gathered from the following list in which the innovations in the Viennese variant of CB [Koekoek 1955: 37–43] are set over against the synchronically corresponding forms of a SB dialect [Kurath 1965: 25–27].

(1)	CB	xĩ	s̆e	bã	mõ	sũ	waĩ ~ wæ̃
	SB	xīn	s̆ēn	pān	mōn	sūn	wain
	SG	hin	schön	Bein	Mann	Sohn	Wein

(2)	CB	tiə	wuəm	wɛəfə	wɔəm
	SB	tīr	wurm	werfn	wɔrm
	SG	Tür	Wurm	werfen	warm

(3)	CB	wüd	ödə	gö̤d	ɔid	hoids
	SB	wilt	ɛltr	gɛlt	ɔlt	xolts
	SG	wild	älter	Geld	alt	Holz

As the result of a change in the articulation of / n, l, r / after vowels, a total of 13 new units are added to the CB system of syllabics:

(1) The loss of / -n / as such produced the 6 nasal vowels / ĩ, ẽ, ã, õ, ũ, ãi ∼ æ̃ /;

(2) the loss of / -r / as such created the 4 ingliding diphthongs / iə, uə, ɛə, ɔə /, the first two of which merged with old phonemes exemplified in lieb / liəb / and gut / guəd /;

(3) the loss of / -l / as such resulted in the 5 new syllabics / ü, ö, ọ̈, ɔi, oi /.

It should further be noted that two new distinctive features are thus introduced in the CB system of syllabics: nasalization and lip rounding. Rounding of the lips was automatic in the older stage of CB, as it still is in SB, i.e., it was confined to back vowels.

We may finally ask this pertinent question: when speakers of South Bavarian give up their native articulation of postvocalic / n, r, l /, as in Styria and Upper Bavaria, do they invariably adopt the new syllabics of Central Bavarian at the same time? No answer can be given until the behavior of speakers belonging to different generations of the several social groups is investigated in the transition belts.

In a recent study, P. Wiesinger [1967] shows that the province of Styria is a typical transition area, graded from northeast (Lower Austria) to southwest (Carinthia) in its phonology. See his Map 1 on page 121. His data are apparently taken from Kranzmayer's collections in Vienna.

8.7 The Southward Diffusion of North Italian Consonants

In Southern Italy and in Tuscany, the medial voiceless plosives / p, t, k / of Latin and the Latin geminate consonants are preserved. In Northern Italy the voiceless plosives of Latin became voiced in this position and the germinates were reduced to short consonants (as also in French and Spanish). The heterophonic lines run in a close-knit bundle along the crest of the northern Apennines, the northern boundary of Tuscany. Along the Adriatic the lines are spaced; and in a corridor leading through the Papal States from the Adriatic (Ancona) to the Tyrrhenian Sea (Rome), they behave in a very complicated way, which points to diffusion rather than indigenous phonological change.

This problem is dealt with in exemplary fashion by R. A. Hall, Jr. [1943], on the basis of the evidence furnished by the linguistic atlas of Italy [Jaberg-Jud: 1928–40]. The location of the heterophones Northern / d / ≠ Southern / t /, as in N fradel ≠ S fratello ∼ frater

(< L fräter "brother"), is shown for ten different words; the course of the heterophone N /g / ≠ S /k /, as in N fig ≠ S fico (< L fīcus "fig"), for ten lexical items, and so forth.

Northern /g / from Latin /k / exhibits the widest dissemination (see Figure 46). It is current in a belt running from the Adriatic

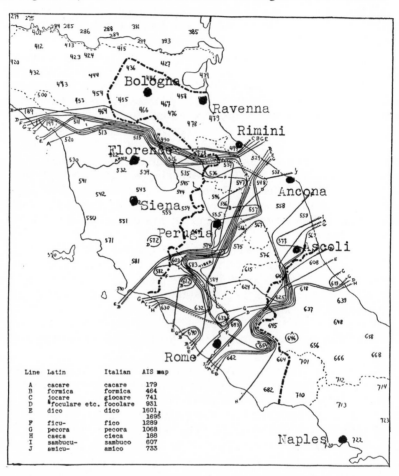

Line	Latin	Italian	AIS map
A	cacare	cacare	179
B	formica	formica	464
C	jocare	giocare	741
D	foculare etc.	focolare	931
E	dico	dico	1601, 1695
F	ficu-	fico	1289
G	pecora	pecora	1068
H	caeca	cieca	188
I	sambucu-	sambuco	607
J	amicu-	amico	733

FIGURE 46: Italy: Southward Diffusion of Northern /g / from Latin /k / Exemplified in Ten Words
From R. A. Hall, Jr., The Papal States in Italian Linguistic History.

(Ancona) to the Tyrrhenian (Rome), all within the confines of the Papal States (Marche, Umbria, Latium), varying somewhat from word to word. Northern / d / from Latin / t / is widely used within this corridor but falls short of Rome and its environs [Hall: Map 4]. Northern / k /, from Latin / kk / as in <u>bucca</u> "mouth," is largely confined to the shore of the Adriatic in the province of Marche [Hall: Map 1]; so is Northern / t /, from Latin / tt / as in <u>catta</u> "cat" [Hall: Map 3].

Divergence in the lexical incidence of the several "shifted" Northern consonants as shown by the behavior of the heterophonic lines and the gradation of the lines from the Adriatic to the environs of Rome unmistakably point to southward diffusion from the Romagna (Ravenna, Bologna)—the northmost of the Papal States—in the direction of Rome. This spreading of northern features follows the Via Flaminia and the Via Salaria, ancient highways connecting Rome with the North.

Hall assumes that the diffusion probably started in the thirteenth century and that with the later rise of Tuscany as the dominant cultural center of Italy the Northern "shifted" consonants receded, especially in sections of the Papal States adjoining Tuscany. No philological evidence is presented in support of this chronology; it is probably not available.

The passive linguistic role of Rome within the political domain of the Papal States may seem surprising. Hall attributes it to the economic superiority of the North and the sharp decline of Rome during the early Middle Ages.

In conclusion, Hall suggests that sporadic Northern consonants in Tuscan, as / g / in <u>pagare</u> "pay" (< L <u>pacāre</u>), <u>ago</u> "needle" (< L <u>acus</u>), spread into Tuscany by way of the Papal States rather than across the northern Apennines.

8.8 Diffusion between Unrelated Languages in India

Structural similarities between genetically unrelated languages spoken in one and the same area or in contiguous areas have been pointed out repeatedly in the last fifty years: in the Amerindian field by F. Boas [1940 < 1917: 202–7] and E. Sapir [1921: 217–20]; in Europe by H. Schuchardt [1928 < 1912: 248–53], and by N. S. Troubetzkoy and R. Jakobson [1949 < 1931: 343–65]. In his article on "India as a Linguistic Area" [1956], M. B. Emeneau discusses this phenomenon in the light of ample linguistic and sociocultural evidence.

The subcontinent of India is indeed an ideal domain for tracing cross influences between languages of different stocks. Indo-Aryan

(Sanskrit and its congeners) is documented both areally and chronologically, and some of the Dravidian languages are well enough known to gage their potential influence upon the Indo-Aryan overlay. For the Munda languages the evidence appears to be sufficient to compare some of its structural features with those of the other two linguistic stocks of India.

As far as Indo-Aryan is concerned, its position in the family of Indo-European languages and the consistent internal developments of its phonemic and morphological structure from Proto-Indo-European onward have been traced in great detail. When features not paralleled in any other Indo-European language make their appearance, the question arises whether they are peculiar indigenous developments or imported from a foreign linguistic system, i.e., from the Dravidian and/or the Munda languages, with which speakers of Indo-Aryan have been in intimate contact through the ages.

Emeneau shows that certain morphological features in which Indo-Aryan deviates from the other IE languages are shared by Dravidian and Munda languages and were in all probability adopted from them. Speakers for whom Indo-Aryan was a "second" language presumably mediated this change.

Four such morphological and/or syntactic features are pointed out [9–19]: (1) Distinct word stems for the singular and the plural of nouns preceding the case morphemes; (2) the extensive use of the so-called "gerund," an uninflected verbal form; (3) a peculiar type of compound consisting of the stem of a past participle and a noun; (4) the formation of so-called echo words. None of these formations actually upsets the basic structure of Indo-Aryan.

A further morphological feature, discussed by Emeneau at some length [10–16], is the use of "classifying" or "quantifying" words or morphemes in certain types of noun phrases, which some branches of all three linguistic stocks of India have in common. Since the "classifying" morphemes occurring in Dravidian and Munda are clearly adopted from Indo-Aryan, the direction of the diffusion of this feature within the linguistic sphere of India is clear. Here the superimposed language is the donor. In Indo-Aryan itself the use of "classifiers" is an innovation modeled on the usage of a vast linguistic sphere comprising "East, Southeast, and South Asia" [16] and such diverse linguistic stocks as Burmese, Chinese, and Japanese.

Emeneau deals briefly with the retroflex consonants / ṭ, ḍ, ṇ, ṣ /, which contrast with the dentals / t, d, n, s / in all three linguistic stocks and characterize India as a "linguistic sphere" (Sprachbund). Since no other branch of Indo-European has these contrastive sets of consonants and Proto-Dravidian had them [7], the retroflex set in Indo-Aryan looks like an importation. But how did it come about? What started it?

The answer is rather clear. In the indigenous vocabulary of Indo-Aryan, the retroflex consonants appear almost exclusively in complementary distribution with the dentals. Thus retroflex / ṣ / occurs only after / i, u, e, o, ṛ, r, k /; / ṭ, ḍ / only after / ṣ, ẓ /; / ṇ / after / ṣ, r, ṛ /. In all other positions / s, t, d, n / are normal [Thumb-Hirt 1930: §§ 83, 122, 147]. The presence of retroflex allophones of the dentals in Indo-Aryan thus facilitated the adoption of retroflex consonants in other positions when words were imported from Dravidian. In the process they became phonemic.

This problem is discussed with extensive documentation and full consideration of the sociocultural setting by F. B. J. Kuiper [1967].

9.

The Adaptation of
Foreign Elements

9.1 Adaptation of French Words to Middle English

During three centuries of bilingualism several thousand word stems were taken into English from socially and culturally dominant French [Baugh 1957: 200–209], but little else was permanently adopted.

The imported word stems were given native inflections.

The phonemes of these word stems were articulated in the English way: thus /p, t, k / before stressed vowels were aspirated; or else they were replaced by phonically similar native phonemes: thus the French rounded mid front vowel / ö / by the unrounded / ē / of ME, as in beef, people. Contrastive vowel length was imposed in accordance with native phonotactic rules: hence ME long vowels in word final and prevocalic positions, as in the ME antecedents of MnE vow, agree, blame, move, robe [Luick 1914–27: 446 ff.].

The stress patterns of the adopted French words were in the course of time also largely adapted to native patterns, as in cíty, énvoy, surface, fore stress replacing end stress [Kurath 1964: 146–48].

Aside from the lexicon, the effect of French upon the English language is thus remarkably slight. Only one French phoneme, the / ɔi / of joy, joint, was added directly to the English inventory; another, the / ž / of vision, measure, developed via / zj / from a French sequence. Initial / g̃, v, z /, as in joy, veal, zeal, which in

ME occurred only medially and finally, is the only other contribution of French to English phonology.

The behavior of English in its confrontation with French, the culturally dominant language of Great Britain for several centuries, may seem to be unusual, but is, in fact, rather typical. The well integrated grammatical and phonological system of a language and its prosodic features strongly resist remodeling under foreign influence, whereas word stems are freely adopted and adapted to the native system phonologically, prosodically, and morphologically.

9.2 Phonological Adaptation in South Bavarian

The persistence of the native system of phonemes and phonotactic rules is strikingly shown in the behavior of a South Bavarian dialect (Carinthian), spoken on the southern slope of the Austrian Alps, in its confrontation with a regional type of Standard German taught in the schools.

This folk dialect has four ingliding diphthongs, as in / liəb / "lieb, dear," / guət / "gut, good," / rɛəstn / "rösten, roast," / prɔəsn / "brosamen, bread crumbs." Of these, / iə / and / uə / are stable, but / ɛə / and / ɔə / were being replaced, word by word, at the turn of the century, the former by / ē / or / ɛ̄ / and the latter by / o /. Thus rustic / grɛəsr / "grösser, greater" was being replaced by refined / grēsr /; / wɛə / "weh, ache" by / wɛ̄ /; / grɔəs / "gross, great" by / grōs / [Kurath 1965: 56–57].

This replacement of the diphthongs is prompted by school-taught German, which lacks ingliding diphthongs and has long monophthongs in such words, i.e., / ē /, / ȫ /, and / ō /. However, the choice of the replacement depends solely upon the resources of the dialect, which has the monophthongs / ē, ɛ̄, ō / from other sources, as in / lēbm / "leben, live," / pɛ̄tn / "beten, pray," / xōfn / "hoffen, hope," and lacks rounded front vowels. Hence no alien phoneme is adopted in these cases. The "induced" changes conform to the indigenous system of vowels; only their lexical incidence is changed.

The "tyranny" of phonotactic rules is also well exemplified in this South Bavarian dialect. With few exceptions resulting from rather recent changes—the late indigenous shortening of the earlier geminates / pp, kk / and the replacement, under the influence of standard German, of final / -nkx / by / -ŋ /—vowels are long before single consonants, short before consonant clusters [Kurath 1965: 5–6]. When a word is adopted from Standard German or from Viennese—which, like other Central Bavarian dialects, has a different positional regulation of vowel duration [Koekoek 1955: 35–36; Kufner 1957: 175–84]—this rule is regularly imposed. Thus Standard German

/ knoxən / "bone" becomes / kxnōxn / (the native term is / pān /,
corresponding to E bone); and Viennese inflected / nɛttə / "nette,
neat" and / fɛššə / "fesche, fashionable, handsome" appear in this
dialect as / nētə / and / fɛ̌šə /.

9.3 The Adaptation of English Words to Norwegian Word Tones

That the tonal patterns of words are imposed by monolinguals
upon words adopted from a foreign language is shown in full detail
by E. Haugen in his investigation of the Norwegian spoken in some
of the Midwestern states [1953: 416–19].

It is a characteristic feature of Norwegian that the stress pattern
of polysyllabic words is invariably combined with one of two tonal
patterns, one of them simple, the other complex. The simple word
tone consists of a rise or a fall in pitch (the former in the eastern
and the latter in the western dialects of Norway), and the complex
word tone of a rise-fall-rise. The tonal pattern extends from the
stressed syllabic to the end of the word or phrase.

When English words are adopted, one of the Norwegian tonal
patterns is imposed upon them, the choice depending primarily upon
Norwegian morphological types. The onset of the tonal pattern is
determined by the location of the main stress of the English word.

Symbolizing (a) the simple tonal pattern by the acute and (b) the
complex tone by the circumflex, this process of adaptation can be
illustrated by the following examples cited by Haugen: (a) héndel <
handle, bísnes < business, píknik < picnic, fóttbål < football,
lármklokka < alarm clock; (b) fârmar < farmer, hômmstedd <
homestead, bêsment < basement, bêbi < baby, hârvista < harvest v.,
fênsapåst < fence post.

9.4 Adaptation of Latin to Celtic Speech Habits in Northern Italy

Since the latter part of the nineteenth century, possible influences
of underlying pre-Latin languages upon Italian regional dialects have
been proposed and vigorously debated. In a stimulating paper published in 1930, G. Rohlfs [1952 < 1930: 61–79] reviewed the several
problems and came to the following decisions. (1) In southern Italy
several syntactic constructions and the survival of the Latin perfect
as a preterit can be attributed to the Greek substratum; some Greek
words have been adopted, but no phonological features. (2) Oscan-
Umbrian and Etruscan influence cannot be demonstrated and must be
rejected; (3) in Northern Italy, the Celtic substratum has produced
some striking changes in the Italian dialects.

Rohlfs' discussion of the effects of the Celtic underlay is summarized below.

The dialects of northern Italy differ markedly from those spoken
in other parts of the peninsula. The bundle of heterophones that
follows the Apennines from Spezia-Luca in the west to Rimini-Ancona
on the Adriatic is the most prominent dialect boundary within Italy.
Not only that: it outranks the dialect boundary between Italy and
France, and is conventionally recognized as the dividing line between
the Western and the Eastern Romanic languages.

Rohlfs cites the following well known groups of heterophones that
set the North Italian dialects off from Tuscan:

(1) The loss of final unaccented vowels, except a, as in gros ≠
Tuscan grosso "big, thick," nas ≠ naso "nose";

(2) the syncopation of pretonic and posttonic vowels, as in slar ≠
sellaio "saddler," vedva ≠ vedova "widow";

(3) the elimination of double consonants, as in boca ≠ bocca
"mouth," spale ≠ spalle "shoulders";

(4) the voicing of voiceless phonemes between vowels, as in
ortiga ≠ ortica "nettle," fradel ≠ fratello "brother," cavei ≠ capelli
"hair";

(5) the occurrence of nasal vowels, as in pã ≠ pane "bread."

Since these features of North Italian have parallels in all of
France, he attributes them "without hesitation" to the Celtic substratum shared by northern Italy with France. The fact that the
earliest written documents exhibit these innovations is taken to support the inference from the areal congruence of these linguistic
subareas of Western Romanic with the originally Celtic domain.

Rohlfs does not comment on the phonemic background of these
alleged substratum effects beyond stating that Insular Celtic exhibits
the loss of initial and final unstressed vowels, which (following H.
Pedersen 1909: 1.260) he attributes to the strong primary stress.
This is clearly a weakness in his treatment of the presumed influence
of Celtic on the Romanic overlay.

Rohlfs [77–78] rejects the widely held view that the fronting of
Latin ū in northwestern Italy resulted from the Celtic substratum on
the following all but irrefutable grounds:

> It is important to note that the boundary of innovation that
> has so generally been attributed to Celtic influence—the
> shift of L ū to ü—does not coincide with the prominent bundle
> of heterophones that runs along the Apennines. As a matter
> of fact, its course is completely different. It runs from
> Lake Garda (whose western shore has ü and ö) southward to
> the Apennines. This line coincides very closely with the one
> that separates western ö from eastern o, as in Lombard kör

≠ Venetian kor (< L cor "heart")—a line that in its northern
sector agrees rather closely with the ancient boundary
between Lombardy and Venetia, as well as with that between the old dioceses of Mediolanum (Milan) and Aquileia.
The agreement between these two heterophones suggests
that they are approximately coeval. Now, it is worth noting
that the old documents of Milan do not yet have ȫ from o . . .
and that within the ü area u (from L ū) survives even now in
some highly conservative mountainous districts—on the
slopes of Monte Rosa and in the Bergamask Alps. If, as it
seems, the shift of u to ü is relatively recent, the assumption
that it resulted from the Celtic substratum must be decidedly
rejected—at least as far as northern Italy is concerned.
Wherever L ū is fronted to ü on Romanic soil, other [back]
vowels are apt to be shifted in the same direction: in northern France, in Raetia, in Apulia, as well as in northwestern
Italy. These innovations are usually later than the consonant
changes. They result from trends that came into being in
more recent times.

9.5 Adaptation of Latin to Celtic Speech Habits in
West Romanic

Several phonological changes in the Western Romanic languages
have been attributed to the influence of the Celtic substratum and
vigorously debated [A. Kuhn 1951: 52–57], among them the "weakening" of word-medial Latin / p, t, k /, as in Latin piper "pepper" >
Provençal pebre, French poivre; Latin sēta "hair, bristle" > North
Italian seda, Spanish seda, French soie "silk"; Latin lacus "lake" >
North Italian lago, Spanish lago, Old French lai. Whether this
development resulted from the persistence of Celtic speech habits
in the acquired Latin or from phonemic or prosodic "drives"
inherent in Latin itself is by no means easy to decide with anything
like finality. Even a brief consideration of some of the circumstances
should make that clear.
    Influence of Celtic speech habits upon the Latin overlay is possible
on ethnological grounds, since northern Italy and most of Western
Europe, conquered by the Romans between 200 B.C. and A.D. 100, was
Celtic territory at the time of the conquest. Thus there is areal congruence between the old Celtic language area and the West Romanic
area in which Latin medial / p, t, k / were "weakened"—a fact that
suggests possible influence of Celtic upon Romanic.
    Evidence for the appearance of "weakened" reflexes of proto-

Indo-European / p, t, k / in Celtic and in West Romanic is skimpy and circumstantial. For Gaulish (Continental Celtic), which was submerged by Romanic between 200 B.C. and A.D. 400, there is no spelling evidence for the "lenition" of / p, t, k / in the inscriptions. Insular Celtic "lenition" is fully established when written documents first make their appearance—ca. A.D. 700 in Irish, later in Welsh. It is with reference to the British branch of Insular Celtic that H. Pedersen [1909: 1 242, 436, 462] assumes the "strong" ∼ "weak" positional allophones / pʿ ∼ p, tʿ ∼ t, kʿ ∼ k / for Gaulish. If Pedersen's assumption stands, these positional variants could have been carried over into Romanic by speakers of Gaulish, the "weaker" allophones later yielding / b, d, g /, whence the further changes illustrated in the examples given above.

It is of considerable importance to point out that "lenition" of / p, t, k /—as also the shortening of all geminate consonants—is confined to word medial position in West Romanic, whereas in Insular Celtic it occurs also in phrase medial position. "Strong" / t, k / thus survive in Celtic only as phrase initials and in certain clusters of obstruents. This distribution of the reflexes of earlier / t, k / results in contextual variation of the initial consonants of words in Celtic for which West Romanic has no parallel.

It should further be noted that "lenited" / t, k / appear as the voiced plosives / d, g / only in the British branch of Insular Celtic (e.g., Welsh). The Goidelic branch (e.g., Irish) has the voiceless fricatives / θ, x / from this source [Pedersen 1909: 1.429].

For "weakened" reflexes of medial Latin / p, t, k / in West Romanic there is no spelling evidence before ca. A.D. 750. Hence the time of their first appearance is unknown.

The tangible evidence that has, or may have, a bearing upon the interpretation of the positional weakening of Latin / p, t, k / in West Romanic can be briefly summarized as follows.

(1) In the Romanic languages this development is largely confined to an area in which Romanic was superimposed upon Celtic.

(2) The positional phonemic split of / p, t, k / is shared by West Romanic with Insular Celtic, as shown by spelling evidence from ca. A.D. 750 onward.

(3) West Romanic differs from Celtic in the distribution of the weakened reflexes of / p, t, k / in that they are confined to word medial position.

(4) Within Insular Celtic, lenited / t, k / yield voiced plosives, / d, g /, in British but voiceless fricatives, / θ, x /, in Goidelic.

(5) Continental Celtic (Gaulish) is assumed to agree with the British branch of Insular Celtic.

(6) A further factor, usually not taken explicitly into account, is

the practical identity of the system of simple and geminated plosives in Proto-Celtic and Proto-Italic, which might lead to parallel development.

Under these circumstances it is difficult to decide with finality whether the treatment of word medial Latin /p, t, k / in West Romanic resulted from internal trends of Latin or whether it was introduced by speakers of Gaulish. Most scholars in the Romanic field take it as a reflex of the Celtic substratum, as does Rholfs (see above).

A. Martinet [1952: 216], who might be expected to champion indigenous development in West Romanic, concludes his discussion of this intricate problem as follows:

> "We have refrained from categorically rejecting the assumption that Celtic "lenition" and Western Romance consonantal development resulted from parallel evolution determined by structural analogy; but it must be clear that there exist potent arguments in favor of interpreting the Western Romance development as ultimately due to Celtic influence."

9.6 An Etruscan Phonological Reflex in Tuscany?

This phonological change, the so-called gorgia toscana, has been widely attributed to the Etruscan substratum of this part of Italy, where the Etrusian language was spoken no later than A.D. 200. This explanation was emphatically rejected by G. Rholfs [1952 < 1930: 71–75], who pointed out that Etruscan phonological evidence is at best highly ambiguous, that Dante makes no mention of it, and that on the evidence of the Linguistic Atlas of Italy [Jaberg-Jud 1928–40] this phenomenon is now restricted to western Tuscany, including Florence and Siena.

In a short article, R. A. Hall, Jr. [1949] brings the full evidence of the LAI to bear upon this problem, which should dispel the ghost of the survival of Etruscan speech habits for ever. He maps the dissemination of affricates and fricatives derived from intervocalic /p, t, k / in 12 words for each of the three phonemes and makes the following discoveries:

(1) affrication of /k / is fully established in northwestern Tuscany, including the cities of Florence, Siena, and Pisa; (2) affrication of /t / is regular in Florence-Siena and environs, but increasingly sporadic farther west (as in Pisa); and (3) the affrication of /p / is largely confined to central Tuscany, being most frequent in Florence and Siena (see Figure 47).

From the behavior of the isoglossic lines Hall draws these inferences: (1) Florence is the center in which the affrication originated and from which it has been spreading southward via Siena and westward down the valley of the Arno in the direction of Pisa. (2) The affrication (aspiration) of the velar, being most widely disseminated, must be earlier than that of the dental, and that of the labial lags far behind. (3) Diffusion of this phonological feature from Florence-Siena is still in progress.

The unmistakable areal evidence for a rather recent shifting of

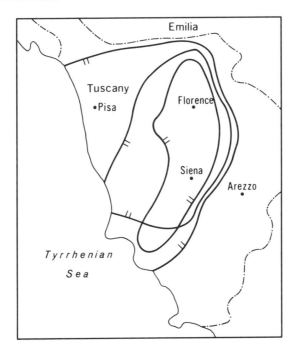

FIGURE 47: Tuscany: Affricated and Fricative Reflexes of Latin /p, t, k /

1. [kh ∼ x ∼ h] in fuoco "fire"
2. [th ∼ θ] in marito "husband"
3. [ph ∼ f] in rapa "turnip"

Based on Maps 1, 2, 3 in R. A. Hall, Jr., A Note on "Gorgia Toscana."

the intervocalic voiceless plosive / p, t, k / to affricates or fricatives is supported by the fact that there is no evidence for this
development before the sixteenth century and that the literary
language of Italy, based upon the Tuscan dialect, completely lacks
this phenomenon.

Hall concludes: "We must therefore abandon any idea of correlation between the present-day extent of the 'gorgia toscana' and
the boundaries of ancient Etruria."

10.

Parallel Development
or Diffusion?

10.1 Introduction

In diachronic investigations of genetically related languages, the relationships established by the comparative method between the several members of the family prepare the ground for an interpretation of these relationships in sociocultural terms.

Innovations shared by some, but not by all, of the languages belonging to the group seem to be the most significant linguistic guide posts to a historical interpretation. The relative chronology of shared changes should be established for each language, if at all possible; and the geographic domains occupied by languages sharing certain innovations must be taken into consideration in preparation for a decision whether a shared innovation developed independently in the languages that have it in common, or whether it was indigenous to one of them and spread to the other(s). Geographic proximity might speak for diffusion rather than parallel development; remoteness in space might favor the assumption of like indigenous development emanating from trends inherent in the shared system. Two examples may serve to illustrate the relevance of areal data in dealing with problems of this kind.

10.2 The Germanic Language Family

The grouping of the Germanic Languages on the basis of regionally restricted phonological and morphological features has been
under discussion for a century and a half, beginning with J. Grimm
[1819–37] and R. Rask [1818]. A brief history of divergent views, a
listing of relevant features with comments, and a useful bibliography
has recently been published by W. P. Lehmann [1965], which the
reader will want to consult along with the several comparative
grammars of the Germanic stock and the histories of individual
languages.

The grouping of the Germanic languages can be exhibited effectively by focusing the attention on structurally and/or statistically
important innovations shared by two or more, but not all, of the
languages of this family. For the sake of simplicity, only the five
languages for which sufficient written evidence is available between
ca. 350 and ca. 900 A.D. have been included in the scheme: Gothic,
Old Norse, Old English, Old Saxon, and Old High German. This
simplification will, I believe, not seriously distort the actual situation.

Shared Innovations in the Germanic Languages

OHG	OS	OE	ON	GO	REGIONAL INNOVATIONS
			X	X	1. pret. sing. 2 in -t: Go nam-t
			X	X	2. intrans. verbs in -na: Go full-na-
			X	X	3. pres. ppl. fem. in -in: Go nimand-ein-
			X	X	4. plosives in Go twaddje, ON tweggia
X	X	X	X		5. unreduplicated pret.: OE het, hleop
X	X		X		6. lowering of PGc æ to a: OHG sat
X	X	X	X		7. allophonic palatalization of back vowels
X	X	X			8. pret. sing. 2 in -i: OHG nam-i
X	X	X			9. *j assim. to preceding cons.: OE biddan
X	X	X			10. merging of PGc z with r: OE mara
X	X	X			11. loss of final unstressed r: OE wulf
	X	X			12. pres. pl. 3 in -þ: OE ber-aþ
	X	X			13. uniform pres. pl. inflection
	X	X			14. loss of *-r in pers. pron.: OE we, me
	X	X			15. dat. = acc. in pers. pron.
X					16. shifting of PGc p, t, k

1. Generalization of the inflection -t (of the PIE perfect) in the pret. sing. 2 of ablaut verbs: Go nam-t "took," ON halp-t "helped." Cp. 8 below.

2. Formation of intransitive verbs in -na to match transitive verbs in -ja: Go full-na- "become full" ≠ full-ja- "make full, fill."

3. Replacement of the stem suffix *-jō by -īn in the feminine of the present participle: Go nimand-ein "taking."

4. Development of long plosives in clusters of laryngeal plus *j or *w; Go twaddje, ON tveggia "two" (gen. pl.); Go triggwa, ON tryggva "troth."

5. Elimination of reduplication in ablaut verbs of class VII, either by complicated phonological developments of old reduplicated forms of the perfect or by descendants of old aorist forms: OE hēt, OHG hiez (Go haihait) "bid, ordered"; OE hlēop, OHG liof (Go haihlaup) "ran." Relics of reduplication are found in ON and OE. See Hirt 1932: 140–59; Prokosch 1939: 176–82.

6. Lowering of PGc ǣ (< PIE ē) to ā, except in Anglo-Frisian: ON sāð, OHG sāt "seed, seeding."

7. Allophonic palatalization of back vowels before *j, i, ī, which after the loss of these position markers yielded contrastive vowel phonemes: OE fyllan (< *full-ja) "fill," settan (< *satja-) "set," fēt (< *fōt-i) "feet." See Twaddele 1957 < 1938: 85–87.

8. Generalization of the inflection -i < PGc -iz (of the PIE aorist) in the pret. sing. 2 of all ablaut verbs: OHG nām-i "took," OE hulp-e "helped." Cp. 1 above.

9. The assimilation of *j to a preceding consonant: OE biddan "beg, ask," hliehhan "laugh," fiellan "fell."

10. Merging of PGc z with PGc r: OE māra "more" (Go maiza), faran "fare" (Go faran). Though merged in OIcel, Runic Norse preserves the contrast until ca. 700 A.D.

11. Loss of final *-r (< PGc -z) in unstressed syllables: OE wulf "wolf" (ON ulf-r, Go wulf-s); OE hulp-e "(you) helped" (see 8 above).

12. Generalization of voiceless -þ in the inflection of the pres. pl. 3: OE ber-aþ "bear" (Go -and, OHG -ant).

13. Spreading of the inflection of the pres. pl. 3 to the first and second person: OE sing-aþ (we, you, they) "sing"; OS hori-að "hear."

14. Loss of final *-r (< PGc -z) in personal pronouns: OE wē "we" (OHG wir), OE mē "me," dat. (OHG mir).

15. Loss of contrastive dative ≠ accusative forms in the personal pronoun: OE mē, þē, ūs, ēow; OS mī ~ me, thī, ūs, eu. However, Old Anglian and OS preserve distinct acc. forms ending in -k to some extent.

16. Shifting of the PGc voiceless plosives p, t, k to fricatives in medial position and to affricates initially: OHG offan "open," wazzar "water," mahhōn "make"; pfad "path," zehan "ten," chalp "calf."

The regional innovations presented above are of different dates and of varying importance.

Included are innovations shared by two or more Germanic languages as attested by early texts or inscriptions: Gothic 350–600 A.D.; Runic Norse 350–800; Old English, Old Saxon, Old High German 800–1000; Old Icelandic 1100–1200. The appearance of these shared innovations cannot be dated absolutely. Some may have occurred in the first centuries of the Christian era, others as late as 800–900. Their relative chronology can be inferred with some probability from their regional dissemination.

Reading the table presented above from top to bottom, we travel from the Baltic in a southwesterly direction through central and western Germany to the Alps. On the shores of the Baltic, Gothic and Norse developed some innovations before the Goths migrated southeastward to the Black Sea (features 1–4). In central Germany, along the North Sea, and in southern Germany other innovations are shared by English, Old Saxon, and High German (features 8–11). Some West Germanic innovations (features 5–7) appear also in Old Norse, which shares other innovations with Gothic. In the northern section of the West Germanic area, Old Saxon, Old English, and Frisian jointly introduced some innovations (features 12–15). In the south, a far-reaching shifting of consonants (feature 16) is shared by all of the High German dialects.

On the basis of shared regional innovations one can construct this family tree:

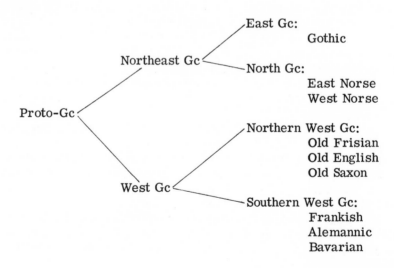

East Gc:
 Gothic

Northeast Gc
 North Gc:
  East Norse
  West Norse

Proto-Gc

 Northern West Gc:
  Old Frisian
  Old English
  Old Saxon

West Gc
 Southern West Gc:
  Frankish
  Alemannic
  Bavarian

This plan neglects the features shared by North Germanic with West Germanic. However, such a simplified scheme, taken as such, has its useful function in orienting the discussion of the history of a family of languages. It must not be taken too literally.

The regional innovations presented above are of very uneven value from the structural and/or the statistical point of view. Among the most important ones are features 1, 5, 8, and 13, which involve the morphology of large classes of verbs. These can be taken as convenient diagnostic features of the several language groups, each of which is characterized by three or four of the regionally restricted innovations displayed in the table. The fact that their dissemination is coextensive with other regionally restricted innovations makes them representative of the several language or dialect groups.

The regional grouping of innovations poses diachronic problems. For example: (1) What is the relative chronology of innovations 8 to 11 shared by all West Germanic languages? (2) Did these features develop independently in prehistoric stages of Old English, Old Saxon, and Old High German, or did they originate in one of these dialects and spread to the others?

In dealing with innovations of recent times, dated localized documents can furnish evidence for establishing the chronology; knowledge of the precise areal spread of an innovation as established by selective sampling can help us decide whether a shared innovation developed independently in the several dialects or was diffused from dialect to dialect. Finally, and most importantly, the location of a dominant sociocultural center may enable us to determine with some probability the focal area in which the innovation originated and from which it spread. When evidence of these types is lacking, no probable answer can be given to the questions raised above. This is one of the important findings of modern area linguistics, which should discourage hasty decisions in dealing with shared prehistoric innovations.

In passing, it is of interest to note that some shared regional retentions of Proto-Germanic features fall into the same areal patterns as shared innovations. Thus, the sequence -ngw- is preserved in Gothic and Norse: Go siggwan, OIcel syngva "sing"; OE gān "go," dōn "do" have corresponding forms only in OS and OHG; and OE hē, hēo, hit "he, she, it" have counterparts only in Old Frisian and Old Saxon.

10.3 The Indo-European Language Family

Structurally important innovations shared by two or more languages of the Indo-European family form the chief basis for establishing degrees of kinship between them and tracing their diachronic filiation. The evidence for such joint innovations, gathered from texts far apart in time, has been accumulated by scholars for a century and a half and was conveniently summarized by K. Brugmann [1904: 2–27] and by A. Meillet [1907] at the turn of the century.

Chief among shared innovations are the following:

1. Sibilation of the PIE palatals / k̂, ĝ, ĝh / in Indo-Iranian and Balto-Slavic (the so-called satəm languages), and merging of the PIE labio-velars / kʷ, gʷ, gʷh / with the pure velars / k, g, gh /.

2. Merging of the PIE palatals with the pure velars and the preservation of contrastive labio-velars in Greek, Italic, Celtic, and Germanic (the so-called centum languages).

3. Merging of the aspirated voiced stops / bh, dh, gh / of PIE with the simple voiced stops / b, d, g / in Iranian and Balto-Slavic; also in Celtic.

4. Development of the "augment" as a verbal prefix in the formation of a past tense in Indo-Iranian and in Greek.

5. Unvoicing of the PIE aspirated stops / bh, dh, gh / to affricated stops in Greek (written φ, θ, χ) and to fricatives in Italics (written f, h).

6. Merging of PIE perfect and aorist forms in a past tense form in Italic, Celtic, and Germanic, thus eliminating the category of aspect.

	Shared Innovations					
Languages	1	2	3	4	5	6
Indic	x			x		
Iranian	x		x	x		
Balto-Slavic	x		x			
Germanic		x				x
Celtic		x	x			x
Italic		x			x	x
Greek		x		x	x	

A striking aspect of these innovations is their areal patterning, which is shown in the accompanying table. Feature 1 is shared by all of the eastern, feature 2 by all of the western languages. The other features are common to two or three contiguous language areas: 3 to Balto-Slavic and Iranian, 4 to Indo-Iranian and Greek, 5 to Greek and Italic, 6 to Italic, Celtic, and Germanic.

This areal patterning of regionally shared innovations furnishes the most important leads for the consideration of the relationships between the Indo-European dialects and their filiation in prehistoric times.   Did proto-Indo-European first split into an eastern and a western branch, as is traditionally assumed by inference from the areal behavior of features 1 and 2? Did innovation 3 develop independently in Balto-Slavic and in Iranian, or did it spread from one to the other through intercommunications? Did the augment (feature 4) arise independently in Indo-Iranian and in Greek after their geographic separation or while they were still in contact? Is the formation of a past tense out of earlier perfect and aorist forms in Italic, Celtic and Germanic evidence for an early common development or does it arise independently in the three languages?

Such are the problems raised by the areal evidence. To answer them is not so simple. Regionally shared retensions of PIE features must be taken into consideration to propose probable solutions and the behavior of the several languages during their historical period may shed some light on earlier processes.

11.

The Social Dimension in Area Linguistics

11.1 Social Dialectology

Until rather recently the techniques of area linguistics have been brought to bear almost exclusively on folk speech. All of the European atlases have, in principle, restricted their selective sampling to this social level of usage. Nevertheless, the sociocultural interpretation of the geographic patterning of variants in folk speech has inevitably led to the recognition of prestige dialects, whether geographic or social, as a potent force of diffusion within the several subareas as well as from area to area. Lacking detailed information on regional variation in prestige dialects, scholars resorted to written records of the literary language to buttress their theories. The chief weakness of this procedure results from the fact that innovations in folk speech are usually not prompted directly by cultivated speech but are mediated by middle class usage, about which so little is known. Only systematic sampling of middle class and upper class speech will provide the evidence for dealing with diffusion realistically.

In the United States, the very first linguistic survey undertook the sampling of usage on three social levels: that of the folk, the middle class, and the cultured. In principle, folk speech and middle class speech were sampled in every community chosen for investigation, cultivated speech in about one out of five. This sampling plan is described in Kurath 1933: 90–95 and Kurath-Bloch 1939: 41–44.

164

The cartographic presentation of two or three social levels community by community offered no serious problems, as one may gather
from the maps of the Linguistic Atlas of New England [Kurath-Bloch-
Lowman 1939–43: Preface to Vol. I].

Limitation in the number of cultured speakers seemed justified
on the ground that their usage might be expected to vary less from
place to place because they have wider contacts than the folk and the
middle class and are more strongly influenced by literary English.
To obtain some insight into differences existing between cultivated
persons in larger urban communities, 5 were interviewed in New
York City, 4 in Charleston, S. C., 3 each in Philadelphia, Baltimore,
and Richmond, and 2 in Boston. These informants include old and
middle-aged men and women, members of different professional
groups, social organizations, and religious denominations.

Despite the rather small number of cultured speakers included
in the American survey, the evidence gathered proved to be
sufficient for the following purposes:

(1) to establish the phonemic system of cultivated speech region
by region and to convey in synoptic tables the phonic realization of
the phonemes by individual speakers [Kurath-McDavid 1961: 31–
100];

(2) to point out some of the more salient features in which
cultivated pronunciation differs from the usage of the folk and the
middle group, region by region [Kurath-McDavid 1961: Maps 28
mountain, 69 can't, 72 rather, 77 calm], or agrees with it [ibid.:
Maps 38 stairs, 97 creek, 113 root];

(3) to trace the diffusion of certain features on the level of
cultivated speech from focal areas to surrounding areas [Kurath in
Lunt 1964: 135–44; Van Riper 1957];

(4) to establish the important fact that in the several regions of
the Eastern United States the phonemic system of folk speech is in
essential agreement with that of cultivated speech; that the differences between them are largely nonstructural, consisting as they do
in divergent lexical incidence and in the phonic realization of shared
phonemes;

(5) to orient the intensive investigation of social dialects in
urban centers and their environs, as several recent studies discussed below have clearly demonstrated.

11.2 The Investigation of Urban Speech

No systematic survey of urban speech comparable with surveys
of folk speech in extent or in scientific technique has been undertaken as yet. Not that the importance of urban speech has been

ignored or underrated. The dominant influence of urban centers upon the speechways of the countryside and the "vaulting" of urban speech forms from major centers to subordinate centers have been fully recognized. See Chapter VIII above.

The preoccupation with the speechways of the folk as such and as a source for tracing the development of standard or literary usage accounts in part for the neglect of urban speech on the part of dialectologists. But the chief reason would seem to be the bewildering complexity of the linguistic situation in the major cities, most of which have grown like mushrooms since about the middle of the nineteenth century, drawing their population not only from their surrounding but from other dialect areas and from remote countries. These complexities demand refinements in the sampling technique and in the analysis of the field data that are yet to be developed. Tape recording and the computer are devices that will have to be brought to bear upon this important task.

In the United States the investigation of city speech has barely begun, but the importance of it has come to be rather sharply felt. The realization that three-fourths of the American people now live in urban areas, that the cities inevitably dominate the countryside socioculturally, and that the effective teaching of English in the city schools demands reliable information on socially marked differences in everyday speech are three factors that have brought this about [Kurath in PADS No. 49 (1970)].

Fortunately we are not entirely unprepared to face this urgent task. The wide-meshed linguistic surveys of three social levels in large parts of our country, notably the East, the Midwest, and the Pacific states, provide the background for singling out features that vary regionally and by social class and may therefore be expected to have currency within a given city. Preliminary sampling of such features should lead to the construction of effective questionnaires that within the means at our disposal would yield reliable data on significant differences in the speechways of the several social and age groups in the various subdivisions (quarters) of the urban area and its rural surroundings. Inclusion of the adjoining countryside in urban surveys is important because of the rather recent growth of American cities. The linguistic historian will want to determine what features are indigenous to the area in which the city is located, what usages have been imported from other areas, and what elements can be attributed to the literary language studied in the schools.

Recent investigations of the social structure of various cities or some of their subdivisions are another asset to the student of urban speech. Instead of making a more or less intelligent guess as to social types and their interrelations within the urban community he can in such cases be guided by the findings of the sociologists in his choice of informants and, in some instances, even interview the very same socially representative individuals.

A critical analysis of some of the studies devoted to problems of urban speech in North America and in Europe will make it clear that the investigation of the speech of any major urban area is a difficult task. Even when elements of the population whose first language is other than that of the dominant groups are set aside, the problems of adequately sampling the usage of the social groups from generation to generation and from section to section of the urban complex are formidable.

11.21 The Speech of New York City

A succinct summary of the phonological features of the speech of New York City (NYC) is presented by Kurath-McDavid [1961: 14–15; 55–57], based upon the evidence gathered from 25 informants in 1941. Three social levels are represented in this sample, which is deliberately restricted to native-born New Yorkers and favors the older generation. Of the 25 informants 6 are cultured, 7 belong to the middle class, and 12 to the lower class; 12 represent the oldest living generation, 8 the middle-aged, and 5 the younger set.

In 1948, Yakira H. Frank, a native of NYC, completed a detailed study of the evidence provided by this sample of the Linguistic Atlas. To gain perspective, she included in her investigation the field records of 21 informants living in the surrounding area—the counties of Nassau and Westchester in New York State and the New Jersey counties adjoining the Hudson River, the bedchamber of many a New Yorker.

It is of some importance to note that the 5 boroughs of NYC— Manhattan, the Bronx, Queens, Brooklyn, and Staten Island—cover some 300 square miles and had a population of nearly 8,000,000 in 1941. Under the circumstances it is obvious that the evidence furnished by 25 informants is hardly sufficient for revealing regional differences within this huge urban complex with its sharply divergent economic and sociocultural subdivisions. For this reason, Frank's treatment is focused on social and age differences within the urban complex as a whole.

The 25 informants interviewed in the five boroughs of NYC— whatever their social standing or age—have essentially the same system of phonemes. They share 6 "checked" syllabics, as in bit, bet, bat, hot, hut, foot; 8 "free" syllabics, as in bee-beat, bay-bait, buy-bite, bar-heart, and do-boot, no-boat, law-bought, and now-bout; and 24 consonants. The phonic realization of some of these phonemes

and their lexical incidence vary by social and/or age groups, as
pointed out below.

The only clear-cut systemic difference occurs in the syllabics
of boy, coil, loin, and burr, curl, learn. Here the cultured speakers
have contrastive / ɔi ≠ 3 /, as in coil ≠ curl, while in lower class
speech the two phonemes are merged in / 3ɪ /, so that coil and curl,
loin and learn are homophonous. Usage of the middle class varies
and fluctuates in a complicated manner.

The chief social differences in the articulation of shared phonemes
and their lexical incidence revealed by the sample can only be briefly
pointed out.

On the folk level, (1) the syllabics in such words as bag and law
are raised and prolonged in a majority of the test words; (2) the
syllabic of buy-bite has a backed beginning; (3) the suffix of laughing,
morning usually ends in / n /; (4) the fricative in three, moth is
sometimes replaced by an affricated plosive and that in the, without
by / d /.

The following phonological features are largely confined to cultivated speech: (1) the monophthongal articulation of the syllabic in
burr, burn, i.e., [3˙]; (2) the centered beginning of the diphthong in
no, boat; (3) the occurrence of [ɑ˙] not only in bar, heart but also—
though not consistently—in aunt, can't, calf and in vase, tomato; (4)
the use of [ai] in either; (5) the sequence / ju / in due, new, Tuesday.

Several phonological features are disseminated by age groups.
Thus relics of lowered / ɔ /, as in law, and the incidence of the
checked vowel / ʊ / in root, broom occur only among the old informants. On the other hand, a rather open beginning of the syllabics
of bee, do, no characterize some of the young speakers.

Two phonological phenomena call for further comment: (1) the
varying reflexes of postvocalic / r /, and (2) the merging of the
syllabics in loin and learn.

In words like chair, car, door, poor, 14 of the 25 New York City
informants had no trace of / r / in 1941, 9 of them had an occasional
weakly constricted / r /, and 2 informants living on the periphery
(northern Queens and southern Staten Island) used / r / with some
frequency, thus agreeing with the usage of the surroundings of NYC,
where the incidence of / r / increases with the distance from the city.

The evidence for this variable feature of the speech of New York
City and the surrounding area is effectively displayed by Frank in
tables IXA and IXB of her dissertation. It is indeed a challenge to
further investigation.

The phoneme / ɔi / of boil, join is sharply distinguished from
the / 3 / of learn, girl in cultivated NYC speech. At the lower end
of the social scale, the / ɔi / is just as regularly merged in / 3 /,

mostly articulated as an upgliding diphthong, so that <u>loin</u> and <u>boil</u> rhyme with <u>learn</u> and <u>girl</u>. Usage of the middle class varies. Though merging predominates, there is a trend to introduce the distinction, presumably under the influence of the schools.

The sampling of the speech of New York City for the <u>Linguistic Atlas of the Eastern States</u> has raised questions that can only be answered by more extensive sampling. That, indeed, is one of the functions of a large scale survey, which provides the data for designing effective plans for the investigation of specific problems.

11.22 Stratification on the Lower East Side of Manhattan

Twenty years after the sampling of New York City speech for the <u>Linguistic Atlas</u>, William Labov undertook a systematic investigation of six variable features in the speech of the Lower East Side of Manhattan for his doctoral dissertation at Columbia University (1964). The project was suggested and directed by U. Weinreich. With minor changes, the text of the dissertation has been published under the broad title <u>The Social Stratification of English in New York City</u> (1966). Its publication was sponsored by the Clearinghouse for Social Dialect Study of the Center for Applied Linguistics in Washington, D. C.

The choice of informants was guided by a previous survey of the social structure of the Lower East Side of Manhattan by social scientists whose findings are based upon 988 representatives chosen from a population of about 100,000 inhabitants. For the linguistic survey the sample was reduced from 988 to 81 as follows: 488 were dropped because their native language was not English; 180 had moved out; 125 of the remaining 320 were eliminated by "random" procedure; of the remaining 195, 157 could be reached, and 122 of them were interviewed at length, whereupon 41 of them were eliminated because they were born outside New York City. This left the 81 informants—45 of Jewish, 19 of Italian parentage—who "provided the main body of data."

To what extent the sample of 81 selected in this manner from the sample of 988 used by the social scientists is representative of the social types inhabiting the Lower East Side is hard to tell. Nevertheless, no other investigation of social gradation in urban speech, in this country or abroad, has been in a position to chose its informants with comparable information and circumspection. Readers of this stimulating and provocative study must of course be aware of the fact that the determination of correlations between speech behavior and social class depends upon the degree to which the informants selected reflect the social structure of the community.

Labov's immediate purpose is to determine the social dissemination of variant pronunciations and the incidence of these variants in several "styles" of speaking on the part of the social types represented by his sample population. From such data he hopes to infer trends in usage within the community—the Lower East Side of Manhattan—and to gain insight into the social dynamics underlying them.

To secure information on the behavior of the informants under varying circumstances, the author investigates five "styles" of utterance: (A) casual (informal) speech, (B) careful (formal) speech, (C) reading of texts, (D) reading of isolated words, (D^1) reading of minimal pairs.

The variable features chosen for investigation are: (1) the occurrence or loss of postvocalic /r/, as in here, hair, hard, four, sure; (2) the syllabic of bad, half, hand, found to vary all the way from [æ ~ æ·] to [eə ~ ɪə]; (3) the syllabic of law, off, more, said to vary from [ɔ· ~ ɒ] to ɔə ~ ʊə]; (4) the consonants of thin and then, articulated as fricatives or as plosives.

The occurrence of the variants among speakers representing the upper middle class, the lower middle class, the working class, and the lower class, and the incidence of these variants in the "styles" of the several social classes are summarily presented in a set of graphs [222, 238, etc.].

The major findings are: (1) postvocalic /r/, as in hard, is increasingly more frequent from "low" to "high" class and from "styles" A to D. (2) Raised variants of the vowel in bad, represented by the digraph /eh/, are less frequent among the middle class than among the lower classes and decrease from "style" A to D. (3) Fricatives in thin and then are consistently more frequent from "low" to "high" class and from "style" A to D. (4) The social stratification of the raised variants of the syllabic of law, off, represented by the digraph /oh/, is less clear; but this variant is clearly more frequent among the lower classes than among the middle class and its frequency drops off sharply from "style" A to D.

If the statistics on which the graphs are based are accepted at face value, the inhabitants of the Lower East Side of Manhattan, whatever their social class, tend to break away from pronunciations current in their casual speech. They introduce the /r/ in postvocalic position, tone down or abandon the raised vowels in bad and in law, and avoid the plosive consonants in thin and then. This trend is especially marked among the lower middle class.

Labov suggests that New Yorkers are on the defensive [Bright 1966: 100] and adopt other people's pronunciations when they want to appear to advantage. That is surely true of the stigmatic plosives

in thin and then, the only non-English features. But the adoption of
postvocalic / r / may have a more complicated background. Not
only is / r / rather regularly heard both before and after syllabics
over the radio and seen in print, but also nearly half of the 81
informants seem to be bilingual, speaking Yiddish or Italian in their
homes and with friends, languages in which / r / occurs in all positions.

The author attaches great importance to the consistent correlation of the relative frequency of the variants with social class and
to the regularity with which the variants either decrease or increase
from casual to careful speech, and further to the reading of texts
and minimal pairs. The behavior of the informants in "styles" of
utterance (or levels of diction) betrays in part an awareness of
prestigeous variants and in part the influence of the written word.
These findings should stimulate scholars to apply Labov's technique
to other speech communities, so that his view of linguistic change
could be tested by other evidence.

Whether linguistic usage in other sections of Manhattan and in
the other four boroughs of NYC exhibits the same social and stylistic
patterning, as Labov claims, is more than doubtful. To be sure,
some of the same "variables" have been observed in other parts of
New York City by earlier investigators—from Babbitt [1896] to the
Linguistic Atlas [1941; Frank 1948], and from C. K. Thomas [1942]
and A. F. Hubbell [1950] to A. Bronstein [1962]. But their social
dissemination still remains to be investigated. The very fact that
Labov found such a striking correlation between the dissemination
of these variables with social indices on the Lower East Side suggests that other sections of Manhattan, characterized by very
different social structure, can hardly conform to the same linguistic
pattern. Only investigation comparable in method will give us
reliable information on other sections of Manhattan—say Harlem
and Washington Heights—and on the other boroughs of NYC. There
is no substitute for informed carefully planned selective sampling.
Until that is done, scholars will do well to set aside Labov's
enthusiastic assertions couched in these words [Bright 1966: 107]:

> Internal and external evidence leads us to think that our
> results apply generally to New York City, and that the
> patterns of social stratification which we studied are
> quite general.

It is the great merit of Labov's investigation to have taken full
advantage of the results of a systematic sociological sampling
operation of a limited section of Manhattan, to have drawn upon

this sample of informants to obtain linguistic evidence for establishing correlations between phonological "variables" and social factors, and thus to determine trends in usage in that section of Manhattan. This is a remarkable achievement, destined to be a model for future investigations of urban speech communities. Wherever comparable sociological surveys become available, linguistics will have a golden opportunity to make significant contributions to our understanding of the complex social forces underlying linguistic change in urban areas.

11.23 Social Gradation of Negro Speech in Washington, D. C.

Wide-meshed sampling of Negro speech for the Linguistic Atlas of the South Atlantic States provided evidence for the following statement [Kurath 1949: 6]:

> By and large the Southern Negro speaks the language of the white man of his locality or area and of his level of education. But in some respects his speech is more archaic or old-fashioned: not un-English, but retarded because of less schooling.

The Gullah dialect spoken along the coast of South Carolina and Georgia appears to be the only exception to this rule (see Section 7.4 above).

That marked social dialects in Negro speech were current long before the abolition of slavery is clear enough: houseservants, separately quartered from the field hands, acquired the language of their masters. The problem of the interrelations between the speech ways of Negroes and Whites has been discussed by the McDavids [1951], with appropriate comments on popular misconceptions.

The social gradation in present-day Negro speech has recently been investigated experimentally by G. N. Putnam and E. M. O'Hern [1955]. Seventy observers were asked to rate the speech behavior of 12 Negroes who had retold a short fable read to them. Recorded separately on tape, the 12 versions of the story were transferred to a master tape in a random order determined by lot. The observers were instructed to place each speaker on a one-dimensional social scale from "high" to "low." Of the 70 "judges," 54 were graduate students and 16 teachers; 55 were White and 15 Negro. Few of them were trained in linguistics.

The 12 speakers, of whom 3 were university professors, 2 secretaries, 2 masons, 2 maids, and 3 inhabitants of a slum area in Washington, D. C. had previously been ranked socially by the investigators with reference to an "index of status characteristics" (I. S. C.) based on 4 factors: occupation, source of income, house type, and dwelling area [25–26].

The ranking assigned to the 12 speakers by the "judges" corresponded very closely to that based upon the "index of status characteristics." In the words of the investigators: "The product-moment correlation between the I. S. C. scores of the twelve speakers and the mathematical equivalents of the judges' ratings was +0.80." This striking correlation is graphically presented in Figure 7 [27].

It is of importance to emphasize the fact that the only information the "judges" had about the 12 speakers was their performance in retelling a short story. Their judgments are based upon a variety of factors, probably in this order of importance: skill in describing the sequence of events, "styling" of the story, prosodic features, syntactic features, verb forms, features of pronunciation. Some insight into the cues on which the judges may have relied can be gained by reading the 12 versions of the story presented in phonetic notation [30–32].

One can readily agree with the concluding remarks of the authors:

> The most remarkable result of the study was the discovery that untrained judges could rate the social status of speakers so accurately after listening to a very short speech selection in the absence of all irrelevant cues.
> . . . The importance of speech as a mark of social status . . . is a matter of great significance.

11.24 The Negro Community in Memphis, Tenn.

An important contribution to our knowledge of Negro speech in an urban community has been made by J. V. Williamson in her study of the speechways of the Negro community in Memphis, Tenn. [1961]. In this city one-third of the population of half a million belongs to this race, which at the time of the field work had its segregated school system leading from grade school to Le Moyne College, where Miss Williamson teaches. Drawing its population, White and Black, largely from the cotton-growing Delta along the Mississippi, Memphis has had a phenomenal growth, doubling its population every 20 years: a city of 65,000 in 1890, it had reached 500,000 by 1960.

The sampling plan conforms to that of the Linguistic Atlas, but is significantly extended to bring social classes and age groups into relief. Of the 24 informants, 6 are cultured, 10 belong to the middle class, and 8 to the folk; 9 are under 45, 5 over 65, and 10 middle-aged. The evidence gathered shows that nonstandard verb forms are largely confined to the folk level and are matched by forms used by Southern Whites. On the other hand, the cultured Negroes employ only the standard literary verb forms, while the usage of the middle class informants varies. A similar situation obtains in phonological matters. There is not a single feature of pronunciation or grammar that lacks its counterpart in the speech of Southern Whites as recorded for the Linguistic Atlas.

Miss Williamson did not investigate the speech of the White population of Memphis, which would indeed be a difficult task for a Negro scholar. One suspects that the socially marked forms of Negro speech are also current among the Whites of the same social level. We shall see that in Chicago, where the Negro population represents a recent mass immigration, the linguistic situation is radically different.

11.25 Negro Speech in Chicago, Ill.

Two sampling surveys of certain aspects of the speech of Chicago have been carried out in recent years. L. A. Pederson's The Pronunciation of English in Chicago [1964] deals with the usage of the White population in its social gradation and forms the background to the investigation of the speech of the large Negro community within the city carried out by a group of scholars under the general direction of R. I. McDavid, Jr. [1966] and published in mimeographed form under the title Communication Barriers to the Culturally Deprived.

The latter study, supported by the U. S. Office of Education, undertook to establish the existing differences between the speech of Whites and Negroes, to determine the social evaluation of these differences on the part of Chicago Whites and Negroes, and thus to pinpoint those features of Negro speech to which the schools might direct their attention for the good of the Negro.

The director of the project, a native of South Carolina and long a resident in the Midwest, was uniquely qualified to design this research project after years of fieldwork both in the South and in the Midwest. His long interest in social dialect as a reflection of social structure and its implication for the life of the individual [1946, 1948, 1951, 1965, 1966] made him fully aware of the problems to be met. Moreover, he was fortunate in having as his associates a number of excellent linguists.

Previously gathered dialect evidence for the Midwest and the South—the former as background for the usage of the dominant White population of Chicago, the latter as background for the practices of the newcomers—made it possible to select 160 critical items from the worksheets of the Linguistic Atlas to determine the more striking phonological and grammatical differences between the usage of Whites and Negroes.

Thirty Negroes were interviewed, 16 by L. A. Pederson and 14 by J. Willis, a Negro graduate student in anthropology. Pederson, who had previously investigated the usage of Chicago Whites [1964], recorded the responses to the 160 items in phonetic notation, Willis on tapes.

The informants range in age from 30 to 70 and represent all social classes. Six of them were born in Chicago (aged 30 to 60), 22 in the South, chiefly in the South Central States. Of those born in the South, 12 had lived in Chicago at least 20 years.

The Negro respondents are ranked from high to low in accordance with a complex sociocultural index, and in the 10 tables of variants their responses are consistently entered in the established sequence. In the tables, agreement with the usage of the Whites and deviations from it are identified by distinct symbols, so that any marked differences in the behavior of upper-class and lower-class Negroes can readily be seen. So can the complexities of the actual situation.

We may take as an example the reflexes of postvocalic / r /, as in beard, chair, horse, four, which are presented by Pederson in Table 2. As is well known, in the Midwest / r / survives in that position as a constricted consonant [ɚ], while it appears as an unsyllabic [ə] in the speech of Whites and Negroes in the coastal South and large parts of the south-central states. With 2 exceptions, the 17 lower-class informants born in the South rather consistently have [ə] in these words, even the 7 that have lived in Chicago for more than 20 years. This is what one might expect. The surprising fact is that 4 of the 6 Negroes born in Chicago (age 30 to 60) rather consistently follow this Southern practice. Only 1 of them, a 30-year-old clerk, has adopted the postvocalic / r /. Residential segregation would seem to account for this situation.

The divergent behavior of 3 upper class informants who came to Chicago after age 30 raises some interesting questions: a lawyer born in western Tennessee, aged 57, consistently uses [ə]; a social worker born in eastern Virginia, aged 69, has constricted [ɚ] with fair consistency; a minister born in Arkansas, aged 69, uneasily fluctuates between [ə] and [ɚ]. Personal attitudes as well as certain contacts conditioned by professional activities are surely involved.

The rating on the part of Chicago Whites of existing differences in pronunciation can be expected to identify features that stigmatize the Negro and thereby put him at a disadvantage within the urban community. In turn, the identification of such "inferior" features furnishes the necessary leads for planning the teaching of the

socially superior variants to the Negro, variants that he can use at
will when the situation requires it.

In a carefully planned experiment, V. S. and C. H. Larsen undertook to determine an evaluation of some of the more striking phonological differences between the speech of Negroes and Whites. White
observers were asked to record on a five-point scale their reaction
to specific items, presented to them on tapes, along such dimensions
as upper class–lower class, educated–uneducated, pleasant–
unpleasant, urban–rural, White–Negro. The essential agreement in
the judgments of the White observers leaves no doubt about the social
standing among Chicago Whites of the variants tested. See, for
instance, "exhibits" 1.12 four and 1.14 poor. Negro observers, the
Larsens found, largely agree with the reactions of the Whites,
although they are less sure of their judgments.

On the assumption that preferred usage tends to spread, one
feels tempted to say that tests of this kind could be used to determine probable trends in usage within a speech community.

The magnitude and the difficulty of the task confronting the
teaching of a prestigeous type of English to the children of the
Chicago Negro community are formidable. Family and neighborhood
tradition in a residentially segregated Negro population of 800,000—
built up largely since the First World War—are powerful, as this
investigation has shown. To make headway at all, the identification
of stigmatized features is a necessary preliminary to the teacher's
problem.

11.26 The English of the Mexican Community in San Antonio, Texas

Using a modified version of the Linguistic Atlas questionnaire,
J. B. Sawyer interviewed 7 informants of Anglo-American stock and
7 of Mexican extraction in the city of San Antonio, Texas. She discovered that "Anglos" and "Latins," speaking their vernaculars and
living lives apart, do not influence each other to any extent.

Miss Sawyer's findings, briefly summarized in Word [15.270–
781], are presented in a doctoral dissertation written under the
direction of E. B. Atwood (University of Texas, 1957).

The speech of the "Anglos" is characterized by phonological
features derived from the Southern and/or the South Midland dialects
as described in Kurath-McDavid [1961: 18–22], among them an upgliding diphthong in law, fog; [æu] in cow, house; monophthongal [aˑ]
in five, night; and contrastive vowels in hoarse ≠ horse. None of
these features has been adopted by those whose family language is
Spanish, not even by those who speak English with ease.

In similar fashion, Southern regional words used by the "Anglos,"

such as clabber "curdled milk," corn shucks "corn husks," light-
bread "white bread," pulley bone "wishbone," snap beans "string
beans," are unfamiliar to most of the "Latins," who acquire the
literary terms taught in the schools.

The same situation obtains with regard to regional folk forms of
the verb current among the lower classes of San Antonians of English
descent.

Although Spanish is now spoken by nearly half the population of
the city, there is no evidence of recent Spanish influence on the
English spoken by the "Anglos," not even in the vocabulary. Such
terms as arroyo "dry creek," mesa "table land," corral "horse pen,"
remuda "group of saddle horses" were adopted during early contacts
(ca. 1850) and survive in San Antonio as elsewhere in Texas [Atwood
1962: Maps 15, 19, 21, 22].

Flocking into the city in ever increasing numbers since 1900,
chiefly as laborers, San Antonians of Mexican descent constitute a
world apart, maintaining contacts with Mexico and preserving their
folk culture in their quarters of the city. On the other hand, the
English-speaking stock keeps aloof.

11.27 The Relations between Urban and Rural Speech in Two Swiss Cities

The social stratification of urban speech in two Swiss cities is
discussed with fine discrimination and careful documentation by
H. Baumgartner [1940], associated with Hotzenköcherle in drawing
up the plans for the Sprachatlas der deutschen Schweiz. His native
city of Biel and the city of Bern, where he conducted his seminars
on dialectology, are his two chief observation posts for accumulating
the large body of evidence that enabled him to place urban usage in
its regional setting, to characterize the behavior of the several
social groups, and to outline trends in urban usage.

According to Baumgartner, all social groups in Biel and in Bern
speak variants of one and the same regional dialect of Swiss German,
that of the Seeland and the Mittelland of the canton of Bern. The
speech of the city-born leading families normally has a larger
number of words adopted from literary German (taught in the schools)
than that of the other social groups, but its systemic phonological and
morphological features and the basic vocabulary are essentially the
same as those current in the Bernese countryside.

Baumgartner distinguishes three social layers in Swiss urban
communities, separates the old stock from the newcomers on all
three levels, and points out their linguistic peculiarities in some
detail.

In the city of Biel, the speech of the lower class, agreeing with
that of the countryside, differs from that of the upper class in such
phonological items as chaub ≠ chalb "calf," fingə ≠ fində "find,"
döiff ≠ dieff "deep," föif ≠ füf "five" [21].

The upper class uses some French and Standard German words
that are not current on the lower levels, articulates the /r/ in the
French way as a velar fricative, replaces the suffix -ig, as in tsitig
"zeitung, newspaper" and meining "meinung, opinion" by Standard
German -ung, and introduces some "refined" verb forms [22–33].
The middle group, less clearly definable and less sure of itself,
wavers between "high" and "low."

Despite such "class markers" all varieties of the speech of Biel
and Bern are mutually intelligible, and many a native is bidialectal
and able to shift his "style" with the circumstances [36–38]. Children
of the upper class usually learn the speech forms of the lower groups
from their playmates in the schoolyard.

Diffusion from "high" to "low" is clearly observable in features
first adopted by the upper class from Standard German, as pinsel for
pämsel "brush," chirchə for chilchə "church," sōn for sūn "son,"
buttər for ankchə, schinkchə for hammə "ham" [41–42].

Spreading from "low" to "higher," though deliberately resisted
by the upper class, is not unknown, especially in recent times. Thus
the phonological type of miuch is replacing milch "milk," fingə is
encroaching upon fində "find," and i gā is taking the place of i gangə
"I am going" among the middle class. Even the children of the upper
class are adopting these "low" variants, which are supported by the
usage of the countryside [44–46]. For the dissemination of two of
these features in Swiss folk speech see Hotzenköcherle 1965: Maps
2.148 folge and 2.119 finden.

Baumgartner summarizes the linguistic dynamics of the Mittelland
and the Unterland of the canton of Bern in an interesting diagram
[102]. From the city of Bern, with a population of 125,000 in 1940,
upper class features spread in all directions to the upper classes in
the smaller cities—northward to Biel and Solothurn, southward to
Thun, and westward to Freiburg. In these subsidiary centers they
infiltrate the lower social levels and may ultimately find their way
into the surrounding villages.

11.28 Recent Phonological Innovations in Vienna

The popular speech of Vienna (Wiernerisch), a variety of Central
Bavarian similar to that of Munich, has been the object of careful
analysis from the structural point of view for half a century. It is
spoken in the homes of most native Viennese, regularly used in

public by the lower and middle classes, and of course familiar to those among the upper classes who no longer speak it in their homes. This vernacular, often referred to fondly as echt Wienerisch, has been the vehicle of popular plays and songs for many years.

In the schools of Vienna a very different kind of German has been taught since the middle of the nineteenth century: the literary language (Schriftsprache), which is based upon the dialects spoken in east central Germany. As a result, all Viennes are bidialectal in one way or another. Some normally speak the vernacular but readily understand school-taught German; others have full mastery of both dialects and use them at will in accordance with the circumstances; others again understand the vernacular but habitually speak a variety of Standard German. All of them read the Schriftsprache in the daily press and other publications, however they may pronounce the printed word.

The phonological structure of the Viennese vernacular has been briefly outlined above [8.6]. Here we shall consider some of the changes in the system of syllabics that have occurred since the turn of the century or are now taking place. They are discussed by E. Kranzmayer in a spirited article entitled Lautwandlungen und Lautverschiebungen im gegenwärtigen Wienerischen [1953].

At the turn of the century, the Viennese vernacular had a symmetrical four-level system of oral monophthongs. The author calls this stage of the dialect Altwienerisch [209]. By the time of the First World War, the monophthongization of the syllabics in weit, Maul, Haus among the younger generation produced the five-level system of oral monophthongs described by A. Pfalz [1918] and reported by B. J. Koekoek [1953: 12] as characteristic of the older generation in midcentury.

The Five-level System of Oral Monophthongs

high	i	ü	u	/ widə	ghü	dsux /
				"again	cool	train"
mid close	e	ö	o	/ bet	hö	offm /
	ɨ	ɨ		"bed	hell	open"
mid open	ȩ	ọ̈	ọ	/ sȩŋ	šdọ̈n	họs /
				"see	steal	hare"
over open	æ	œ	ɔ	/ wæd	mœ	hɔs /
				"wide	mouth	house"
low		a		/ has /		
				"hot"		

A generation later—at the time of the Second World War—the symmetry of this five-level system was "shattered." While contrastive close / o / and open / ǫ / were preserved, the close front vowels / e / and / ö / were merged in the open vowels / ę / and / ö̧ /, respectively, as shown by the arrows in the vowel diagram above. How this asymmetry, this "hole" in the system, was mended is discussed at length by the author [219ff.].

Kranzmayer attributes the merging of the two sets of mid front vowels to the influence of Standard German (Hochsprache), taught in the schools of Vienna, but without analyzing the complicated background. A simple listing of the conflicting correspondences between Standard German (SG) and the Viennese vernacular (W) in typical words reveals the problems faced by the teacher of SG:

SG / e /:	Bett	Brett	Hexe	recht	Eltern	stellen	helfen	hell
W	e	ē	ę	ę̄	ö	ȫ	ö̧	ȫ̧

SG / ē /:	Segen	sehen	betet	Seele
W	ē	ę̄	ę	ȫ̧

SG / ö /:	Köpfe	Hölle
W	e	ȫ

SG / ȫ /:	schön	Flöhe
W	ē	ę̄

Under the circumstances the teacher would presumably tell his pupils to pronounce the vowels in accordance with the spelling, sounding the graphemes e, eh, ä, äh without rounding the lips and the graphemes ö, öh with rounding. In the process the distinction between close and open mid front vowels would be eliminated in reading Standard German texts—whence ultimately also in the vernacular of the younger generation.

Two other changes in the phonemic structure of Wienerisch were in progress by 1950: denasalization of nasal syllabics as in hin / hĩ /, schön / šẽ /, Bein / bã /, Sohn / sũ / [231].

Kranzmayer is inclined to attribute denasalization to "Czech infiltration" [233]; and yet, a similar change has recently taken place in the Central Bavarian dialect of Munich [Kufner 1962: 71–73], where such an influence is unthinkable. Why not simply the effect of school-taught Standard German?

The merging of the strong postvocalic fricative / ff, ss, xx /, as in offen, wissen, machen, with their weak counterparts, as in Ofen, Wiesen, weihen, is even more recent. It is said to occur in the speech of less than 15 percent of persons under 25 and to vary from word to word [227–28].

Kranzmayer links these striking changes in the phonology of Wienerisch since ca. 1900 to the social upheavals resulting from the two World Wars. The impoverishment of the linguistically conservative upper classes are said to have given free rein to trends inherent in the Wienerisch of the lower classes and to the intrusion of features of Standard German. This seems plausible enough as a general theory. And yet, some of the author's attributions to specific social forces and to certain inherent linguistic drives, advanced with no little enthusiasm, fail to carry conviction. Disagreeing sharply with the views of the Sprachatlas group at Marburg, he underrates diffusion through communication and overstates the case of parallel spontaneous phonological change emanating from drives inherent in the phonological system, which he calls "polygenesis."

The author's challenging presentation of striking phonological changes in the former capital of the Austro-Hungarian Monarchy lays the foundation for planning a systematic sampling survey of the speech of Vienna in its social and regional manifestations. The 500 informants interviewed by the author over a three-year period [200]—representing different age groups and several social classes in the 21 wards of the metropolis—could hardly provide the evidence required for a detailed description of the varieties of German current among social and age groups in the several wards (Bezirke) of the city. A set questionnaire levelled at known or expected variants and a systematic selection of representative speakers are essential in dealing with complex linguistic situations.

11.29 Phonological Variants in the Speech of Young Parisians

In 1957 R. Reichstein sampled the usage of 556 girls enrolled in public and private schools of 5 of the 20 wards (arrondissements) of Paris with respect to three variable phonological features: (1) preservation or loss of contrastive low front and low back $/ \acute{a} \neq \grave{a} /$, as in pattes "paws" vs. pâtes "pastries"; (2) preservation or loss of contrastive short and long $/ \varepsilon \neq \bar{\varepsilon} /$, as in belle "beautiful" vs. bêle "bleats"; (3) preservation or loss of contrastive unrounded and rounded $/ \tilde{\varepsilon} \neq \tilde{œ} /$, as in brin "stalk" vs. brun "brown."

The examples were presented to the informants on slips in such sentences as il march à quatre pattes "he walks on all four" and il mange des pâtes "he eats pastries." They read the sentences and then repeated them by heart.

The informants were assigned to three social levels on the basis of the occupations of their fathers [84]. In the statistical treatment of the responses only the usage of the daughters of "professionals" and of "workingmen" are taken into account, the middle group being set aside. Even with this drastic simplification of the statistical problem the results of the investigation are highly significant.

These are Miss Reichstein's chief findings:

(1) The preservation of the three contrastive pairs of syllabics differs markedly from ward to ward, being consistently highest in Ward 16 and lowest in Ward 18 [71].

(2) In the total sample of 556 informants, the preservation of contrastive / á ≠ à / ranges from 72 to 43 percent; that of / ɛ ≠ ɛ̄ / from 58 to 23 percent; that of / ɛ̄ ≠ œ̃ / from 30 to 10 percent. It is suggested that the isolated quantitative distinction represented in / ɛ ≠ ɛ̄ / and the small "functional load" of / ɛ̄ ≠ œ̃ / favor the loss of these two contrasts.

(3) There are marked differences between the social extremes and between pupils in public and private schools [85–86], but without any clear-cut pattern from ward to ward.

(4) The preservation of contrastive / á ≠ à / varies from word to word, being 50 percent in pattes vs. pâtes but only 10 percent in rat "rat" vs. ras "shaved" [61].

This may be enough to suggest the complexity of the social and regional behavior of the variants of the three Parisian features investigated by the author. It is more than likely that phonological changes in progress in such cities as Vienna and New York exhibit similar complexities in their social and regional dissemination.

Reichstein rests content with a statistical analysis of the linguistic data in their relation to social groups and schooling in the 5 wards of Paris she chose for investigation—and wisely so. As A. Martinet points out in his concluding remarks to this article [96–99], all of the 20 wards of Paris as well as the suburbs will have to be investigated before the social drives and the controlling structural factors can be established with some degree of probability.

11.3 Concluding Remarks

In recent years there has been a quickening interest in social dialects and the relations between different languages spoken within political domains, and in determining their relations to social structures and sociocultural forces. In America such publications as those of C. A. Ferguson [1959], D. Hymes [1964], J. Gumperz and D. Hymes [1964], and W. Bright [1966] bear witness to a spirited discussion of a field of research that lay all but dormant for the two or three decades devoted to the structural analysis of a great variety of languages and the refinement of appropriate theories and techniques for the pursuit of purely synchronic studies.

The results achieved in structural linguistics will be an invaluable asset in dealing with the complicated problems of social dialectology. It is obvious that the differences between the dialects current in a community or area must be identified as structural and substructural, and that incidental variants must be evaluated as such if the description of the dialects is to be meaningful, i.e., scientifically sound. Whether the study of language in a variety of social settings will lead to modifications of some of the concepts underlying synchronic structural linguistics remains to be seen.

The student of social dialects has also at his disposal the theories and the results of diachronic linguistics, a major achievement of the nineteenth century. Here the central concept is the regularity of phonemic change as finally formulated by the Neo-Grammarians. Based upon regular phonemic correspondences existing between several stages of one and the same language or between languages of the same linguistic stock, it implies the recognition of the fact, so clearly demonstrated by synchronic linguistics, that every language or dialect is structured phonemically. Being so structured, it is to be expected that the units of the phonemic system will change in the same way in all the morphemes in which they occur, unless prosodic factors or cross influences in the grammatical or derivational system interfere. Deviations from the normal change of a phoneme that cannot be accounted for by such internal processes are attributable to external influence, i.e., to adoption from another language or dialect. Unless the student of social dialects chooses to be content with a purely synchronic description, he will rely upon the theory of the regularity of phonemic change to distinguish between internal developments and importations.

Since the adoption or adaptation of features of another dialect is a common phenomenon, the dialectologist is in a strategic position to elucidate the nature of such processes and the social conditions underlying them. He may even be able to demonstrate that under certain circumstances regular phonemic change can result from consistent replacement of a native phoneme by that of a dominant dialect.

Some of the techniques that have been employed in determining the geographic (spatial) dissemination of dialect features and their interpretation are directly applicable to research in social dialectology, and others can be rather easily adapted, such as preliminary sampling, the construction of a questionnaire, the conduct of the interview, the determination of correlations between speech areas and sociocultural domains leading up to historical interpretation. But some innovations and refinements in procedure are required, especially a prior investigation of the social structure of the area or community on which the choice of representative informants must be based. Recording on tape of elicited responses as well as spontaneous conversation or narration will play a major part in coping with the usage of bidialectal speakers.

Although little systematic work has been done in social dialectology, awareness of the currency of two or more social dialects in one and the same community or geographic area has of course not been wanting. In German-speaking Europe three major levels, more or less clearly defined area by area, are generally recognized [Henzen 1938: esp. 179–94; Moser 1960]: (1) cultivated speech (Hochsprache), which tends to approximate the national standard taught in the schools; (2) folk speech (Mundart), peculiar to the farming population and to country folk in general, which is used in the home and in dealing with one's neighbors; (3) regional colloquial speech (Umgangssprache, Verkehrssprache), which serves as the medium of informal public communication within a major dialect area or political domain.

The relation between these three social levels of speech varies strikingly from area to area. Thus in Switzerland regional colloquial speech is rather clearly set off from cultivated and from folk speech. Here many a native is tridialectal, using each dialect in its proper social setting. In Württemberg, Bavaria, and Austria the situation is similar, although folk speech is not as widely used as in Switzerland. Also in Scotland three social dialects are current: folk speech, standard Scots, and standard English [Grant 1921: xx–xxii; McIntosh 1952: 28–33].

Many of the problems with which research in social dialectology is faced are also encountered by the student of bilingual communities, such as the correlation between the several languages with social groups, the conditions that prompt the choice of the medium of communication on the part of bilingual speakers, and diffusion from one medium to the other.

Since the lines are more sharply drawn between languages than between dialects, the student of bilingual areas has certain advantages in dealing with such problems. For this reason it seems highly probable that the social dialectologist can improve his techniques and interpretations by keeping in touch with research now underway in the field of bilingualism.

Bibliography

The bibliography is highly selective. Included are (1) the many works to which reference is made in the text; (2) publications in which methodological principles are discussed or applied to specific problems; (3) books and articles on the several language areas containing a wealth of bibliographical information.

Abbreviations

ACLS:	American Council of Learned Societies
AS:	American Speech
BSLP:	Bul. de la Soc. de Linguistique de Paris
DDG:	Deutsche Dialektgeographie
JEGP:	Journal of English and Germanic Philology
Lang.:	Language, Journal of the Linguistic Society of America
Orbis:	Bulletin International de Documentation Linguistique
PADS:	Publications of the American Dialect Society
PBB:	Beiträge zur Geschichte der deutschen Sprache
PMLA:	Publications of the Modern Language Association of America
SSRC:	Social Science Research Council
TAPA:	Transactions of the American Philological Association
TPS:	Transactions of the Philological Society (London)
Word,	Journal of the Linguistic Circle of New York
ZMF:	Zeitschrift für Mundartforschung
ZRP:	Zeitschrift für Romanische Philologie (Halle)

Allen, H. B., Minor Dialect Areas of the Upper Midwest. PADS 30.3–16 (1958).

-----, The Primary Dialect Areas of the Upper Midwest: Readings in Applied English Linguistics (ed. Allen), 31–41. New York, 1964.

Arndt, W., Ein Ansatz zur strukturellen Gliederung der deutschen Dialekte. Phonetica 9 (1963).

Atwood, E. B., A Survey of Verb Forms in the Eastern United States. Ann Arbor, Mich., 1953.

-----, The Regional Vocabulary of Texas. Austin, Tex., 1962.

-----, The Methods of American Dialectology. ZMF 30.1–30. [Transl. by F. Schindler: pp. 565–600 in L. E. Schmitt, Germanische Dialektologie, 1968.]

Avis, W. F., The Mid-back Vowels in the English of the Eastern United States. U. of Mich. diss., 1955.

-----, The New England "Short o": A Recessive Phoneme. Language 37.544–58 (1961).

Babbitt, E. H., The English of the Lower Classes in New York City and Vicinity. Dialect Notes 1.459–64 (1896).

Babington, M. and E. B. Atwood, Lexical Usage in Southern Louisiana. PADS No. 36 1–24 (1961).

Bach, A., Deutsche Mundartforschung: Ihre Wege, Ergebnisse und Aufgaben. Heidelberg, 1950.

Baldinger, K., Die Herausbildung der Sprachräume auf der Pyrenäenhalbinsel. Berlin, 1958.

Bartoli, M., Introduzione alla neolinguistica. Geneva, 1925.

Baugh, C. A., A History of the English Language. New York, 1957.

Baumgartner, H., Stadtmundart und Landmundart: Beiträge zur bernischen Mundartgeographie. Bern, 1940.

Bertoni, G., Profilo linguistico d'Italia. Rome, 1940.

Beranek, F. J., Die Umgangssprache und ihre Erforschung. Muttersprache 1950: 65–71.

Birnbaum, H. and J. Puhvel, Conference on Indo-European Linguistics: Ancient Indo-European Dialects. Berkeley, Calif., 1966.

Blancquaert, E., Na meer dan 25 jaar dialect-onderzoek op het terrein. Tongeren, 1948.

-----, Taalgeografie. Grootaers Album, 71–80. Leuven, 1950.

Bloch, B., The Treatment of Middle English Final and Preconsonantal R in the Present-day Speech of New England. Brown Univ. diss., 1935.

-----, Interviewing for the Linguistic Atlas. AS 10.3–9 (1935).

-----, see Kurath-Bloch 1939 and 1939–43.

Bloomfield, L., Language. New York, 1933.

Boas, F., Race, Language and Culture. (Pp. 199–225 contain reprints of papers on language). New York, 1940.

Bohnenberger, K., Über die Ostgrenze des Alemannischen:
Tatsächliches und Grundsätzliches. PBB 52.217–91 (1928).
-----, Die schwäbisch-fränkische Sprachgrenze um Jagst und
Kocher. Würtembergische Jahrbücher 1932–33.
-----, Die alemannischen Mundarten. Tübingen, 1953.
Bonfante, G., The Neolinguistic Position. Lang. 23.344–75 (1947).
-----, History and the Italian Dialects. Pp. 84–108 in Dialektologen-
kongress (1967–68).
Bottiglioni, G., Atlante Linguistico Etnographico Italiano della
Corsica. Pisa, 1933–42.
-----, Linguistic Geography. Pp. 255–67 in Martinet-Weinreich
1954.
Bremer, O., Politische Geschichte und Sprachgeschichte. Hist.
Vierteljahrschrift 5.315–46 (1902).
Bright, W., ed., Sociolinguistics: Proceedings of the UCLA Socio-
linguistic Conference. The Hague, 1965.
Bronstein, A., Let's Take Another Look at New York City Speech.
AS 37.13–26 (1962).
Brugmann, K., Kurze vergleichende Grammatik der indogermanischen
Sprachen. Strassburg, 1904.
Brunot, F. and C. Bruneau, Précise de grammaire historique de la
langue française. Paris, 1949.
Cassidy, F. G., Some New England Words in Wisconsin. Lang.
17.324–39 (1941).
Catalan, D., ed., see Estructuralismo e historia.
Catford, J. C., Vowel Systems of Scots Dialects. TPS 1958: pp.
107–17.
-----, The Linguistic Survey of Scotland. Orbis 6.105–21 (1957).
Cochran, G. R., The Australian English Vowels as a Diasystem.
Word 15.69–88 (1959).
Cohen, M., Pour une sociologie du language. Paris, 1956.
Conference on Non-English Speech in the United States, ed. H. Kurath.
ACLS Bulletin No. 34. Washington, 1942.
Congrès de Dialectologie, ed. A. J. Van Windekens. Louvain, 1964.
Coseriu, E., La geografía lingüistica. Montevideo, 1956.
Dauzat, A., La géographie linguistique. Paris, 1922.
-----, Les patois: évolution, classification, étude. Paris, 1927.
Davis, A. L., A Word Atlas of the Great Lakes Region. Univ. of
Michigan diss., 1948.
----- and R. I. McDavid, "Shivaree": an Example of Cultural
Diffusion. AS 24.249–55 (1949).
----- and -----, Northwestern Ohio: A Transition Area. Lang.
26.264–73 (1950).
Dearden, E. J., Dialect Areas of the South Atlantic States as Deter-
mined by Variation in Vocabulary. Brown Univ. diss., 1943.

Debus, F., Die deutschen Bezeichnungen für die Heiratsverhältnisse. Deutsche Wortforschung, ed. L. E. Schmitt, 1.2–116. Giessen, 1958.

DeCamp, D., The Speech of the San Francisco Metropolitan Area. Univ. of Calif. (Berkeley) diss., 1953.

Devoto, G., Profilo di storia linguistica Italiana. Florence, 1960.

Dialektologenkongress, see Schmitt 1967–68.

Dillon, M., Linguistic Borrowing and Historical Evidence. Lang. 21.12–17 (1945).

Doroszewski, W., Pour une représentation statistique des isoglosses. BSLP 36.28–42 (1935).

-----, Structural Linguistics and Dialect Geography. Proceedings of Intern. Congress of Ling., ed. E. Sivertsen. Oslo, 1958.

Downer, J. W., Features of the New England Rustic Pronunciation in James Russell Lowell's Biglow Papers. Univ. of Mich. diss., 1958.

Dozier, E. P., Linguistic Acculturation. Pp. 509–20 in Hymes 1964.

Eliason, N. E., Tarheel Talk. Chapel Hill, N. C., 1956.

Emeneau, M. B., India as a Linguistic Area. Lang. 32.3–16 (1956).

-----, Bilingualism and Structural Borrowing. Proc. Am. Philosophical Society 106.430–42.

Entwistle, W. J., The Spanish Language together with Portuguese, Catalan and Basque. London, 1936.

Espinosa, A. M., Estudios sobre el español de Nuevo Méjico. Buenos Aires, 1930.

Estructuralismo e historia: Miscelánea homenaje a André Martinet, ed. D. Catalan. Madrid, 1957–58.

Ettmayer, K., Über das Wesen der Dialektbildung, erläutert an den Dialekten Frankreichs. Ak. der Wiss. in Wien, phil.-hist. Klasse, vol. 66, Abh. 3 (1924).

Ferguson, C. A., Diglossia. Word 15.325–40 (1959).

-----, Directions in Sociolinguistics: Report on an Interdisciplinary Seminar. SSR Council: Item 19 (1965).

Firth, J. R., On Social Linguistics. Pp. 66–70 in Hymes, Culture and Society. New York, 1964.

Fishman, J., Readings in the Sociology of Language. 1968.

Flórez, L., El español en Colombia y su Atlas Lingüístico. Thesaurus 18.268–356 (1963).

For Roman Jakobson, ed. E. Pulgram. The Hague, 1957.

Forschungsinstitut für deutsche Sprache: Jahresberichte. Marburg, 1961– .

Fourquet, J., Linguistique structurale et dialectologie. Fragen und Forschungen: Festgabe Frings, 190–203. Berlin, 1956.

-----, Phonologie und Dialektgeographie. ZMF 26.161–73 (1958).

Fragen und Forschungen: Festgabe Frings. Berlin, 1956.

Frank, Y. H., The Speech of New York City. Univ. of Mich. diss., 1948.

Fries, C. C., American English Grammar. New York, 1940.

Frings, T., Germania Romana (Mitteldeutsche Studien, Heft 2). Halle, 1932.

-----, Grundlegung einer Geschichte der deutschen Sprache, ed. 2. Halle, 1950.

-----, Sprache und Geschichte, parts I–III. Halle, 1956. [Contains reprints of papers published 1922 ff.]

Gamillscheg, E., Romania Germanica. Berlin, 1934–36.

-----, Die Sprachgeographie und ihre Ergebnisse für die allgemeine Sprachwissenschaft. Bielefeld-Leipzig, 1928.

Gauchat, L., Gibt es Mundartgrenzen? Arch. f. d. Studium d. neueren Sprachen 111.365–403 (1904).

-----, L'unité phonétique dans le patois d'une commune. Halle, 1905.

Gauchat, L., J. Jeanjaquet and E. Tappolet, Tableaux phonétiques des patois swisses romands. Neuchâtel, 1925.

Geiger, P., and R. Weiss, Atlas der schweizerischen Volkskunde. Zurich, 1950 ff.

Germanische Dialektologie, see Schmitt 1968.

Gilliéron, J., Généalogie des mots désignant l'abeille. Paris, 1918.

-----, Patologie et thérapeutique verbale. Paris, 1918.

-----, La faillite de l'étymologie phonétique. Paris, 1919.

----- and E. Edmont, Atlas linguistique de la France. Paris, 1902–10.

Gladwin, T. and W. C. Sturtevant, eds., Anthropology and Human Behavior. Washington, D. C., 1962.

Goossens, J., Zur Geschichte der niederländischen Dialektologie. Pp. 180–208 in Germanische Dialektologie.

Grammont, M., Traité de phonétique. Paris, 1933.

Grant, W., and J. M. Dixon, Manual of Modern Scots. Cambridge, 1921.

Greenberg, J. H., Essays in Linguistics. Chicago, 1957.

Griera, A., Cinquante années de dialectologie romane. Orbis 7.347–56 (1958).

Grootaers Album. Leuven, 1950.

Gumperz, J. and D. Hymes, eds., The Ethnography of Communication. American Anthropologist, Special Publications, vol. 66, no. 6, part 2.

Haag, K., Sieben Sätze über Sprachbewegung. ZfhdMa 1.138 (1900).

-----, Sprachwandel im Lichte der Mundartgrenzen. Teuthonista 6.1–35 (1929).

Haden, E. F., and E. A. Joliat, Le genre grammatical des substantifs en Franco-Canadien empruntés à l'anglais. PMLA 55.839–54 (1940).

Haeringen, C. B. van, Dialectologie en Etymologie. Grootaers Album 107–15 (1950).

Hall, R. A. Jr., The Papal States in Italian Linguistic History. Lang. 19.125–40 (1943).

-----, The Linguistic Position of Franco-Povençal. Lang. 25.1–14 (1949).

-----, A Note on "Gorgia Toscana." Italica 26.65–71 (1949).

-----, Pidgin and Creole Languages. Ithaca, N. Y., 1966.

Hankey, C. T., A Colorado Word Geography. PADS 34 (1960).

Hanley, M. L., "Serenade" in New England. AS 8.24–6 (1933).

Harris, R. S., New England Words for the Earthworm. AS 8.12–17 (1933).

-----, The Speech of Rhode Island. Brown Univ. diss., 1937.

Haugen, E., Problems of Linguistic Research among Scandinavian Immigrants in America. Conference on Non-English Speech 35–57 (1942).

-----, The Analysis of Linguistic Borrowing. Lang. 26.210–31 (1950).

-----, The Norwegian Language in America: A Study in Bilingual Behavior. Philadelphia, 1953.

-----, Bilingualism in the Americas: A Bibliography and Research Guide. PADS 26 (1956).

Hawkins, J. D., The Speech of the Hudson River Valley. Brown Univ. diss., 1941.

Heeroma, K. H., Dialectologie en Taalgeschiedenis. Grootaers Album 187–203 (1950).

----- and K. Fokkema, Structuurgeografie. Amsterdam, 1961.

Hempl, G., Language Rivalry and Speech Differentiation in the Case of Race Mixture. TAPA 29.31–47 (1898).

Henzen, W., Schriftsprache und Mundart. Zurich-Leipzig, 1938 (ed. 2, 1954).

Hertzler, J. O., A Sociology of Language. New York, 1965.

Hirt, H., Handbuch des Urgermanischen, vol. II. Heidelberg, 1932.

Hoff, I., Historisch-phonematische Mundartkarten. Pp. 373–87 in Dialektologenkongress (1967–68).

Höfler, O., Stammbaumtheorie, Wellentheorie, Entfaltungstheorie. PBB 77 and 78 (1955–56).

Hoenigswald, H. M., Language Change and Linguistic Reconstruction. Chicago, 1960.

Hoijer, H., Linguistic and Cultural Change. Lang. 24.335–45 (1948).

-----, ed., Language in Culture, Am. Anthrop. Assn. Memoir No. 79. Menasha, Wis., 1954.

-----, Anthropological Linguistics. Pp. 110–27 in Trends in
European and American Linguistics, ed. Mohrman. Utrecht-
Antwerp, 1961.

Hotzenköcherle, R., Zur Raumstruktur des Schweizerdeutschen.
ZMF 28.207–27 (1961).

-----, Einführung in den Sprachatlas der deutschen Schweiz. Bern,
1962.

----- and others, Sprachatlas der deutschen Schweiz. Bern, 1962ff.

Hubbell, A. F., The Pronunciation of English in New York City. New
York, 1950.

Hymes, D., ed., Language in Culture and Society. New York, 1964.

Iordan, I., Einführung in die Geschichte und Methoden der
romanischen Sprachwissenschaft. [Transl. of original of 1932,
revised and supplemented by W. Bahner.] Berlin, 1962.

Ivic, P., On the Structure of Dialectal Differentiation. Word 18.33–
53 (1962).

Jaberg, K., Sprachtradition und Sprachwandel. Bern, 1932.

-----, Aspects géographiques du language. Paris, 1936.

----- and J. Jud, Transkriptionsverfahren . . . bei Mundartenauf-
nahmen. ZRP 47.171–218 (1927).

-----, Der Sprachatlas als Forschungsinstrument. Halle, 1928.

-----, Sprach- und Sachatlas Italiens und der Südschweiz. Zofingen,
1928–40.

Jakobson, R., Sur la théorie des affinités phonologiques entre les
langues. Appendix, 351–65, in Troubetzkoy 1949.

-----, Principes de phonologie historique. Appendix, 315–36, in
Troubetzkoy 1949.

Jensen, M., Regionalism in America. Madison, Wis., 1951.

Jespersen, O., A Modern English Grammar, part I. Heidelberg,
1909 [reprinted 1922].

-----, Nation and Individual from a Linguistic Point of View. Oslo-
Leipzig, 1925.

Joos, M., Readings in Linguistics. Washington, 1957.

Jud, J., La valeur documentaire de l'Atlas Linguistique de l'Italie.
Rev. de Ling. Romane 15–16. 251–89 (1928).

-----, see Jaberg-Jud.

Kahane, H. R., Designations of the Cheek in the Italian Dialects.
Lang. 17.212–22 (1941).

Keniston, H., Notes on Research in the Spanish spoken in the United
States. Pp. 63–67 in Conf. on Non-English Speech (1942).

Kiddle, L. B., The Spanish Language as a Medium of Cultural
Diffusion in the Age of Discovery. AS 27.241–56 (1952).

Kimmerle, M. M. and R. I. McDavid, Jr., Problems of Linguistic
Geography in the Rocky Mountain Area. Western Humanities
Review 5.249–64 (1951).

Kloeke, G. G., De Hollandsche Expansie. The Hague, 1927.
-----, Taalatlas van Noord- en Zuid-Nederland. Leiden, 1939 ff.
-----, Herkomst en Groei van het Afrikaans. Leiden, 1950.
Kloss, H., Die Entwicklung neuer germanischer Kultursprachen von 1800 bis 1950. Munich, 1952.
Kluge, F., Von Luther bis Lessing. Leipzig, 1918.
Koekoek, B. J., Zur Phonologie der Wiener Mundart. Giessen, 1955.
Kolb, E., Linguistic Atlas of England: Phonological Atlas of the Northern Region. Bern, 1966.
Krahe, H., Sprache und Vorzeit. Heidelberg, 1954.
Kranzmayer, E., Die Namen der Wochentage in den Mundarten von Bayern und Österreich. Wien-München, 1929.
-----, Lautwandlungen und Lautverschiebungen im gegenwärtigen Wienerischen. ZMF 21.197–239 (1952).
-----, Historische Lautgeographie des gesamtbairischen Dialektraumes. Wien, 1956.
Kranzmayer Festschrift, see Schmitt 1967.
Krapp, G. P., The English Language in America. New York, 1925.
Kretschmer, P., Wortgeographie der deutschen Umgangssprache. Göttingen, 1918.
Kroeber, A. L., ed., Anthropology Today. Chicago, 1953.
Krüger, F., Die Hochpyrenäen. Hamburg, 1935–39.
Kufner, H. L., Zur Phonologie einer mittelbairischen Mundart. ZMF 25.175–84 (1957).
-----, Strukturelle Grammatik der Münchner Stadtmundart. München, 1961.
-----, Lautwandel und Lautersatz in der Münchner Stadtsprache. ZMF 29.67–75 (1962).
-----, Lautbibliothek No. 35. Göttingen, 1964.
Kuhn, A., Sechzig Jahre Sprachgeographie in der Romania. Rom. Jahrbuch 1.25–63 (1947–48).
-----, Die romanischen Sprachen. Bern, 1951.
Kuiper, F. B. J., The Genesis of a Linguistic Area. Indo-Iranian Journal 10.81–102 (1967).
Kurath, H., The Linguistic Atlas of the United States. See Schrijnen 1933: 90–95.
-----, New England Words for the Seesaw. AS 8.14–18 (1933).
-----, Dialect Areas, Settlement Areas, and Culture Areas in the United States. In C. F. Ware, ed., The Cultural Approach to History, 331–45. New York, 1940.
-----, ed., Conference on Non-English Speech in the United States. ACLS Bull. No. 34. Washington, 1942.
-----, German Relics in Pennsylvania German. Monatshefte für deutschen Unterricht 37.96–102 (1945).

-----, A Word Geography of the Eastern United States. Ann Arbor, Mich., 1949 [reprint 1966].

-----, Linguistic Regionalism. In Jensen 1951: 297–310.

-----, Middle English Dictionary: Plan and Bibliography. Ann Arbor, Mich., 1954.

-----, The Binary Interpretation of English Vowels. Lang. 33.111–22 (1957).

-----, Review of Mitzka, Deutscher Wortatlas, vols. 1–4. Lang. 34.428–34 (1958).

-----, Review of L. E. Schmitt, Deutsche Wortforschung in europäischen Bezügen. Lang. 36.441–50 (1960).

-----, Phonemics and Phonics in Historical Phonology. AS 36.93–100 (1961).

-----, Interrelation between Regional and Social Dialects. Ninth Intern. Congress of Linguists, ed. H. G. Lunt, pp. 135–44. The Hague, 1964.

-----, British Sources of Selected Features of American Pronunciation: Problems and Methods. In Honor of Daniel Jones, ed. Abercrombie, pp. 146–55. London, 1964.

-----, A Phonology and Prosody of Modern English. Heidelberg and Ann Arbor, 1964.

-----, Die Lautgestalt einer Kärntner Mundart und ihre Geschichte. Wiesbaden, 1965.

-----, Contributions of British Folk Speech to American Pronunciation. Studies in Honor of Harold Orton, ed. Stanley Ellis, pp. 129–34. Leeds, 1968.

-----, The Investigation of Urban Speech. PADS No. 49 (1970).

----- and B. Bloch, Handbook of the Linguistic Geography of New England. ACLS and Brown University, Providence, R. I., 1939.

-----, M. L. Hanley, B. Bloch, G. S. Lowman, Jr., and M. L. Hansen, Linguistic Atlas of New England. 734 Maps in 3 vols. ACLS and Brown University, Providence, R. I., 1939–43.

----- and R. I. McDavid, Jr., The Pronunciation of English in the Atlantic States. Ann Arbor, Mich., 1961.

Labov, W., The Social Motivation of a Sound Change. Word 19.273–309 (1963).

-----, The Social Stratification of English in New York City. Washington, 1966.

-----, Hypercorrection by the Lower Middle Class as a Factor in Linguistic Change. Pp. 84–113 in W. Bright, Sociolinguistics. The Hague, 1966.

Ladefoged, P., The Value of Phonetic Statements. Lang. 36.387–96 (1960).

Lambert, M. B., A Dictionary of the Non-English Words of the
    Pennsylvania German Dialect. Norristown, Pa., 1924.
Lane, G. S., Notes on Louisiana French. Lang. 10.323–33 (1934).
Larsen, V. S., A Working Bibliography of English Dialect Geography
    in America. Mimeograph. Chicago, 1961.
Lautbibliothek der deutschen Mundarten, ed. E. Zwirner. Heraus-
    gegeben vom Deutschen Spracharchiv. Göttingen, 1958 ff.
Lerch, E., Über das sprachliche Verhältnis von Ober- zu Unter-
    schicht. Jb. f. Philologie 1.70–124.
Lehmann, W., The Grouping of the Germanic Languages. In H.
    Birnbaum and J. Puhvel, eds., Ancient Indo-European Dialects,
    13–27. Calif. University Press, 1966.
le Roux, T. H., Afrikaanse Taalstudies (ed. 4). Pretoria, 1946.
Lindgren, K. B., Die Ausbreitung der neuhochdeutschen Diphthongie-
    rung. Helsinki, 1961.
Lowman, G. S. Jr., Sampling Survey of the Southern Counties of
    England, 1937. [Collections of the LA of the USA.]
Luick, K., Historische Grammatik der englischen Sprache. Leipzig,
    1914–27.
Lunt, H. G., ed., Proceedings of the Ninth International Congress of
    Linguists. The Hague, 1964.
Malkiel, Y., Distinctive Traits of Romance Linguistics. In Hymes
    1964: pp. 671–88.
Malmberg, B., L'español dans le nouveau monde. Studia Linguistica
    1.79–116, 2.1–36 (1947–48).
Marckwardt, A. H., Review of H. Kurath and others, Linguistic Atlas
    of New England, vol. I, and Handbook of the Linguistic Geography
    of New England. Lang. 16.257–61 (1940).
-----, Principal and Subsidiary Dialect Areas in the North-Central
    States. PADS 27.3–15 (1957).
-----, American English. New York, 1958.
-----, ed., Studies in Languages and Linguistics in Honor of Charles
    C. Fries. Ann Arbor, Mich., 1963.
Martinet, A., Celtic Lenition and Western Romance Consonants.
    Lang. 28.192–217 (1952).
-----, Diffusion of Languages and Structural Linguistics. Rom. Phil.
    6.5–13 (1952).
-----, Economie des changements phonétiques. Bern, 1955.
----- and U. Weinreich, eds., Linguistics Today. New York, 1954.
Maurer, F., Volkssprache. Beiheft 9 of Wirkendes Wort. Düsseldorf,
    1964.
McDavid, R. I. Jr., Dialect Geography and Social Science Problems.
    Social Forces 25.168–72 (1946).
-----, Postvocalic /r/ in South Carolina: A Social Analysis. AS
    23.149–203 (1948).

-----, The Relationship of the Speech of American Negroes to the
Speech of Whites. A̲S̲ 26.3–17 (1951).

-----, / h / before Semivowels in the Eastern United States. Lang.
28.41–62 (1952).

-----, The Dialects of American English. In W. N. Francis, The
Structure of American English, 480–543. New York, 1954.

-----, The Position of the Charleston Dialect. PADS 23.35–49
(1955).

-----, The Second Round in Dialectology of North American English.
JCLA 6.108–15 (1960).

-----, Structural Linguistics and Linguistic Geography. Orbis 10.
35–46 (1961).

-----, Dialectal Differences and Social Differences in an Urban
Society. In Bright 1965.

-----, Sense and Nonsense about American Dialects. PMLA 81.7–
17 (1966).

-----, see A. L. Davis 1950.

-----, see M. M. Kimmerle 1951.

-----, see Kurath-McDavid 1961.

-----, see H. L. Mencken 1963.

-----, W. M. Austin and others, Communication Barriers to the
Culturally Deprived: Research Project 2107 of the Office of
Education. Typescript. Chicago, 1966.

McDavid, Virginia, Regional and Social Differences in the Grammar
of American English. Univ. of Minn. diss. (1950).

McIntosh, A., An Introduction to a Survey of Scottish Dialects.
Edinburgh, 1952.

-----, A New Approach to Middle English Dialectology. English
Studies 44.1–11 (1963).

Meillet, A., Les dialectes Indo-Européens. Paris, 1907.

-----, La méthode comparative en linguistique historique. Oslo,
1925.

-----, Linguistique historique et linguistique générale. Paris, 1965
[reprint].

Mencken, H. L., The American Language. Abridged, annotated, and
supplemented by R. I. McDavid, Jr. New York, 1963.

Menéndez Pidal, R., Manual de gramática histórica española.
Madrid, 1905. [Ed. 6, 1941.]

-----, Orígenes del español. Madrid, 1926. [Ed. 3, 1950.]

Menner, R. J., Linguistic Geography and the American Atlas. A̲S̲
8.3–7 (1933).

-----, Review of H. Kurath and others, Linguistic Atlas of New
England, vol. II. Lang. 18.45–51 (1942).

-----, Review of H. Kurath, A Word Geography of the Eastern United
States. A̲S̲ 25.122–26 (1950).

Merlo, C., Il sostrato ètnico e i dialetti italiani. L'Italia dialettale.
    9.1–24 (1933).
-----, Saggi linguistici. Pisa, 1959.
Migliorini, B., Lingua e Cultura. 1948.
-----, Storia della lingua italiana. Florence, 1960.
Millardet, G., Linguistique et dialectologie romanes: Problèmes et
    méthodes. Montpellier-Paris, 1923.
Mitzka, W., Grundzüge nordostdeutscher Sprachgeschichte. Halle,
    1937.
-----, Deutsche Mundarten. Heidelberg, 1943.
-----, Handbuch zum deutschen Sprachatlas. Marburg, 1952.
-----, Wortgeographie und Gesellschaft: Festgabe für L. E. Schmitt.
    Berlin, 1968.
----- and L. E. Schmitt, Deutscher Wortatlas. Giessen, 1951 ff.
Mitzka Festschrift, see Schmitt 1968.
Möhn, D. Sprachwandel und Sprachtradition in der Industrielandschaft.
    Pp. 561–68 in Dialektologenkongress, 1967–68.
Moore, S., S. B. Meech, and H. Whitehall, Middle English Dialect
    Characteristics and Dialect Boundaries. Ann Arbor, Mich., 1935.
    [In Essays and Studies in English and Comparative Literature.]
Moser, H., Stamm und Mundart. ZMF 20.129–45 (1952).
-----, Sprachgrenzen und ihre Ursachen. ZMF 22.87–111 (1954).
-----, Umgangssprache. ZMF 27.215–32 (1960).
Moulton, W. G., The Short Vowel Systems of Northern Switzerland.
    Word 16.155–82 (1960).
-----, Lautwandel durch innere Kausalität: die ostschweizerische
    Vokalspaltung. ZMF 28.227–51 (1961).
-----, Dialect Geography and the Concept of Phonological Space.
    Word 19.23–32 (1962).
-----, Phonologie und Dialekteinteilung. In Sprachleben der Schweiz,
    ed. Zinsli, Bern, 1962.
-----, Phonetische und phonologische Dialektkarten. In Congrès de
    Dialectologie, pp. 117–28. Louvain, 1964.
-----, Die schweizerdeutsche Hiatusdiphthongierung in phonologi-
    scher Hinsicht. Philologia Deutsch, pp. 115–29. Bern, 1965.
-----, The Mapping of Phonemic Systems. Pp. 574–91 in Dialek-
    tologenkongress (1968).
-----, Structural Dialectology. Lang. 44.451–66 (1968).
Naumann, H., Über das sprachliche Verhältnis von Ober- zu Unter-
    schicht. Jb. für Philologie 1.55 ff (1925).
Navarro Tomás, T., The Linguistic Atlas of Spain and the Spanish
    of the Americas. In Kurath, ed., 1942: pp. 68–74.
-----, El Español en Puerto Rico. Rio Piedras, P. R., 1948.
Neumann, J. H., The Dutch Element in the Vocabulary of American
    English. JEGP 44.274–80 (1945).

Newman, S., L. Spier, and A. I. Hallowell, eds., Language, Culture, and Personality: Essays in Memory of Edward Sapir. Menasha, Wis., 1941.

Oberdeutsche Dialektologie: see Schmitt 1967.

Orbeck, A., Early New England Pronunciation as Reflected in Some 17th Century Town Records of Eastern Massachusetts. Ann Arbor, Mich., 1927.

Orton, H., Survey of English Dialects: Introduction. Leeds, 1962.

----- and W. J. Halliday, Survey of English Dialects: The Six Northern Counties. Leeds, 1962-63.

----- and M. F. Wakelin, Survey of English Dialects: The Southern Counties. Leeds, 1967.

Paris, G., Les Parles de France. Rev. des Patois Gallo-Romans 2.161-75 (1888).

Paul, H., Prinzipien der Sprachgeschichte. Halle, 1937. [Reprint of ed. 1909, a revised ed. of 1886.]

Paullin, C. O. and J. K. Wright, Atlas of the Historical Geography of the United States. Washington, 1932.

Pedersen, H., Vergleichende Grammatik der keltischen Sprachen. Göttingen, 1909-13.

-----, Linguistic Science in the Nineteenth Century. Transl. by J. W. Spargo. Cambridge, Mass., 1931.

Pederson, L. A., The Pronunciation of English in Chicago. Univ. of Chicago diss., 1964.

-----, Phonological Indices of Social Dialects in Chicago. In McDavid and Austin 1966.

Penzl, H., The Development of Middle English a in New England. Univ. of Vienna diss., 1934.

-----, The Vowel Phonemes in father, man, dance in Dictionaries and New England Speech. JEGP 39.13-32 (1940).

Petty, J. J., The Growth and Distribution of Population in South Carolina. Columbia, S. C., 1943.

Pfalz, A., Die Mundart des Marchfeldes. Ak. der Wissenschaften in Wien. Vienna, 1913.

-----, Grundsätzliches zur deutschen Mundartenforschung. Germanistische Forschungen: Festschrift des Wiener Akademischen Germanistenvereins. Vienna, 1925.

Philipp, M., Transfer du système phonologique de Blaesheim sur une autre langue, le Français. Pp. 392-97 in Lunt, ed., 1964.

-----, Le système phonologique du parler de Blaesheim. Nancy, 1965.

Pisani, V., Geolingistica e indo-europeo. Rome, 1940.

Pop, S., La dialectologie, 2 vols. Louvain, 1950-51.

-----, see Puscariu 1938.

Prokosch, E., A Comparative Germanic Grammar. Philadelphia, 1939.

Puhvel, see Birnbaum.

Pulgram, E., Prehistory and the Italian Dialects. Lang. 25.241–52 (1949).

-----, The Tongues of Italy. Cambridge, Mass., 1958.

-----, ed., For Roman Jakobson. The Hague, 1957.

Puscariu, S., Der rumänische Sprachatlas. Arch. für vergleichende Phonetik 2.107–17 (1938).

-----, S. Pop, and E. Petrovici, Atlasul linguistic roman. Clui-Sibiu, 1938 ff.

Putnam, G. N. and E. M. O'Hern, The Status Significance of an Isolated Urban Dialect. Lang. Diss. No. 53 (LSA). Baltimore, Md., 1955.

Pyles, T., Words and Ways of American English. New York, 1952.

Read, A. W., Bilingualism in the Middle Colonies. AS 12.93–100 (1937).

Read, W. A., Louisiana French. Baton Rouge, La., 1931.

Redard, G., Le renouvellement des méthodes en linguistique géographique. Pp. 253–58 in Lunt, ed., 1964.

Reed, C. E., The Gender of English Loan Words in Pennsylvania German. AS 17.25–9 (1942).

-----, The Adaptation of English to Pennsylvania German Morphology. AS 23.239–44 (1948).

-----, The Pennsylvania German Dialect Spoken in the Counties of Lehigh and Berks. Seattle, Wash., 1949.

-----, The Pronunciation of English in the State of Washington. AS 27.186–89 (1952).

-----, Washington Words. PADS 25 (1956).

-----, Word Geography of the Pacific Northwest. Orbis 6.86–93 (1957).

----- and L. W. Seifert, A Linguistic Atlas of Pennsylvania German. Marburg, 1954.

Reed, D. W., Eastern Dialect Words in California. PADS 21 (1954).

----- and J. A. Spicer, Correlation Methods of Comparing Dialects in a Transition Area. Lang. 28.348–60 (1952).

Regionale Dialektologie der deutschen Sprache: Arbeitsbericht der Forschungsunternehmen. ZMF 32.101–69 (1965).

Reichard, H. H., Pennsylvania German Dialect Writings and their Writers. Proceedings, Pa. Ger. Society, vol. 26, 1918.

Reichstein, R., Etudes des variations sociales et géographiques des faits linguistiques. Word 16.55–99 (1960).

Remacle, L. and E. Legros, Atlas linguistique de la Wallonie. Liège, 1953 ff.

Robacker, E. F., Pennsylvania German Literature. Philadelphia, 1943.

Roedder, E., Schriften zu Mundartforschung und Wortgeographie.
   JEGP 36.408–25 (1937).
Rogers, E. M., Diffusion of Innovations. New York-London, 1962.
Rohlfs, G., Sprachgeographische Streifzüge durch Italien. Munich,
   1947.
-----, Historische Grammatik der italienischen Sprache und ihrer
   Mundarten. Bern, 1949.
-----, An den Quellen der romanischen Sprachen. Halle, 1952.
   [Reprint of earlier papers.]
Rona, J. P., Aspectos metodológicos de la dialectología Hispano-
   americana. Montevideo, 1958.
Rosenblat, A., La lengua y la cultura de Hispanoamérica. Paris,
   1951.
Ross, A. S. C., Linguistic Class Indicators in Present-Day English.
   Neuphilologische Mitteilungen 55.20–56.
Rousselot, L'Abbé, Les Modifications phonétiques du language
   étudiées dans le patois d'une famille de Cellefrouin. Paris, 1892.
Rush, B., An Account of the Manners of the German Inhabitants of
   Pennsylvania. Reprint in Pa. Ger. Soc. Proceedings, 1910.
Sache, Ort, und Wort: Festschrift J. Jud. Romania Helvetica, vol.
   20. Geneva and Zurich, 1943.
Sandfeld, K., Linguistique balkanique. Soc. Ling. de Paris, No. 31.
   Paris, 1930.
Sapir, E., Language. New York, 1921.
-----, Selected Writings. D. G. Mandelbaum, ed. Berkeley-Los
   Angeles, 1949.
Saussure, F. de, Cours de linguistique général. Eds. Bally,
   Sechehaye, Riedlinger. Paris, 1915.
Sawyer, J. B., A Dialect Study of San Antonio, Texas: A Bilingual
   Community. Univ. of Texas diss., 1957.
-----, Aloofness from Spanish Influence in Texas English. Word
   15.270–81 (1959).
Schach, P., Semantic Borrowing in Pennsylvania German. AS 26.
   257–67 (1951).
Scheuermeier, P., Observations et expériences personnelles faites
   au cours de mon enquête. Soc. Ling. de Paris 33.93–110 (1932).
Schirmunski, V., Sprachgeschichte und Siedlungsmundarten. Germ.-
   Rom. Monatsschrift 18.113 ff and 171 ff (1930).
-----, Zur vergleichenden Formenlehre der deutschen Mundarten.
   PBB 82.297–311 (1961).
-----, Deutsche Mundartkunde, Berlin, 1962. [Transl. by W.
   Fleischer from the Russian edition of 1956.]
Schmidt, J., Die Verwandtschaftsverhältnisse der indogermanischen
   Sprachen. Weimar, 1872.

Schmitt, L. E., ed., Deutsche Wortforschung in europäischen
    Bezügen. Giessen, 1958 ff.
-----, ed., Beiträge zur oberdeutschen Dialektologie: Festschrift
    E. Kranzmayer. Marburg, 1967.
-----, ed., Verhandlungen des II. Internationalen Dialektologen-
    kongresses. Wiesbaden, 1967–68.
-----, ed., Germanische Dialektologie: Festschrift W. Mitzka.
    Wiesbaden, 1968.
Schmitt Festgabe, see Mitzka 1968.
Schrijnen, J., Essai de bibliographie de géographie linguistique
    générale. Nimègue, 1933.
Schuchardt-Brevier, ed. L. Spitzer. Halle, 1928.
Schwarz, E., Die deutschen Mundarten. Göttingen, 1950.
Sebeok, T. A., ed., Style in Language. New York, 1960.
Seifert, L. W., Lexical Differences between Four Pennsylvania
    German Regions. Pa. Ger. Folklore Society 11.155–76 (1946).
-----, see C. E. Reed 1954.
Siegel, E., Deutsche Wortkarte 1890–1962: eine Bibliographie.
    Giessen, 1964.
Sivertsen, E., ed., Proceedings of the Eighth International Congress
    of Linguists. Oslo, 1958.
-----, Cockney Phonology. Oslo, 1960.
Sommerfelt, A., Sur la propagation des changements phonétiques.
    NTS 4.76–125 (1930).
Sonderegger, S., Schweizerdeutsche Mundartforschung 1800–1959.
    Frauenfeld, 1962.
Sprachatlas, see Wrede-Mitzka 1926 ff.
Sprachleben der Schweiz, ed. P. Zinsli. Bern, 1963.
Springer, O., Dialektgeographie und Textkritik. PMLA 56.1163–78
    (1941).
-----, The Study of Pennsylvania German. JEGP 42.1–39 (1943).
Stankiewicz, E., On Discreteness and Continuity in Structural
    Dialectology. Word 13.44–59 (1957).
Steinhauser, W., 250 Jahre Wienerisch: Zur Geschichte einer Stadt-
    mundart. ZMF 21.159–90 (1953).
Stoeckicht, O., Sprache, Landschaft und Geschichte des Elsass. DDG
    42 (1942).
Strang, B., The Tyneside Linguistic Survey. Pp. 788–94 in Dialek-
    tologenkongress, 1967–68.
Streitberg, W., Die Erforschung der indogermanischen Sprachen,
    vol. 2: Germanisch. Berlin-Leipzig, 1927.
Terracher, L. A., L'histoire des langues et la géographie linguistique.
    Oxford, 1929.

Thomas, C. K., Pronunciation in Downstate New York. AS 17.30–41
   and 149–57 (1942).
Thumb, H., and H. Hirt, Handbuch des Sanskrit. Heidelberg, 1930.
Tourtoulon, C. and O. Bringuier, Etude sur la limite géographique de
   la langue d'oc et de la langue d'oil. Paris, 1876.
Troubetzkoy, N. S., Principes de phonologie. Paris, 1949. (Transl.
   of Grundzüge der Phonologie, 1930, by J. Cantineau, with appen-
   dices.)
-----, Phonologie et géographie linguistique: appendix III in above.
Turner, L. D., Africanisms in the Gullah Dialect. Chicago, 1949.
Utěšený, S., Die Bedeutung der Wortgeographie für die Abgrenzung
   der Mundartlandschaften. Pp. 838–43 in Dialektologenkongress,
   1967–68.
Valkhoff, M. F., Studies in Portuguese and Creole. Johannesburg,
   1966.
Van Riper, M. R., The Loss of Post-vocalic / r / in the Eastern
   United States. Univ. of Mich. diss. 1957.
Vereecken, C., Van slut-ila naar sleutel. Commissie voor Toponymie
   en Dialectologie 12.33–100. Brussels, 1938.
Vogt, H., Dans quelles conditions et dans quelles limites peut
   s'exercer sur le système morphologique l'action du système
   morphologique d'une autre langue? Sixth International Congress
   of Linguists, 1949, pp. 31–45.
Wagner, K., Deutsche Sprachlandschaften. DDG 23. Marburg, 1927.
Wagner, M. L., Lingua e dialetti dell'America Spagnola. Florence,
   1949.
Wartburg, W. von, Die Ausgliederung der romanischen Sprachräume.
   Bern, 1950.
Weijnen, A., De Nederlandse Dialecten. Groningen, 1941.
-----, Dialectologie en Fonologie. Pp. 117–27 in Grootaers Album.
-----, Structurelle factoren in de historische grammatica van het
   Nederlands. Assen, 1966.
Weinreich, U., Languages in Contact: Findings and Problems. New
   York, 1953. [Reprint: The Hague, 1964.]
-----, Is a Structural Dialectology Possible? Pp. 268–80 in Martinet-
   Weinreich 1954.
Weiss, R., Die viersprachige Schweiz im Atlas der schweizerischen
   Volkskunde. Pp. 1–21 in Sprachleben der Schweiz, 1963.
Wenzel, W., Wortatlas des Kreises Wetzlar. DDG 28. Marburg,
   1930.
Werner, O., Welche Stufen phonematischer Reduktion sind für die
   Dialektgeographie sinnvoll? Pp. 861–70, Dialektologenkongress.
Westermann, D. and I. C. Ward, Practical Phonetics for Students of
   African Languages. Oxford, 1933.

Wetmore, T. H., The Low-central and Low-back Vowels in the English of the Eastern United States. PADS 32 (1959).

Whitney, W. D., Life and Growth of Language, chapter IX. New York, 1875.

Wiesinger, P., Mundart und Geschichte in der Steiermark. Pp. 81–184 in Schmitt, ed., 1967.

Williamson, J. V., A Phonological and Morphological Study of the Speech of the Negro of Memphis, Tenn. Univ. of Mich. diss., 1961.

Wilson, H. R., The Dialect of Lunenburg County, Nova Scotia. Univ. of Mich. diss., 1958.

Windisch, E., Zur Theorie der Mischsprachen und Lehnwörter. Sächs. Gesellschaft der Wissenschaften zu Leipzig 49.101–26 (1897).

Winteler, J., Die Kerenzer Mundart des Kantons Glarus. Leipzig, 1876.

Wood, G. R., Dialect Contours in the Southern States. AS 38.243–56 (1963).

-----, Word Distribution in the Interior South. PADS 35 (1961).

Wortatlas, see Mitzka-Schmitt 1951 ff.

Wortgeographie und Gesellschaft, see Mitzka 1968.

Wrede, F., Kleine Schriften. Marburg 1963. [Reprint of papers, 1902–31.]

----- and W. Mitzka, Deutscher Sprachatlas. Marburg, 1926 ff.

Wright, J., The English Dialect Dictionary. London, 1898–1905.

Wright, J. K., New England's Prospect: 1933. New York, 1933.

Zamora Vicente, A., Dialectología española. Madrid, 1960.

Zinsli, P., ed., Sprachleben der Schweiz. Bern, 1963.

Zwirner, E., Lautbibliothek der deutschen Mundarten. Göttingen, 1957 ff.

----- and H. Richter, Gesprochenes Deutsch: Probleme ihrer strukturalistischen Untersuchung. Wiesbaden, 1966.